The Whitewashing of Christianity

A ***Hidden*** Past,
A ***Hurtful*** Present,
and a ***Hopeful*** Future

by Jerome Gay Jr.

THE WHITEWASHING OF CHRISTIANITY. Copyright 2020 by JEROME GAY, JR.. All rights reserved. No part of this publication may be reproduced, distributed, or transmitted in any form or by any means, including photocopying, recording, or other electronic or mechanical methods, without the prior written permission of the publisher, except in the case of brief quotations embodied in critical reviews and certain other noncommercial uses permitted by copyright law.

For permission requests, write to the publisher, addressed "Attention: Permissions Coordinator," 205 N. Michigan Avenue, Suite #810, Chicago, IL 60601. 13th & Joan books may be purchased for educational, business or sales promotional use. For information, please email the Sales Department at sales@13thandjoan.com.

Printed in the U. S. A.

First Printing, May 2021

Library of Congress Cataloging-in-Publication Data has been applied for.

Paperback ISBN: 978-1-953156-02-0
Hardcover ISBN: 978-1-953156-06-8

Praise for *The Whitewashing of Christianity*

JESUS DOES NOT NEED RESCUING, but Christianity does. It's been hijacked and held hostage by a set of racial and cultural attitudes and actions that suggest Christianity belongs to white people or is at least best expressed in white cultural idioms. That, of course, is rarely something people say explicitly. It is, however, a common posture people take in everything from assuming 'good theology' comes only from predominantly white contexts, 'sound churches' primarily exist in those contexts, and there are no meaningful contributions past or present from outside of white Christian society. It's a problem as old as early evangelicalism's equating of 'civilized' with 'European' and 'Christian.' The time for a faithful interrogation of Christianity's captors has come and Jerome Gay provides us with both a tough and hopeful examination. If you sense that something is not quite right in the depictions of the Christian faith dominant in the West, pick up this book to learn more about the whole story and the rest of us.

Thabiti Anyabwile
Pastor of Anacostia River Church
Author, Exalting Jesus in Luke:
Christ-Centered Exposition Commentary

I still vividly remember the first time I saw "Jesus." He was blonde haired. He had blue eyes. He had porcelain skin. His painting hung at the entrance of my family's all-Black Catholic Church. I remember the dissonance, even as a boy, and how I wondered how Jesus could look like that, but be Saviour of the world. This would not be the last time I saw that Jesus, and similar images of David, Goliath, Paul, and Pharaoh—all porcelain, thin lipped, with flowing hair. Many years, and many pains would pass before I would see clearly that Jesus was not white, and that the Bible was replete with image bearers who bore my brown skin. As I read this provocative and powerful work from my friend Jerome, I could but wonder what a help it would have been in those troubling years, as my faith itself teetered, because I could not reconcile a white Jesus, with my very Black experience.

Léonce B. Crump Jr.
Pastor and Founder of Renovation Church
Author, Renovate: Changing Who You Are By Loving Where You Are

This book is more than a compilation of pages filled with information. This book is an answer to an evangelistic crisis in the African American community. It exposes how the whitewashing of our faith excludes African Americans from seeing themselves in the story of Scripture. However, it doesn't stop there. It also provides a balanced and biblical blueprint back to a Christianity for people of every nation, tribe, and tongue. I'm so grateful that Jerome wrote it and it's my prayer that the world will hear it.

Dr. Dharius Daniels
Lead Pastor, Change Church
Author, Relational Intelligence

This is a profoundly helpful book that will guide all people in understanding the Gospel and race in a Christocentric way. Jerome has written this book with a tone of pastoral-care and passionate pursuit of unity and reconciliation. This book will challenge everything you ever understood in the area of the Gospel and race with the truths of scripture, history, and Jerome's experiences that flood every page. After reading this book, I'm sure some will feel confronted; some will feel vindicated, but none will be unclear about Jesus's heart for all people. Get this book, Read it, study it, teach it, heed it.

DR. DOUG LOGAN, JR.
President Grimeké Seminary
Author, On the Block
Associate Director of the Acts 29 Family of Churches

Christianity is not a "white man's religion," for we serve no tribal deity, but the Lord of the nations, Jesus Christ. The history of Christianity is beautifully diverse, and this fact needs to be made known today. My friend Jerome Gay has done some hard work in this area, leaving us with much to process and apply, and much to celebrate.

DR. TONY MERIDA
Pastor for Preaching, Imago Dei Church
Dean of Grimké Seminary
Director for Theological Training for Acts 29

This work is beyond past due. Whiteness has been exalted in the world and unfortunately in the church of Jesus Christ. From painting history white to asserting whiteness by assuming that Jesus is white has had a horrid impact on the Black community. That is why this work by Jerome Gay is extremely vital to the global body. Everyone from Black mystery groups and ideologies to white Christians need this. The 100 year silence is over and Jerome's work will ring heavy to aid generations who will never have to struggle like we did. They will have answers to the reality that Christianity is a global faith for all people rooted in the gospel.

DR. ERIC MASON
Lead Pastor, Epiphany Fellowship
Author, Woke Church

Truth can be wielded either as a knife, which harms, or a scalpel, which heals. The Whitewashing of Christianity is a much needed scalpel, exposing the truth of Christianity, but in a way that fosters true healing and reconciliation. I pray this book, written by my friend Pastor Jerome Gay, gets a wide reading and is used greatly to bring people to Christ, and open the eyes of so many who have been blind to these historical realities.

Dr. Bryan Loritts
Author, The Dad Difference

In confronting cultural narratives, using plain language and retelling Christianity's story, yet doing it all with an eye toward hope and unity, Jerome Gay, Jr., has given the church a gift. Thank God that Christianity is not merely the white man's religion! This one resource compiles and gives us the opportunity to see the foundations of the church in full color, with all of its richness and beauty. We must expose and face the past if we want to make sense of the present, but he does not leave us there. Jerome shows us that there is hope for the future because the gospel of Jesus Christ is good news to all people.

Bill Riedel
Lead Pastor Redemption Hill Church

This is a necessary book that helps correct the false narrative that Christianity is a white man's religion. Jerome Gay did a fantastic job!

Lisa Fields
Founder and President of Jude 3 Project
Author, Through the Eyes of Color

Warning! This book contains industrial strength paint-stripper! Jerome Gay skillfully exposes and removes the "white wash" which has covered up the rich African heritage that nurtured Christianity from the first days of the church to today. Gay methodically applies his knowledge of history, Biblical insight, theology and culture to expose the centuries-old project of whitening Christianity, and in doing so debunks the monumental myth it created: the "Christianity is the white man's religion" narrative. The Whitewashing of Christianity builds on and references previous works with over 100 citations dispelling the deception once and for all. The global reach of this lie, and the images it has created are so widespread, we all have been impacted, and need to read this! If you have considered rejecting Christianity based on the false premise that it could not celebrate Blackness, this book provides truth, renewed perspective and hope. I only wished it would have been around sooner to help me and so many I know we didn't have to choose between being Black and being Christian.

RASOOL BERRY
Teaching Pastor, Bridge Church
Host, Where Ya From? Podcast

Change begins with a conversation. Jerome Gay's The Whitewashing of Christianity is nuanced take on how a global faith has been applied locally across the American landscape. Helping readers navigate through Christianity's hidden past and hurtful present, Gay amplifies the redemptive work of Christ in order to direct our attention towards the hopeful future He promised to His followers.

DAMON A. HORTON
Assistant Professor of Intercultural Studies
Author, Intensional

Acknowledgments

To Crystal, Jamari and Jerome III:
I love you and I'm grateful to God for you.

To my mother and brother:
I love you and thank you for always supporting me.

To Vision Church:
I love all of you and you challenge me to be a better son
of Yeshua and pastor of His church.

Contents

Foreword 1

Close the Subject 5

Chapter 1. What exactly is Whitewashing? 9

Chapter 2. White Jesus 28

Chapter 3. The Danger of White Jesus 53

Chapter 4. Reformed Theology vs Reformed Culture 66

Chapter 5. Whitewashing Africa 78

Chapter 6. Product of his Culture: The Whitewashing of Slavery 87

Chapter 7. Hidden Heroes 105

Chapter 8. Responses to Whitewashing: Liberation 134

Chapter 9. Responses to Whitewashing: Self-Hatred
            the Making of a COON 158

Chapter 10. Responses to Whitewashing: Urban Apologetics 180

Chapter 11. A People From All People 201

Conclusion 216

Afterword 222

Bibliography 225

Scripture Index 231

Subject Index 234

Foreword

BY CHRIS BROUSSARD

I COULD HARDLY CONTAIN MY EXCITEMENT. Newly born-again and basking in the joy and peace I had received since accepting Jesus Christ as my personal Lord and Savior, I called my younger brother Terry to share my story. For 10 minutes I testified and for 10 minutes he ate it up. Soon, he was attending Bible studies and getting to know Jesus at his school, Howard University, the mecca of historically-Black colleges and universities.

But Louis Farrakhan's Nation of Islam was also on campus, and Terry's newfound interest in religion led him to give them a listen. Presenting an undeniably strong image of Black manhood, the Nation highlighted the hypocrisy of American Christianity, railed against the lilly-White images of Jesus, the apostles, the angels, and every other positive biblical character, and they preached that our enslaved ancestors were given Christianity to make us weak and docile. Before long, the brother I had been leading was now seeking to lead me—away from Christianity. This was the same story for one of my closest childhood friends. Like Terry, he attended an HBCU and after initially showing interest in following Jesus, he turned toward Islam because he had come to believe Christianity was the "white man's religion." Every time we spoke, they mocked me, asking questions I couldn't answer and speaking as if Christianity was synonymous with racism. They tore into me like I was some ignorant dupe.

Jerome Gay Jr.

My only retort was, "Jesus ain't racist." A baby Christian with no knowledge of biblical or African church history, I couldn't defend my belief with anything but blind faith. Despite their challenges, I was resolute: There was no way I was leaving Jesus. But I was also curious. I knew the Bible was set mainly in what is now called the Middle East and in Africa. I knew Jesus had to be a man of color and could not have looked anything like the pale-skinned, blue-eyed person I had grown up seeing in pictures and paintings. And I knew the religion practiced by white slave owners and racists, whether in the 17th century or the 20th century, was in direct opposition to the teachings I was reading in the Bible, to the faith that had changed my life.

As I began studying the Bible voraciously, I supplemented it with extra-biblical works, particularly those related to Africa and Black people. What I found amazed me. From the book of Genesis, which associates the Garden of Eden with the Nile River and Ethiopia, to the book of Acts, which reveals African men being present on the day of Pentecost, an African man being baptized by the apostle Philip, Africans preaching Jesus to the Greeks, and African men laying hands on the apostle Paul and sending him out for ministry, the Bible is a treasure trove of Black history. Beyond that, I discovered that renowned, early Christian theologians such as Augustine, Tertullian, Origen, and Athanasius were African, that Ethiopia was one of the first countries to establish Christianity as its state religion, and that Nubia was a thriving Christian nation for approximately 1,000 years. And that isn't even the half of it. Indeed, the Bible and Christian history are so full of Black people and Black nations that to call Christianity "the white man's religion" is the very height of ignorance.

But while my brother and best friend were sorely mistaken in their historical assessment of the Christian religion, they had legitimate reasons for their beef with Christianity as it has been presented since the Trans-Atlantic Slave Trade and European colonialism. After all, they weren't making up their stories about white people oppressing Black people under the guise of Christianity, or whites twisting the Scripture to say Black people were cursed and meant to be slaves. The fact is that white people have been guilty of the egregious sin of presenting Christianity as a white man's religion. Against the mountains of evidence to the contrary (not to mention common geographical sense), they've depicted all biblical and Christian heroes as white. As missionaries throughout the world, they've falsely presented Western and European customs and culture as an essential part of Christianity, even insisting that Africans take on European names upon being

The Whitewashing of Christianity

baptized into the faith. And while many Christians fought to end American chattel slavery as abolitionists, many more sought to provide scriptural justification for the persecution and isolation of Black people through slavery and segregation. Many so-called "Bible-believing" evangelical seminaries have a long history of discrimination against African Americans. And to this day, when teaching church history, some of these schools ignore the church in Ethiopia, Egypt, India, Persia, and other nations of color, acting as if they did not exist. They have taught, and still teach, European church history as the only church history. This is literally a whitewashing of Christianity.

But it's more than that. True biblical Christianity is not the white man's religion, the Black man's religion, or any man's religion. It is God's way of salvation for all mankind. It is God's work, period. For it to be presented as the religion of any single race, for it to be whitewashed, is idolatry. That is why this book is so important. In addressing this critical issue, Pastor Jerome Gay is exposing the counterfeit and the fake so that the legitimate and the real can be accepted, and so the God of the universe can be glorified. As white supremacy dies, and a multicultural worldview becomes more prevalent, it is imperative that Christianity be presented in its true, biblical form, a form that values all races of people equally and displays God's love—both today and historically—for those of every nation, tribe, people, and language (Revelation 7:9). A whitewashed Christianity cannot do that. May this book play a large role in forever killing this false religion that so many, both Black and white, have been fooled into believing is the truth.

Chris Broussard
Television and Radio Broadcaster
Founder and President, The K.I.N.G. Movement

Close the Subject

ON FEBRUARY 15TH, 1974, the show *Good Times* aired an episode called "Black Jesus." *Good Times* was a show that featured a strong Black family with loving parents, creative children, and caring neighbors living in a Chicago housing project. The star of the show was the flamboyant James "J.J." Evans, Jr. with his rousing signature wail, "Dy-no-miiiite!" In this episode, Florida (J.J.'s mother) becomes vehemently upset when Michael (J.J.'s brother) hangs J.J.'s painting of a Black Jesus on the wall next to the family's framed print of a conventional rendering of a white Christ.

Michael was amazed by the picture of Black Jesus and took down the painting of white Jesus as he said, "A Black family should have a Black Jesus on the wall." Once his mother came home, she noticed the switch immediately. A debate ensued wherein Michael pleaded with his mother to at least allow the painting of Black Jesus to hang next to the picture of white Jesus. Florida responded, "The only Jesus I know is him, and the one thing he don't need is a partner. This picture [pointing to white Jesus] has been in my family since I can remember. When I was a baby, I don't know what I saw first: my momma, my poppa, or this Jesus [pointing to white Jesus again]. Now he's the one I know and love, so let's close the subject. If Jesus was Black, the Bible would've said so." Michael responded, "But it does say so." Michael proceeded to grab a large Bible and turned to Revelation 1:14-15. The verses state:

> 14 The hairs of his head were white, like white wool, like snow. His eyes were like a flame of fire, 15 his feet were like burnished bronze, refined in a furnace, and his voice was like the roar of many waters.

Jerome Gay Jr.

Florida grabbed the Bible from Michael with a look of disbelief. "Oh Lord have mercy. It sure do say that, don't it?" his mother cried. Michael took the painting of Black Jesus into his hands to make comparisons and concluded, "Momma, how do we know Jesus wasn't Black? He could've been from the lost tribe of Israel; they were supposed to be Black." J.J. ends the segment with levity as he says in true J.J. fashion, "If ever a people were lost, we're it."

Florida's statements highlight how the American church has responded to the idea of a Black Jesus and how proponents of the white Jesus myth have fought vehemently to perpetuate the Christian faith as almost exclusively influenced by white people. Florida told her son to "close the subject." Closing the subject and refusing to address the subject of whitewashing has been an extremely effective tactic in keeping the white Jesus myth active for centuries. Statements like, "His race doesn't matter," or "Discussions like this take away from the core message," and "I'm colorblind," are deployed to close the subject. Closing the subject only nurtures the delusion of those who think Jesus was white and those making an eternal decision to reject Him based on this grossly incorrect assertion.

When thousands of Black and brown people are turning away from the faith, in part due to the perpetuation of a white Jesus, we should not close the subject. When one community's contributions are highlighted while the contributions of others are neglected, we cannot close the subject. When an entire faith is misrepresented, we cannot close the subject. This book will not allow proponents of the white Jesus myth to close the subject. Instead, this book will address this misconception head-on with the hope of shedding light on a very important subject: whitewashing and its detrimental effects.

While the verses in Revelation that Michael read on the episode of *Good Times* had nothing to do with Jesus' race, and was primarily symbolic about His power and judgment, it's important to note that Jesus' race had already been a concern for centuries at that time. Particularly, the way Christianity has been presented in America. Jesus has been presented as a white man, with white disciples, coming back surrounded by white angels. White Jesus is the elephant in the sanctuary who has been comfortably presented as historically accurate in churches, seminaries, and households for far too long. White Jesus is the beneficiary of centuries of whitewashing, and the American church is His victim. In many cases, America has been a willing victim. It's easy to say that His race doesn't matter, but it's too late to say that once inaccurate depictions of Him have been circulating and erroneously affirmed for centuries.

The Whitewashing of Christianity

The prophet Isaiah is the one who gives us a physical depiction of Jesus and His race isn't mentioned at all. In this depiction, Isaiah says, "For he grew up before him like a young plant, and like a root out of dry ground; he had no form or majesty that we should look at him, and no beauty that we should desire him" (Isaiah 53:2). The Jesus that Isaiah describes isn't the Jesus that has been presented to us, which is why Florida Evans could point to white Jesus and say that He's the only Jesus she knows. He's the only Jesus she knows because He's been the only Jesus presented.

My hope is to expand our view of Jesus and who He's used as part of his plan of redemption. The omission of the African presence in Scripture and history has millions functionally saying that white Jesus is "the only Jesus [they] know." This is a travesty that must not be ignored or dismissed as divisive. What's divisive is presenting nearly every biblical character as white. What's divisive is presenting the brown-skinned, middle eastern, Jewish savior as a white man, presenting it as fact, and labeling those that address this lie as troublemaking dissenters. What's truly divisive is presenting one race of people as the entire representation of the Hebrew nation.

The notion that Christianity is the "white man's religion" is an observation that does not find resonance in biblical or historical reality. Christianity is not a faith that's "becoming" a global religion; it has always been a global religion and will always be a global religion. At every point in history, the Christian faith has found Afrocentric expression, and it is God's heartfelt wish that the gospel takes firm root among all people. He wants to see people "from every nation, from all tribes and peoples and languages, standing before the throne and before the Lamb, clothed in white robes, with palm branches in their hands" (Revelation 7:9).

The proclamation of the psalter that "Kush will soon stretch out her hands to God" (Psalms 68:31) finds unique application in the reality that the descendants of the Kushites—the Nubians—not only embraced Christianity as the national religion as early as the fifth century CE, but fought off Arab Muslim invasion in order to maintain an indigenous, Black Christian kingdom that would flourish for a thousand years. The late antique Kushite kingdom centered at Meroë fell away in the late fourth century. While there is not much evidence to suggest a significant Christian presence in Sudan during its Meroitic Kushite period, it is noteworthy that the "Ethiopian" eunuch mentioned in Acts 8 was likely from Kush, rather than the southern Axumite kingdom of Ethiopia.[1] The queens of Kush were commonly

---

1 Vince Bantu, *Early African Christianity: Nubia* https://jude3project.org/blog/2016/earlychristianitynubia, September 2016.

called Candace (or Kandake), and Ethiopia (or Greek Aithiopia) was often used to refer to Black inhabitants south of Egypt conflating both the Nubian kingdoms of Sudan and the Axumite empire of Ethiopia. The mere reality that facts like this aren't as widely known, shared, or taught is another reason why this subject must be broached and we simply cannot "close the subject."

Depending on your belief system, social experience, or theological disposition, you're either extremely interested in reading about how an entire faith has been whitewashed, disagree with the sentiment, or you don't see a need for the conversation. Wherever you land, my hope is fivefold:

I hope to address the concerns of those who've mistakenly judged Christianity as a white man's religion rooted in slavery, oppression, and white supremacy and have decided that it's not an indigenous faith of people of color.

I hope that after reading this, you'll reconsider making an eternal decision based on erroneous information and realize that Christianity is a faith that thrived in Africa long before slavery, and it's for ALL people that you'll place saving faith in Yeshua.

I hope to lovingly address how Christianity has been whitewashed and highlight some of the damaging effects it has on how Christianity is perceived and received.

I hope to give tips towards correcting the whitewashed narrative of the Christian faith in favor of a more historically-accurate narrative.

I will highlight and accentuate the contributions of Black and brown people to the Christian faith, theology, philosophy and academia.

Throughout the book I'll primarily refer to Jesus as Yeshua. If you're unfamiliar with the Christian faith, these terms are interchangeable and refer to the same person. I hope you will read with an open mind, so put your social and/or theological guards down. If we address this honestly instead of closing the subject, we'll grow together!

1

What exactly is *Whitewashing?*

> *The ones who believe that Christianity is "The White Man's Religion" have actually believed the "White Man's" narrative.*
> — JACKIE HILL PERRY

Why Does Jesus' Race Matter?

This is a good and fair question, but in many cases, it's the wrong question. While Jesus' race doesn't hold any weight as it relates to salvation, it has anthropological and social implications. Rather than simply asking why his race matters, we should ask why he and the entire Christian faith have been whitewashed. Knowing that Jesus was a Jewish man of color, why have we been bombarded with images that present him as a blond-haired, blue-eyed white man? Jesus' color is an integral part of his ontological being, as he was both human and divine (John 8:58, Colossians 1:15, Titus 1:13). This book will explore some of the historical tactics used to hide this truth, address some of the reasons behind the whitewashing of Christianity, and why it must be opposed.

Jerome Gay Jr.

Why Whitewashing Must Be Confronted

There's a growing sentiment amongst people of African descent as well as people across the globe that Christianity is a Western created, European influenced, white-owned religion of oppression. While this is historically inaccurate, there are legitimate reasons why many have adopted this assertion. Dr. Vince Bantu says, "Christianity has been perverted into a mechanism of tyranny by many Western nations." The main reason for this growing sentiment is historical and cultural whitewashing as well as the under-emphasized reality that the gospel took firm root in Africa, the Middle East, and Asia long before even an idea of it traveled to the West. In order to properly present the gospel and the Christian faith accurately, it must be understood that Christianity is not the cultural property of any single racial or ethnic group. On the contrary, it has always existed as a chosen nation comprised of every nation, tribe, and tongue. Because many non-Western groups have been made to feel culturally alienated from the gospel, it is imperative to explore the neglected history of non-Western Christianity.[2] This is one of the many reasons why whitewashing must be confronted. Dr. Carl Ellis addressed this in his sociological and historical masterpiece *Free at Last* when he pointed out how Black militants responded to what he called "White-Christianity-ism," yet failed to distinguish the difference between the true "Christianity of Christ" and the "Christianity of this land." Dr. Ellis says:

When Christianity was rejected, secularism and humanism filled the void. Secularism is the belief that human life is independent of God and his revelation and that the sociological struggles of a people transcend all forms of religion. Humanism is the belief that humans are the final judge of all truth. Ironically, both of these are worldviews, with their own belief system and demands for faith. Since this is the essence of religion, secularism and humanism do not transcend religion. They are religions themselves. Not realizing this, the secular militants ended up merely switching from a God-centered faith to a human-centered religion. They were justified in rejecting "White-Christianity-ism" and asserting that we should replace White definitions of us with definitions of our own.[3]

---

2   Vince Bantu, *Early African Christianity: Egypt* http://www.jude3project.com/blog/2016/8/20/early-africanchristianity-egypt?rq=vince%20bantu, August 2016.

3   Carl Ellis, *Free at Last*, (InterVarsity Press Downer Grove, IL 1996), 20-21.

The Whitewashing of Christianity

Dr. Ellis pointed out how many of the Black militants of the 1960s didn't do their homework and bought into the false narrative that Christianity is the white man's religion. Unfortunately, many are making the same mistake today.

Throughout the pages of this book, we will start our journey by defining whitewashing and addressing some of its effects. We'll see that it must not only be confronted, but also diagnosed within Western evangelicalism, and opposed by all who claim Christianity as their theological home.

The Whitewashing Must Stop

There I was, just sitting at my computer, preparing for a conversation on Christianity and race. I'd read extensively on the subject, and I decided to go to a trusted online source for some additional information that tackles all types of questions regarding Christianity, Scripture, and history: GotQuestions.org. I had referenced them an innumerable amount of times for personal pursuit of knowledge and even recommended them to others. I had never used them for lectures, I primarily used Scripture and other books for that; however, on this day, I decided to see how they engaged the question of Christianity being thought of as a 'white man's religion.' I typed my inquiry into the search bar, hit enter, and sat back in shock as I read these words:

In the past 2,000 years, the vast majority of Christians have been white/European. While Christianity had its beginnings in the Middle East, it spread rapidly to Europe and parts of Asia where Caucasians were the predominant race. The history of Christianity is filled with expansions, but mostly throughout Europe and Asia, then on to the West in the 15th century. Christianity has not had nearly the same success spreading among Middle Easterners, Africans, and Asians, and this led many to declare that Christianity is a religion for white people.[4]

I paused and thought, I paced and thought, and the disheartening nature of the post just wouldn't leave me. I said to myself, *Wow, here we go again. Even trusted sources drop the ball when it comes to Africans, the African Diaspora and their contributions to the Christian faith.* For the past 2,000 years, the vast majority of Christians have been white? Africa was not even a footnote in terms of its influence on the Christian faith? My last thought was loud and clear: THE. WHITEWASHING. MUST. STOP! I aired out my concern on Facebook (I know, but don't judge me) as I typed:

---

4   Got Questions: *"Is Christianity a White Man's Religion?"* https://www.gotquestions.org/Christianity-white-religion.html, accessed June 2018.

Jerome Gay Jr.

> This is from *GotQuestions.org*. They are considered to be a resource for the body of Christ. This opening paragraph is intended to answer the question, "**Is Christianity a white man's religion?**" This opening is not only offensive, but it's laughable. Many of the early Church Fathers were African, most of the people mentioned in Scripture are people of color, the library of Alexandria is in Africa, yet the last 2,000 years of Christianity has been primarily white people? Family, this is what we mean by whitewashing and this assertion contributes to lostness. #gotquestionsMUSTedit #pleaseremove

The post garnered a lot of interaction and most of the dialogue was healthy. Of course, there were voices of dissent, but overall people recognized that there was a problem, which was my goal. I was also hoping that *GotQuestions* would see the damage of a response like this. I knew something had to change. I knew that I wasn't someone who *GotQuestions* knew or possibly even cared to receive feedback from, but I also wouldn't know unless I initiated a conversation about their incomplete reply to a very important and impactful question. A brother of mine by the name of Rasool Berry who serves as a Teaching Pastor with The Bridge Church in Brooklyn, NY and I decided to reach out and engage them with an open and hopeful mind, instead of just assuming that nothing would change.

Here's the letter that Rasool sent to Got Questions:

> Greetings Got Questions!
>
> First, thank you for your tireless efforts to make a defense for the faith. I have come to depend on your website often as I share the Gospel and prepare for sermons. I find your research very helpful much of the time.
>
> Recently, a friend of mine who shares my passion for defending the faith shared your article on Is Christianity A White Man's Religion. I was shocked and disappointed to read the article I believe doesn't meet your usual standards of accuracy.
>
> As a missionary, and pastor, I have done much research on this topic. There is perhaps no greater lie that is leading people of color away

The Whitewashing of Christianity

from the faith in greater numbers than the myth that Christianity is a white man's religion.

The article starts by stating: In the past 2,000 years, the vast majority of Christians have been white/European.

This statement implies that throughout its origins the vast majority of Christians have been white/European. Of course, at the beginning of the church, that wasn't true as is mentioned in the next sentence:

While Christianity had its beginnings in the Middle East, it spread rapidly to Europe and parts of Asia where Caucasians were the predominant race. The history of Christianity is filled with expansions, but mostly throughout Europe and Asia, then on to the West in the 15th century. Christianity has not had nearly the same success spreading among Middle Easterners, Africans, and Asians, and this has led many to declare that Christianity is a religion for white people.

The next statement races so quickly through many important moments in early church history. I list a couple here:

1) Acts 2:10, 13:1, and most notably Acts 8:26-36 record Africans responding to the Gospel. In Acts 13:1, we are even told that Simeon was called Niger (most likely because of his complexion). The Ethiopian Coptic Church, considered the oldest church in the world, traces its origin to the Ethiopian official in Acts 8.

2) The spread of the gospel in Antioch (Asia) was clearly the first dominant hub of Christianity once it spread beyond Jerusalem. More evidence of the dominance of Asia is found in the proliferation of Paul's letters (Galatians, Ephesians, Colossians) and Revelation which is written to Asian churches.

3) The leadership of St. Augustine, Athanasius, and Tertullian—all church fathers from Northern Africa—demonstrate the vibrancy of Christianity in Africa. Ireneus, Ignatius, and others demonstrate the vitality of Christianity in Asia in the first 3 centuries. This history was inadequately represented in the article.

Christianity was never intended for white people only. The first Christians were all Semitic in ethnicity and likely had light- to dark-brown skin. Christianity having been predominantly a white religion in past centuries has nothing to do with the message of Christianity. Rather, it is due to the failure of Christians to take the Gospel of Jesus Christ to the ends of the world (Matthew 28:19-20; Acts 1:8).

While this section offers an effective theological position about the common origin we share as children of Adam and the universality of Christ's atonement for all, it fails to anticipate and capture the primary reason that the claim "white man's religion" exists. It's less about theology and more about history.

The reason most people label Christianity a white man's religion is because of the legacy of the Church's complicity with racist teaching, practices, and oppression. People believe that the Christianity of Christ (to use Frederick Douglass' term) is the Christianity of the Southerners who broke off from the 1848 Triennial Baptist Convention (PCA, Catholics and every major denomination were complicit as well). They defended slavery on theological grounds. The Museum of the Bible recently displayed a Bible that was edited to remove the portions relating Exodus stories or other portions that might give enslaved Africans hope. Throughout the history of our nation, including during Civil Rights, where Christian schools sprung up to resist the integration of public schools, white evangelicalism has been synonymous with oppression. The Letter from a Birmingham Jail even shows how Rev. Martin Luther King, Jr., a pastor, was resisted by white clergy.

Please, I urge you, to remove this article until it is edited to properly treat the topic in a way that will be effective to reach people with the Gospel. I have preached on this message and done much research and would be open to assist you.

I serve with a predominantly white Christian organization and believe in the unity of the church. This is why we must get this right. It's important we deal with the issue head-on and recognizing the history of the contributions of people of color to Christianity from the very beginning is essential.

The Whitewashing of Christianity

Christianity didn't become predominantly "white/European" until the rise of Europe. For the first several centuries until Islamic invasions reversed progress in the Middle East and Africa, Ethiopia, current day Libya, Egypt, and western Asia were all hubs of Christianity as much as Europe was. To say otherwise not only undermines your point, it's inaccurate.

Rasool even provided them a link to a sermon on the topic in order to educate them. To our pleasant surprise, the site edited how they engaged the question, and this time key African leaders were included:

> The charge is sometimes leveled that Christianity is a "white man's religion," due to the historical connections that Christianity had with the rise of European nations and the founding of the United States. This is complicated by the fact that, during the era of the African slave trade, many white slave owners claimed to be Christians and tried to use the Bible to justify their actions. Acceptance of the idea that Christianity is a white man's religion causes some people of color to embrace non-Christian religions such as Islam, animism, and Rastafarianism.
>
> Regardless of world history since the reign of Charlemagne, Christianity was never intended for white people only. The Bible teaches that all people are created in the image of God (Genesis 1:27). The first Christians were all Semitic in ethnicity and likely had light-to-dark-brown skin. Christianity having been predominantly a white religion in recent centuries has nothing to do with the message of Christianity. Rather, it is due to the failure of Christians to take the gospel of Jesus Christ to the ends of the world (Matthew 28:19–20; Acts 1:8). Jesus Christ is the propitiation for the sins of the entire world—all races and nationalities (see 1 John 2:2). Spiritually, men of all races are in need of the Savior because of their shared sinful condition (Romans 5:12).
>
> The idea that Christianity is a white man's religion is countered in the book of Acts. When the church began, there were Africans who responded to the gospel (Acts 2:10). Philip the evangelist was called specifically to share the message of Christ with an Ethiopian official

in Acts 8:26–38. This Ethiopian was saved and baptized, and the last we read of him, he "went on his way rejoicing" (verse 39). The Ethiopian Coptic Church traces its origin to the evangelistic work of the Ethiopian official in Acts 8.

The spread of the gospel in Syrian Antioch—a metropolitan city located in Asia—highlights the varied roots of the church. In fact, Antioch was the first dominant hub of Christianity once it spread beyond Jerusalem. More evidence of the strength of the Asian church is found in the number of Paul's letters (Galatians, Ephesians, and Colossians) that were written to Asian churches, and the letters to the churches in Revelation 2–4, also written to residents of Asia.

Church leaders such as Augustine, Athanasius, and Tertullian—all from Northern Africa—demonstrate the vibrancy of Christianity in Africa. Irenaeus, Ignatius, and others demonstrate the vitality of Christianity in Asia in the first three centuries. Ethiopia, present-day Libya, Egypt, and West Asia remained firmly Christian territory until Muslim invasions in the Middle East and Africa turned it over to Islamic control. Before the arrival of Islam, many African and Asian regions were hubs of Christianity as much as Europe ever was.

Forgiveness of sin through the sacrifice of Christ, the essence of Christianity is offered to all races, colors, creeds, and genders, to all "those who receive God's abundant provision of grace and of the gift of righteousness" through Him (Romans 5:18). In giving His life as a substitute for sin, Jesus Christ purchased for God with His blood "men from every tribe and tongue and people and nation" (Revelation 5:9). No, Christianity is not a white man's religion. Christianity is not a Black, brown, red, or yellow religion, either. The truth of the Christian faith is universally applicable to all people. "How true it is that God does not show favoritism but accepts from every nation the one who fears him and does what is right" (Acts 10:34–35).[5]

---

5   Got Questions: *"Is Christianity a White Man's Religion?"* https://www.gotquestions.org/Christianity-white-religion.html, accessed June 2018.

The Whitewashing of Christianity

Based on this change, I decided to go back to the platform where I aired out my concern to share how GotQuestions not only responded, but was willing to edit their post in a way that included the contributions that people of color have made to the Christian faith:

Earlier this week, I posted a screenshot from *GotQuestions.org* where they made a claim that, for the last 2,000 years, the majority of Christians have been white. This was in response to the question, "Is Christianity a white man's religion?" My intent wasn't to boycott or cast aspersions on them, but rather to engage them with a full historical narrative... I reached out to them with some concerns as well as history, and I'm glad to say that they adjusted their post. I also want to thank Rasool Berry, who engaged them also. This is what happens when we're not too fragile to engage and listen to each other. The goal was not "getting my way," but rather to inform them of how statements like that make it harder for those of us engaging African mystery cults, how it wasn't completely accurate, and how that phrase undermined the rest of the article which was rich in content. #engage #confrontationcanbehealthy

The comments I received when I posted the edited version from *GotQuestions* reminded me of the need to confront whitewashing when it rears its ugly and historically-inaccurate head. *GotQuestions* displayed the humility to listen, an ability that has been missing in much of our dialogue around race, historic whitewashing, and injustice. While the *GotQuestions* article is a reason for writing this book, the gospel is the primary reason, the gospel has been eclipsed in the minds of many who perceive Christianity to be a monolithic faith. I want to address the effects of whitewashing while championing the preeminence of the gospel in hopes that people who've wrongly rejected it based on an inaccurate representation of Christianity, will come to faith. Hopefully, this book will empower others to display the same level of humility by not propagating a narrative that presents Christianity as a faith influenced by only one group of people. As Dr. Eric Mason says, "We must address the things that happen in our culture exegetically, expositionally, theologically, historically, critically, lovingly, passionately, humbly, and with Jesus at the center."[6]

---

6   Eric Mason, *Woke Church: An Urgent Call for Christians to Confront Racism* and Injustice, (Moody Publisher Chicago, IL 2018), 122.

Back to the Term

When we hear the term whitewashing, the responses are vast. Just like the term white privilege, it can drum up vehement ridicule. What I've found with the term whitewashing, as with the term white privilege, is that opponents of the concept rarely ask how we're defining it; they assume a definition and respond based on their assumptions. The term whitewashing has been used in Hollywood in recent years when actress Jada Pinkett Smith accused the Oscars of being "so white." Pinkett Smith was so outraged by the lack of diversity among the Oscar nominees in 2016 that she decided to boycott the Oscars. Not only did she avoid attending the show, but she said she wasn't even going to watch it on television. This move led to a hashtag that ended up being more than a mere twitter movement. It became an actual social movement. The hashtag #OscarsSoWhite, started by April Reign and later posted by Jada, took off and thousands of people joined Jada in her quest to see more diversity as it relates to acknowledging the amount of talented people in film. To keep this from being simply another social media movement that didn't extend beyond hashtags and tweets, Jada Pinkett Smith and her husband Will Smith started *Careers in Entertainment*, a foundation to highlight the steps needed to make entertainment more inclusive as well as to acknowledge the diverse talent that often goes unnoticed. Their goal was not simply to address and express apathy towards whitewashing in Hollywood, but rather to acknowledge and correct the issue. I share the same hope. My goal isn't to simply call out whitewashing. While I will do that, too, my ultimate goal is to acknowledge its effects on how the Christian faith is viewed outside of white evangelicalism and to present a metanarrative of Christian history, one that highlights the reality that God has used and still uses all people in His redemptive plan, not just white people, which are often highlighted the most and sometimes exclusively.

So, what exactly is whitewashing? Like much of the *Christianese*, or religious jargon, used in churches all over the world, definitions are essential to understanding, engagement and transformation. With this thought in mind, I want you to think of whitewashing beyond political propaganda used by "the left" to divide us as many would assert, but rather a historical reality that still affects the way we think about and present the Christian faith. This will help us to engage the concept with a more balanced perspective as we review historical realities that shape how we engage Scripture, humanity, and Christian history. I'm asking you to reject your motivational reasoning; this is what social scientists call the process

The Whitewashing of Christianity

of deciding what evidence to accept based on the conclusion one prefers, despite evidence to the contrary. The evidence is clear both spiritually and historically that many races were used in scripture and Christian history. The evidence also shows that this is not highlighted in churches, seminaries, film and print. Why? Because whitewashing has been an acceptable norm in America.

The Cambridge dictionary defines whitewashing as an attempt to stop people from finding out the truth about a situation.[7] This is essentially hiding facts in order to control or even change a narrative. The secondary definition of whitewashing is using white people to represent people of color in film and history. This helps us to understand the version of Christianity that's been presented for centuries, one void of any ethnic diversity that's significant. So, how do we define whitewashing as it relates to the Christian faith? **Whitewashed Christianity refers to the affinity of white Christian scholars to dominate the Bible, Christian art, literature, and history with white people at the expense of authentic ethnicity and true scholarship in order to resonate most deeply with white audiences, primarily based on their experiences, presuppositions, and worldviews.** As Dr. Ernest Grant says, "Whitewashing occurs institutionally and structurally when the contributions of the African Diaspora to theology, ethics, and culture are largely ignored, and the influence of people groups of European descent are accentuated."[8] Whitewashing wrongly validates and champions the implicit cultural and historical bias within conservative evangelical communities and bolsters the notion that people of color will remain unequal to our white counterparts, regardless of our credentialing or accomplishment.[9]

This doesn't mean that every white scholar is racist, nor does it mean that every white Christian scholar was complicit in the historic whitewashing that plagues Christianity in the West today. However, we must not ignore how the history of white supremacy has affected how the Christian faith has been presented and propagated, especially in the West. When we look at whitewashing historically, we'll find that it was dishonest, deliberate, and oftentimes destructive.

---

7   Cambridge Dictionary *Whitewashing* https://dictionary.cambridge.org/us/dictionary/english/whitewashing, accessed October 2018.

8   Ernest Grant, *Whitewashed Christianity* https://thewitnessbcc.com/whitewashed-christianity/, October 2016.

9   E. B. Lane, *The African American Christian Man: Reclaiming the Village.* (Dallas: Black FAMILY PRESS 1997), 156.

Jerome Gay Jr.

Whitewashing is Dishonest

A tactic of white supremacy has been the intentional removal of any African influence from their presentation of Christianity and its history. Just peruse *Saint Vladimir's Seminary Press*, do a Google search, or look up church fathers on Amazon and you'll see almost every single African church father and African martyr presented as a white man or woman. We see this in artwork wherein Middle Eastern Jewish biblical figures and the African church fathers are portrayed inaccurately as white. "White Jesus has done more harm historically than the Confederate flag," says Dr. Eric Mason, theologian and pastor of Epiphany Fellowship. Sadly, Dr. Mason's statement is true. Learning about church history often starts with the Reformation in Europe instead of Israel and Africa, bypassing African influence. The library of Alexandria of the third century provided the standard of the European university used in practically all of medieval Europe, but Africa and Africans aren't given credit or even acknowledged for their contributions. For instance, people like Basil the Great, Gregory of Nazianzus, and Gregory of Nyssa (all fourth century) are credited with the concept of God the Father, God the Son, and God the Holy Spirit. The reality is that these Cappadocian Fathers were shaped by the exegesis of African scholars like Didymus the Blind and Tyconius and Origen, considered to be one of Africa's greatest scientific investigators of sacred text. Even when mentioned, African fathers like Augustine and the like are presented as white men on almost every piece of literature in seminaries and institutions of higher education. This dishonesty isn't accidental—it is deliberate.

Whitewashing is Deliberate

The historic version of Christianity presented in America often doesn't include the diversity within Scripture and history. This wasn't an accident, and those who were doing the printing, proclaiming, and proselytizing were not aloof to the reality of color in the Bible and the African influence on the Christian faith that precedes the European reformers and Puritans. When examined, Christianity in Numidia, Mauretania, Byzacena, and Libya reveals tons of martyrial oratories, cemeteries, and churches that date back to the fourth and fifth centuries (and some well before Constantinian conquest). Yet this rich history is left out of many of our seminaries, lectures, and literature.[10] Why? Because whitewashing

---

10   Thomas Oden, *How Africa Shaped the Christian* Mind, (IVP Books, 2007), 38-39.

The Whitewashing of Christianity

is deliberate, and to present an accurate narrative of history that includes Africa would undermine a whitewashed narrative of history. Rather than starting Christian history with the Protestant Reformation of the sixteenth century, we should not skip over African martyrdom and philosophy that preceded it, but doing that would cause those who are happy with a whitewashed narrative to lose their power. What power? Power to control and propagate a narrative that favors the idea that Christianity is primarily shaped, influenced by, and the property of white people. While this notion is historically and biblically false, it's functionally true when we look at Christianity in America both historically and presently, which is one of the reasons why whitewashing is destructive.

Whitewashing is Destructive

The destructive nature of whitewashing is seen in high definition when we consider that slave owners painted the Bible white in order to justify chattel slavery. To do so, fallacies like the Curse of Ham, Aristotle's Climate Theory, and the erasure of the Black presence in the Bible were all deployed in an attempt to convince Black people of their tainted identity. Sadly, this hasn't changed much—the myth of a white Jesus and his 12 white disciples are supported when books ignore the African heritage of many within Scripture, and illustrate the myth through whitewashed imagery. What makes whitewashing destructive is not just that it presents one group of people as the exclusive choice of God's use, but the fact that this false notion is actually functionally supported by institutions who hold themselves to high standards of orthodoxy and historical accuracy. Opponents say that the gospel isn't for one group of people and I agree with that, but the gospel wasn't shared, theology taught, catechisms created and philosophies developed by only one group, either. When the Black and brown presence of redemptive history is not acknowledged, it leaves people of color with questions about the role they play(ed) in God's plan. It's a barrier to the message of hope—an unnecessary one at that. What opponents to books and subjects like this miss is that they assume their version of history and their anthropological experience is universal and therefore applies to everyone, which is why they say race doesn't matter after using race in their favor to paint the Bible and Christian history largely white. Additionally, opponents reveal a lack of Christian love when they express apathy towards people who explain how whitewashing affects people of color and the Christian faith in general. You can't support or ignore whitewashing while championing truth, love, and orthodoxy.

Jerome Gay Jr.

Whitewashing is destructive because it's a lie, a blatant, diabolical lie. It's a hermeneutical lie. A historical lie. After reading the Bible and finding white people on every page of Scripture as relates to imagery by most Christian publishers, it's no wonder why many Black and brown people question if the Christian faith is a white man's religion. It's destructive because it hands primarily people of color to BRIC's (Black Religious Identity Cults) and mystics because in the mind of those seeking solace, they don't see a God welcoming them with grace and open arms. They see a God who'll tolerate them and wants them to assimilate to His real chosen people, which are functionally presented as white. I'm not affirming their conclusion to walk away, but it's vital that we enter the mind of unbelievers to examine how many of them affirm their unbelief. It's vital to understand my words as an explanation, not necessarily an affirmation. Whitewashing is an affront to the Christian faith because it presents a truncated gospel that holds one group of people in a higher esteem than others, which contributes to lostness and is a detriment to the Christian mission to depopulate hell through the spread of the authentic gospel that tears down walls of division and welcomes every tribe, tongue and nation (Revelation 7:9).

I will unpack the aforementioned with specificity as we look at how racism not only affects social engagement, but also scholarship, Christian history, and interpretation.

There are two primary aspects to whitewashed Christianity: Historical Whitewashing and Class Whitewashing.

Historical Whitewashing occurs when practically all biblical characters are presented as white men and women in literature, from children's books to textbooks in seminaries and places dedicated to Christian education. This also occurs when nearly every Church father is presented as a white man, despite their African heritage, yet, the same isn't done when someone is of European heritage. It's assumed that Europeans are white and they are presented as such in literature and art, but the same isn't done for their African counterparts. When it comes to someone who has done something significant as it relates to hermeneutics, homiletics, theology, education, and/or scholarship, if the person is from Africa, historians for centuries have comfortably assumed—or worse— rewritten history to present them as white. Athanasius, historically known as the "Black Dwarf" based on his dark skin and short stature, is presented as a white man resembling Saint Nicholas (the nickname Black Dwarf is debated as the author who claims this didn't provide a citation, but Dr. Justo Gonzales does confirm Athanasius being called Black in a derogatory

The Whitewashing of Christianity

manner and having darker skin).[11] This is not only dishonest, it's diabolical. It undermines the faith we claim when we comfortably present a God who is homogenous in whom he uses, and it undermines our claim to be committed to truth. As Christians, we vow to be honest and fair, yet we'll rewrite truth when the truth is that most of Christian history involves people of color.

Class Whitewashing occurs when we relegate people of color in Scripture and history to that of slaves almost exclusively. This is most clearly seen in how scholars present the Cushites in Scripture. A people known for archery, leadership, and diligence are presented as slaves even though they are mentioned more than any other group in the Old Testament in terms of variation.[12] Why would we present an African tribe hundreds of years before the antebellum South as slaves with nothing to contribute but manual labor? Why would this be done without sources in many cases? This is indicative of a subconscious or conscious racial bias that may be unintentional, but also unavoidable because, in most cases, it is indeed intentional. It is inadequate scholarship, and it exposes that African and other ethnic contributions to faith, scholarship, and history are viewed as insignificant and not worthy of scholarly effort or precision.

Historic and Class Whitewashing have contributed to the false narrative that Christianity is a white man's religion wherein God only used white people in Scripture, and it asserts that only white scholars can determine what's scholarly, accurate, and historical for the world to consume. It's dangerous and contributes to lostness by creating opponents to Christianity unnecessarily because it presents our God as one who is guilty of the sin of partiality because, functionally speaking, Black people didn't contribute anything significant to theological and cultural change except Harriet Tubman, the Civil Rights Movements, and a few athletes. While false, it's presented as truth and this is what the world sees: A God who's white, committed to an agenda of salvation that includes all, but only places white people at the helm of leadership, influence, innovation, intelligence and revival.

The hashtag #OscarsSoWhite brought to the forefront decade-long issues, like the fact that 2016 was the second time in 20 years that the nominations list featured exclusively white actors. If one were to go back a little further, they

---

11   Simonetta Carr, *More on The Black Dwarf* http://simonetta-carr.blogspot.com/search?q=black+dwarf, June 2011.

12   J. Daniel Hays, *Racial Bias in the Academy Still?* (Ouachita Baptist University), 316.

would find out that this was the fifth time in 30 years that this has happened. And between the years 1927 and 2012, a staggering 99 percent of women who have won "Best Actress" have been white, and the same is true for 91 percent of men who have won "Best Actor." Not to mention, the fact that 94 percent of voting members are white, which isn't a glaring endorsement of diverse perspectives and appreciation being at the decision-making table.

That's Hollywood. What does that have to do with faith and Christian history? Historically, like the Oscars, white people (namely white men) have been the only ones at the table to determine what is written in history. These men are given free rein to decide what is scholarly, how people looked historically, and they have even gone so far as rewriting history to make it fit a white narrative as it relates to the Christian faith. In other words, the people determining who's significant hasn't been left up to history, but rather how white men have viewed and interpreted history. This has led to and propagated an incomplete narrative to a faith that's filled with people from all backgrounds that have contributed to its expansion, yet this aspect of history is hidden to generations who view Christianity as a monolithic religion based on how it continues to be presented in literature and art.

Whitewashing when not confronted exacts the same vitriol as white supremacy does in our society because, in many ways, whitewashing is an extension of white supremacy. White supremacy is the fanaticism and obsession of "whiteness" which leads to the dehumanization, degradation, and disenfranchisement of those not considered "white," thus making whiteness the standard for all other people groups. This false narrative causes many to embrace an inaccurate biblical framework, which presents false depictions of Eurocentric Bible figures as fact without remorse or repentance. This is why whitewashing is not something that should be ignored but must be confronted with truth and love.

My hope is not simply to expose, but to unify. This is why we must first look at the **hidden past** that whitewashing has created a past that is filled with African church fathers, theologians, monks, and martyrs that have been ignored. Secondly, we'll look at a **hurtful present**, one where whitewashing has infected and affected how people view the Christian faith and how some have responded in iniquitous ways. Lastly, we'll look at a **hopeful future** and how we can move forward together with loving honesty and embrace an accurate narrative which will empower us to move forward in unity and strength because **reconciliation is impossible without confrontation.**

The Whitewashing of Christianity

Paul makes this clear when he confronts Peter in Galatians 2. Peter acted one way around Jewish people and another way around Gentile (non-Jewish) people. He distanced himself from people made in God's image when his Jewish friend showed up. Peter's behavior was so detrimental and unbecoming of someone who claims faith in Christ that he (Paul) had to oppose him to his face in front of others. Paul didn't go behind Peter's back, nor did he ask someone else what they thought about Peter's behavior; he approached him directly and firmly. Something that shouldn't be overlooked is the fact that **a Jewish man confronted another Jewish man on his partiality and prejudice**. What made him do that? One of the reasons was the diverse nature of the team sent with him when he was commissioned for ministry:

- Antioch is where we hear the term Christian used for the first time (Acts 11:26).
- The missionaries that were sent from Antioch were diverse: Barnabas—Jew of the diaspora, Simeon called Niger—most likely African, Lucius of Cyrene—Lucius was a Cyrenian Jew, like John Mark who wrote Mark (don't miss this, an African man wrote the gospel of Mark), Manaen—friend of Herod the Tetrarch and Paul—Jewish (Acts 13:1-3).
- What would make Paul oppose Peter to his face? What would make him go from standing with him in Jerusalem (Galatians 1:18), to standing against him in Antioch (Galatians 2:11)? Duplicity in behavior and deviation from the gospel, which Paul will say later.

If the authenticity of the gospel is to be upheld and unity is to be achieved, you and I can't shy away from confrontation. We must not be afraid of **intra-racial** confrontation as in Galatians we see Jew-on-Jew confrontation. We must see and apply intra-racial confrontation by confronting people within our racial group about prejudice and whitewashing.

We must confront a one-sided narrative of the Christian faith by admitting that whitewashing is indeed a thing: a destructive ideology that must be confronted with the gospel. We must have honest conversations about how whitewashing continues when churches, seminaries, publishers and productions almost exclusively use white people to represent people of Scripture. We must change the imagery used in books from as early as school-aged children to institutions of higher learning and we must change the narrative from the pulpit, pastors of all colors must not passively contribute to whitewashing with displaying white images throughout their churches and only highlighting the accomplishments and contributions of white people in history. In essence, we must stop ignoring the Black and brown presence in Scripture and throughout the world which has played an integral part in God's plan of redemption. As we confront the divisive and destructive nature of whitewashing with truth, we're then given a firm foundation toward authentic unity and glorifying God, who welcomes everyone to His table by grace and through faith. Dr. Vince Bantu addresses the need to reclaim the often forgotten and ignored aspects of African Christianity, and in order to do this, we must trace our history long before the slave trade, colonialism and whitewashing.

> "We… have to go back and reeducate our people and our community… and also to help people understand the last five centuries that we have experienced are not the beginning of the story… if someone was only to look at the last five centuries, then it (Christianity) would seem like it's the white man's religion and it's a mechanism of oppression. When you go back to the early church, roughly 2000 years ago, you find out that Christianity was growing in Africa before it was ever growing in Europe. When Europeans were still worshipping Oden and Thor, African Christians in Egypt, North African Africa, Ethiopia, and Nubia were worshipping Jesus as Lord and Savior before Islam even existed."[13]

The primary issue of whitewashing isn't the inclusion of white people, but rather the exclusion of Black and brown people.

Discussion Questions

1. How can addressing whitewashing foster unity?
2. How have you seen Christianity whitewashed in your own experience?

---

13 Vince Bantu, *"Is Christianity a White Man's Religion?"*, [audio podcast] retrieved from http://www.jude3project.com/podcast/whitemansreligion?rq=vince%2-bantu. The Jude 3 Project June 2016.

The Whitewashing of Christianity

3. What are some of the dangers of presenting a one-sided narrative of history?
4. What are some ways to stop your church, organization or school from presenting a whitewashed version of Christianity?
5. What makes it hard for people to see the ways Christianity has been whitewashed?
6. What work needs to be done in your own heart based on what you have learned?

2

White Jesus

Jesus was a white man, too.
— MEGYN KELLY

IT WAS ALMOST TOO FUNNY to be real. I mean, she didn't say that and mean it, did she? In 2013, then-Fox-news-anchor Megyn Kelly responded to a woman by the name of Aisha Harris who contended that Santa should not be presented as white. Harris concluded that, in order to spare children of color from the insecurity that stems from presenting Santa as white, Santa should be presented as a penguin. That's right, a penguin. But what baffled me wasn't Ms. Harris' presentation, but rather Kelly's assurance that Jesus was, and is, a white man. The Sphenisciformes origin of the fictitious man who is omnipresent and can fit through any chimney is more probable than a Middle Eastern Jew from Bethlehem with four out of five women mentioned in his genealogy being of Hamitic descent (Matthew 1:1-6) being a blond-haired, blue-eyed white man. We can easily point to Jesus' Jewishness to realize that he was a brown-skinned Middle Eastern man, most likely with curly hair.[14] Yet, Kelly spoke with a confidence and dismissiveness that is both harmful and outrageous, but not surprising:

---

14 Sarah Pruitt, *The Ongoing Mystery of Jesus's Face*, https://www.history.com/news/what-didjesus-look-like, March 2019.

The Whitewashing of Christianity

"You know, I've given her, her due. Just because it makes you feel uncomfortable doesn't mean it has to change," Kelly said. "Jesus was a white man, too. It's like we have, he's a historical figure that's a verifiable fact, as is Santa. I just want kids to know that. How do you revise it in the middle of the legacy in the story and change Santa from white to Black?"[15]

I agree with Megyn; just because it makes you uncomfortable doesn't mean it has to change. Jesus wasn't white, and that makes many people uncomfortable, but it doesn't change the fact that, as a Middle Eastern Jew, the Lord Yeshua had melanin in his skin. I also think that even if it makes you uncomfortable, if change is true, then change must be something that we embrace. We must change the historical notion that Jesus was a white man. This is historically, geographically, and biblically inaccurate, yet Megyn and millions of evangelicals aren't willing to be uncomfortable when it comes to the myth that Jesus was a white man. Whiteness is where whitewashing Christianity starts because it presents whiteness as superior and eventually assumes that God in the flesh was a white man, while ignoring the biblical record of his Jewish ethnicity. Before looking at Jesus' ethnicity, it's vital that we examine Eurocentrism, ethnocentrism, race and racism.

Eurocentrism

To understand whitewashing and how it leads to painting the Bible white, we must understand Eurocentrism. Oftentimes, when the idea of ethnocentrism is broached, the focus is on how Blacks need to place Christ at the center of their identity and not their Blackness, this is true, but I rarely hear how Eurocentrism needs the same attention because it's equally as dangerous and more prevalent in America.

Eurocentrism is placing the experience, culture, and philosophy of people of European descent at the center of personal understanding and culture.[16] Essentially, it's making whiteness universal. Eurocentrism is a particular kind of ethnocentrism that elevates and, in most cases, deifies whiteness based on the false belief

---

15 Hadas Gold, *"Megyn Kelly: Jesus and Santa were white."* https://www.politico.com/blogs/media/2013/12/megyn-kelly-jesus-and-santa-were-white-179491, Politico December 2013.

16 Skot Welch, *Plantation Jesus*, (Herald Press 2013), 57.

that whites are superior and other races are inferior. This is what led (past tense) and leads (present tense) to the whitewashing of the Christian faith and painting it with one broad stroke and contributes to lostness as people look at God as homogenous in whom he uses in his redemptive plan. This isn't just a race issue, it's a soul issue. The world sees our faith as monocultural and Christians should care about that. The truth is when it comes to race, while we all may not share the same color (Psalms 139:14), our varying colors are an expression of God's creative genius, and while our colors differ, we do all share the same ancestry:

> Acts 17:26 (CSB)
>
> 26 From one man he has made every nationality to live over the whole earth and has determined their appointed times and the boundaries of where they live. This means that the very notion of racial superiority is foolish.

Eurocentrism not only functions as if white is better, it makes white the default race of nearly all significant contributions to every field of study and influence.[17]

White Is Better Myth

The idea of whiteness being superior to all other races has its roots in the sin of racism (partiality). Typically, when racism is addressed it's dismissed by the phrase, "racism isn't a skin problem, it's a sin problem." Agreed, but sin has names like murder, stealing, cheating and racism. Even though there is truth to this phrase, it fails to acknowledge the importance of identifying a sin by name. Naming a sin by its specific name doesn't eliminate the validity of it being an issue of internal sin. Racism has been defined in many ways. In his book, *The Color of Compromise*, Jemar Tisby refers to Beverly Daniel Tatum's definition of racism as a system of oppression based on race,[18] while others say that racism is simply *prejudice plus power*. I'm in favor of a merger of the two: racism is a systematic and/or individual oppression of one group for the preservation of the perceived dominant group, primarily based on race but can also include class and is rooted in sin. Racism is

---

17 Skot Welch, *Plantation Jesus*, (Herald Press 2013), 57.
18 Beverly Daniel Tatum, *Why Are All the Black Kids Sitting Together in the Cafeteria? And other Conversations about Race* (New York: Basic Books 1997).

the sin of partiality or favoritism (James 2:9) and hatred for humanity (1 John 4:20). When we think of race, it's vital to think of it on a spectrum to avoid loosely labeling everyone a racist when there could be other factors that are applicable.

- Racial Ignorance
- Racial Indifference
- Racial Insensitivity
- Racism

Race Spectrum

When we think of race, it's vital to think of it on a spectrum to avoid loosely labeling everyone a racist when there could be other factors that are applicable.

Racial Ignorance—don't know

Racial ignorance deals with proximity and experience. Since the Civil Rights Act of 1964, laws have changed, but not much in terms of interracial relations. Even amongst Christians, we're functionally integrated, but very much still relationally isolated and segregated as it relates to our social, professional, and worship experiences. In other words, we're still living, schooling, and worshipping in homogenous settings even though we are "free" to do otherwise. This means that our interaction with each other is often event-driven: work, sporting events, and maybe a worship gathering. Generally speaking, Black people don't have much of a choice of interacting with white people in America while, generally speaking, whites have options as it relates to who they interact with interpersonally. Black people make up around 13 percent of the U.S. population and aren't readily afforded relational options.[19] When we stay in homogenous settings, we forsake experiences that could destroy our assumptions and enhance our understanding; thus, racial ignorance continues to run rampant because we don't know each other. And we don't know each other because we're not in relationships with each other, and the interactions we do have rarely go beneath surface-level cordiality. If we're not in authentic relationships, we don't know what's offensive, or what our individual and collective experiences are, so we forfeit the opportunity for real understanding and growth with each other. Racial ignorance isn't willful in most cases, but it isn't any less dangerous when it comes to how one view can affect an individual or an entire group of people.

Racial Indifference—don't care

While racial ignorance is not knowing, racial indifference is not caring. This can be summed up by those who view race as an unnecessary discussion topic or people who refuse to cross the cultural aisle. The people who adopt this attitude are likely to say, "You live your life and I'll live mine." This is also seen in how many respond to racial issues in order to deflect from having to deal with it. Skot Welch and Rick Wilson address this in their book, *Plantation Jesus*. They address some of the common responses of those that I would say fall under the racially indifferent crowd. This may sound familiar if you're trying to converse with or

---

19   Kristen Bialik, *5 Facts About Black Americans* https://www.pewresearch.org/fact-tank/2018/02/22/5-facts-about-blacks-in-the-u-s/, February 2018.

The Whitewashing of Christianity

educate someone about the experience of Black and brown people in America and abroad. Tell me if this sounds familiar: "I never owned a slave. Slavery is in the Bible, so it has to be right. Some people were nice to their slaves," and my personal favorite: "I don't see color. I see people." These people assume that colorblindness equals godliness. The aforementioned are common responses of people who may or may not care about the injustices that others endure because, frankly, it doesn't affect them. They care only if it hits home or if there are stats to convince them. One person being affected isn't enough; it must be systemic, and systemic to them is usually subjective. When one is racially indifferent, it's easy to not care about the issues that affect others, which is why whitewashing is a non-issue for them. In *Divided by Faith: Evangelical Religion and the Problem of Race in America*, Michael Emmerson addresses how many white evangelicals' social worlds are homogenous and have very few interracial contacts. He interviewed many white evangelicals and out of those interviewed, most of them lived in worlds that were 90 percent white in their daily experience. Many acknowledged being unexposed to racial diversity and insulated in their own small world, yet still felt that they understood the issue with Black people while not having close interactions with Black people. Emmerson says that, according to many of the white evangelicals interviewed, the issue with Black people was that Black people were being misled by Black leaders. These said leaders had an ax to grind and wanted to maintain the problem because they made a living from it. And because Black leaders were stuck in the past, Black people are taught to mistrust white people.[20] It's interesting that they had the temerity and unmitigated gall to diagnose Black people when most of them weren't around Black people. In fact, a 2013 survey by the Public Religion Research Institute found that the social networks of white Americans are 91 percent white and that "fully three-quarters (75 percent) of whites have entirely white social networks without any minority presence."[21] This mindset is a display of racial indifference and leads to the next category: racial insensitivity.

---

20 Michael Emmerson, *Divided by Faith: Evangelical Religion and the Problem of Race in America*, (Oxford University Press, 2000), 81-82.

21 Christopher Ingram, "*Three Quarters of Whites Don't Have Any Non-White Friends*," Washington Post, August 25, 2014, www.washingtonpost.com/news/wonk/wp/2014/08/25/three-quarters-of-whites-dont-have-any-non-white-friends/?utm_term=.b994b0930aa1.

Racial Insensitivity—careless

Former President Donald Trump has demonstrated, at a minimum, consistent racial insensitivity as he lumped Mexicans as rapists, drug dealers, and disease-carrying people that need to be kept from crossing the border. He also ranted about "shithole" African countries all the while claiming that, "Two Corinthians" is his favorite verse on love when speaking at Liberty University (1 Corinthians 13).[22] Too many white evangelicals and politicians can say racially charged and insensitive things and simply dismiss it by saying, "I'm not racist." They truly think that that's enough to absolve them of their harmful statements. Racially insensitive people don't care who they offend or hurt because it's their First Amendment right. They appeal more to the law than they do Scripture, even if they claim Christianity as their theological home. What's worse is when people with this attitude who claim to be followers of Christ fail to display the great commandment of love of God and love of neighbor (Matthew 22:36-40). Isn't the greatest commandment to love your neighbor as yourself (Mark 12:31)? I guess the question is, *Who's my neighbor?* For a lot of white evangelicals, their neighbor can be Black, but they will only grant them love if they agree with their views on race, justice, and the Bible. Oftentimes this leads to racial habits that demean and devalue others when not checked. As Eddie Glaude writes, our racial habits are "the ways we live the belief that white people are valued more than others. They are the things we do, without thinking, that sustain the value gap. They range from the snap judgments we make about Black people that rely on stereotypes to the ways we think about race that we get from living within our respective communities."[23] This typically isn't biblical Christianity, but rather secular conservatism presented as faithfulness to God. In reality, it's the deification of patriotism. Racial insensitivity is one hair strand away from racism, and, to be clear, it is sinful because it breaks the greatest commandment and ignores what Paul says about placing the needs and cares of others above your own (Philippians 2:3).

---

22 Jessica Taylor, *Citing 'Two Corinthians,' Trump Struggles To Make The Sale To Evangelicals* https://www.npr.org/2016/01/18/463528847/citing-two-corinthians-trump-struggles-to-make-the-sale-to-evangelicals January 2016.

23 Eddie S. Glaude, *Democracy in Black*, (New York: Crown Publishers, 2016), 55.

The Whitewashing of Christianity

Racism—willful hatred

This is willful hatred of an entire group of people based on race; it's the sin of partiality (James 2:1-13). Many evangelicals never think to look within to recognize racism or xenophobia in their hearts. This is because they've internally raised the bar of racism so high that they can never reach it and therefore never have to look within to confront themselves. They can simply say, "I'm not racist. I've never used the n-word." The reality is that believers should actively be trying to work against racism because *racism is a sin against humanity and the God of humanity.*

For centuries, there has been a racial divide about racism because in most cases no one listens. Oftentimes, whites assume victimization without exploring the reality that there are actual victims. Additionally, the assumption is that Black people want to make everything about race, while not taking into account that Blacks are forced to talk about and address it when we experience racial profiling, or our children are told by white children that their parents don't like Black people. Situations that many Blacks experience yearly aren't to be addressed, and when we speak against being dehumanized, we are labeled victimizers. Perhaps, whites with this assertion should look in the mirror and see that a response like that is both inhumane and barbaric, but since the label of victim is often given without knowing or caring to know individual stories, hatred persists, and is supported through the neglect of evangelicals who remain both willfully silent and willfully aloof. They assume that because none of their "Black friends" are experiencing what others are that their "Black friends'" experience is the universal Black experience. Sadly, it doesn't stop there. Many evangelicals seem to have embraced the myth that talking about or preaching against racism is somehow a distraction from the gospel. Dr. Esau McCaulley addresses this:

> Today, there are a host of issues clamoring for the attention of this generation. If a pastor commented on every single event, little else would be done on Sunday. Although the news cycle shouldn't overcome the liturgical cycle of the church, nonetheless, our people need theological resources to think through these issues. Both majority white and majority Black and brown churches need to know in no uncertain terms where the church stands on racism and white supremacy. And majority white churches need opportunities to discuss and repent of the myths they might harbor about Black and

brown people. Pastors also need to educate themselves. I have often found that the most superficial discussions of race occur among my white Christian friends, who repeat platitudes that are deeply offensive and historically inaccurate. Accordingly, I am exhorting pastors and other leaders to apply the truths of the gospel to the issues of the day and to call their congregants to higher ground.[24]

Dr. McCaulley exposes both a cultural and scriptural hole. Paul can confront Peter, but many evangelicals simply don't want to be confronted, and look for spaces where they won't be confronted. The reality is that they can find spaces; homogeneous spaces where these issues aren't addressed, and they can live with the illusion that racism no longer exists, or that since things "aren't as bad," that is good enough. Willful ignorance is as dangerous as willful hatred, which is why racism must be confronted. While it may not be the subject every Sunday, it shouldn't be avoided every Sunday, either.

How do we combat racial ignorance, indifference, insensitivity and racism? James, Yeshua's half-brother, addresses this in his letter:

James 2:1

1 My brothers and sisters, do not show favoritism as you hold on to the faith in our glorious Lord Jesus Christ.

James is clear in this verse that favoritism dishonors God and demeans mercy. Favoritism?

Favoritism is the Greek word *prosopolempsia*, and it means to turn face or to lift up someone's face; it carries the idea of judging based on appearance.[25] Christians are supposed to be unstained by the world by not valuing people the way the world does. While America claims to be more and more progressive and welcoming, the reality is we still base a person's value externally: looks, income, weight,

---

24 Esau McCaulley, *Preaching Against Racism is Not a Distraction from the Gospel* https://www.christianitytoday.com/pastors/2019/august-web-exclusives/racism-preachingagainst-not-distraction-from-gospel.htl, August 2019.

25 Sermon Index: *Partiality* https://www.sermonindex.net/modules/articles/index.php?view=article&aid=34571, accessed March 2021.

The Whitewashing of Christianity

and in many cases, race. This is done both by people who hold a spiritual view and those that don't. External judgment is done universally.

If James had to deal with this during his day, we must ask, how does favoritism dishonor God? Matthew 15:24 and John 4:22 are where Yeshua tells a Canaanite woman that He's been sent to the lost sheep of Israel and a Samaritan woman that salvation is from the Jews. These verses are used by some groups like orthodox Jews and the Hebrew Israelites to assume that salvation is for the Jews only. In Jeremiah 50:6, God calls Israel His people and "lost sheep." The Messiah, spoken of throughout the Old Testament, was seen as the one who would gather these "lost sheep" (Ezekiel 34:23-24; Micah 5:4-5). Jesus presenting Himself as a shepherd to Israel is simply Him claiming to be the fulfillment of Messianic prophecy, not a God who excludes people based on ethnicity or nationality (Mark 6:34, 14:27; John 10:11-16; see also Hebrews 13:20; 1 Peter 5:4).

Yeshua's words to the Canaanite woman also show an awareness of Israel's place in God's plan of salvation. God revealed through Moses that the children of Israel were "a holy people to the LORD ... chosen ... a special treasure above all the peoples on the face of the earth" (Deuteronomy 7:6). It was through the Jews that God issued His Law, preserved His Word, and sent His Son, but as Paul said, the gospel is first to the Jew and also for the Greek (Romans 1:16). We're made in the image of a God who has no favorites because His creation is sinful and in need of salvation and He's the Savior. The playing field is level at the foot of the cross, so no one can look down on someone, because we're all sinners in need of grace. Paul echoes James' sentiments:

Romans 2:6-11

6 He will repay each one according to his works: 7 eternal life to those who by persistence in doing good seek glory, honor, and immortality; 8 but wrath and anger to those who are self-seeking and disobey the truth while obeying unrighteousness. 9 There will be affliction and distress for every human being who does evil, first to the Jew, and also to the Greek; 10 but glory, honor, and peace for everyone who does what is good, first to the Jew, and also to the Greek. 11 For there is no favoritism with God.

Notice how James connects holding on to the faith not by showing favoritism, but instead by seeking to glorify the Lord Jesus Christ, and Paul does the same. We do this by seeing the image of God in ALL people. When we devalue people by judging them externally, we're acting like we're not recipients of mercy ourselves missing the entire point of redemption. James didn't simply say, don't show favoritism, he gave a few specific instances and examples to show what it looks like:

> James 2:2-5
>
> 2 For if someone comes into your meeting wearing a gold ring and dressed in fine clothes, and a poor person dressed in filthy clothes also comes in, 3 if you look with favor on the one wearing the fine clothes and say, "Sit here in a good place," and yet you say to the poor person, "Stand over there," or "Sit here on the floor by my footstool," 4 haven't you made distinctions among yourselves and become judges with evil thoughts? 5 Listen, my dear brothers and sisters: Didn't God choose the poor in this world to be rich in faith and heirs of the kingdom that he has promised to those who love him?

James is calling out their hypocrisy regarding how they treat people who come to their gathering. The bigger point is that we're all poor, which is a necessity when it comes to eternity (James 2:4).

> Matthew 5:3
>
> 3 "Blessed are the poor in spirit, for the kingdom of heaven is theirs.

We're blessed when we realize our spiritual poverty and need of salvation. If we realize this it'd be impossible to look down on anyone, especially based on what we see externally.

- Class—we're not to judge people based on economic status, whether rich or poor, in fact, we're supposed to remember our spiritual poverty and that it's only through Christ that we're made spiritually rich.
- Race—this has been one of the most consistent in the church, sadly. Jemar Tisby wrote an excellent book that addresses this called *The Color of Compromise*, and he says this: "The failure of many Christians in the South and across the nation to decisively oppose the racism in their families,

The Whitewashing of Christianity

communities, and even in their own churches provided fertile soil for the seeds of hatred to grow. The refusal to act in the midst of injustice is itself an act of injustice. Indifference to oppression perpetuates oppression."[26] This still exists today when we judge and separate based on preferences and prejudices against people who bear God's image.

- Gender—many people today view the Bible as misogynistic, which is the wrong label because misogyny means to hate women. While the Bible affirms roles, it never demeans women, which is one of the reasons Jesus presented Himself to women first when He resurrected. While the Bible doesn't do it, the Bible does record men in particular demeaning women simply for being women. Toxic masculinity shouldn't be celebrated; it should be shunned.
- Age—Scripture consistently assumes generational diversity within the church. It's important that we never associate usage and value with age.

In order to avoid operating in racial ignorance, indifference, insensitivity and racism, we should ask ourselves:

1. Do I judge based on external appearances?
2. Have my experiences caused me to wrongly judge an entire group of people?
3. Am I comfortable with internal prejudice as long as I don't say it?
4. Do I value people based on their contribution or their Creator?

Pharaoh gives us a framework of the mechanics of oppression in his dealings with the Israelites: people of an array of colors oppressed for their beliefs by another group of color. While Pharaoh's oppression wasn't based on race, he gives us a framework for how oppression and partiality work.

Exodus 1:9-10:

And he said to his people, "Behold, the people of Israel are too many and too mighty for us. 10 Come, let us deal shrewdly with them, lest they multiply, and, if war breaks out, they join our enemies and fight against us and escape from the land."

---

26 Jemar Tisby, *The Color of Compromise: The Truth about the American Church's Complicity in Racism*, (Zondervan, Grand Rapids, MI 2019), 15.

Notice how Pharaoh presents the people of Israel to his constituents:

- They are (the Jews) a threat numerically and structurally.
- They (the Jews) will overtake us, so we must oppress them.
- We (Egyptians) must see them as a threat (socially and economically) to justify our oppressive acts.
- They are not worthy to be treated as humans. They are a commodity (Exodus 5:6-9).
- Goal: **Control** and **Domination**.

It's interesting that white supremacists have used the same tactics in order to justify their oppressive acts against Black and brown people throughout history.

- They are (Black people) a threat to us numerically and structurally, so we must move them from their native land.
- They (Black people) will overtake us and steal our women, so we must enslave them.
- We (white people) must see them as a threat to civilization and devoid of souls in order to justify our oppressive acts.
- They are (Black people) incapable of salvation, so making them slaves in perpetuity is actually doing them a favor.
- German supremacists deployed the same tactics in their oppression of Jewish people, too.

The roots of white supremacy are consistent with Pharaoh's tactics of oppression and superiority. Racism is not unique to the United States nor to the modern world as many would assert. In many ways, racism has its roots in Greco-Roman philosophy, literature, and culture—or Romanitas. Philosophers who laid the foundation of what would become Roman identity argued for social hegemony rooted in biological determinism. Roman authors also made it plain that a central aspect of determining social superiority and inferiority was skin color: "Let the straight-legged man laugh at the club-footed, the white man at the Black man."[27] To understand the roots of the white superiority myth throughout history, we

---

27 Juvenal Satire II, *Moralists without Morals*, ed. G.G. Ramsay (London: William Heinemann, 1918), 19.

The Whitewashing of Christianity

must look no further than the Roman historian, Publius Cornelius Tacitus, and his work *Germania*. This is the origin of what Kelly Brown Douglas calls the Anglo-Saxon Myth.[28] In *Germania*, Tacitus describes Germanic tribes as aboriginal people "free from the taint of intermarriage." In other words, he purported that whites were pure and superior, and the source of their superiority was in their blood.[29] Tacitus' perspective on human value and purity spread rapidly, and his views weren't restricted to Rome.[30] In fact, Thomas Jefferson referenced him in a letter to his granddaughter, heralding him as "the first writer of the world without exception." He not only embraced Tacitus' writings, but his ideology as well, which informed his view of white people as superior and others as inferior. Jefferson saw himself and other Anglo-Saxons as chosen by God to implement systems of government, and he also considered Americans to be the New Israelites. To be clear, in Jefferson's eyes, white Americans were the new Israelites. Douglas references John Adams' letter to his wife in which he says, "Mr. Jefferson proposed. The Children of Israel in the Wilderness, led by a Cloud by day, and a Pillar of fire by night, and on the other Side Hengist and Horsa, the Saxon Chiefs, from whom we claim the Honour of being descended and who political principles and Form of Government We have assumed."[31] Notice how Jefferson uses the ideology of Tacitus to make the original Hebrew people Anglo-Saxons? This is the historic pattern of white supremacy and whitewashing. If God's chosen people are exclusively white, then all others must be inferior and even cursed, which many would assert. This should come as no surprise from a man who revised the Gospel to fit his commitment to enlightenment ideologies in what was called, *The Life and Morals of Jesus of Nazareth*.[32]

What Tacitus, Jefferson, many puritans, many missionaries, and scholars have intentionally ignored is the overwhelming presence of diversity in the Bible. But this is the point—in order for whitewashing to continue, the Black and brown

---

28   Kelly Brown Douglas, *Stand Your Ground*, (Orbis Books, 2015), 4.
29   Kelly Brown Douglas, *Stand Your Ground*, (Orbis Books, 2015), 6.
30   Reginald Horsman, *Race and Manifest: Destiny The Origins of American Racial Anglo-Saxonism*, (Cambridge, MA: Harvard University Press, 1981).
31   Kelly Brown Douglas, *Stand Your Ground*, (Orbis Books, 2015), 13.
32   Thomas Jefferson, Harry R. Rubenstein, Barbara Clark Smith, and Janice Stagnitto Ellis, *The Jefferson Bible: The Life and Morals of Jesus of Nazareth*, (Washington, DC Smithsonian Books 2011).

presence in Scripture must be ignored in order to perpetuate a false narrative. Whitewashing opened the door for artistically making Adam and Eve, Abraham, Moses, David, Ruth, Mary, and—of course—Jesus white. There are countless examples of people of color in Scripture that were connected to Jesus' earthly lineage. We must ask, why isn't this highlighted?

A Broad White Stroke

One of whitewashing's biggest supporters has been art, specifically white artists, from children's books that illustrate just about everyone in Scripture as white to paintings like Michelangelo's painting on the ceiling of the Sistine Chapel that present God and Adam and Eve as all white, artists have historically been monolithic in their presentation of people in Scripture. However, none stands out more to me than the 1956 movie The Ten Commandments. This movie presented Charlton Heston as Moses and tons of other white people as the Egyptians and the Hebrew people. I remember watching the movie and wondering where did all the Africans go? Pharaoh was white, his African queen was white, and Moses, Joshua, and Aaron were all white. This is what people of color are referring to when they talk about unfair, and, in this case, unbiblical underrepresentation of people of color as it relates to the Christian faith. It's actually impossible to read the Bible and think that everyone in it is of European descent, yet this truth has been ignored in art, literature, and film for years. Thankfully, the Bible presents an authentic reality of God including and using people of color for His divine plan.

Biblical Israel Was Not Ethnically Monolithic

In order to whitewash the Bible, scholars consistently whitewash the Jewish people. If we study Scripture and geography using the markers of language, land, faith, clothing, appearance, and ancestral origins, we can clearly see that the ancient people primarily consist of four major ethnic groups:

1. The Cushites (Black Africans that resided along the Nile River). Often referred to as Nubians or Ethiopians (we'll discuss the Cushites and how they've been handled more in Chapter 5: Whitewashing Africa).
2. The Egyptians (north African and Asiatic).

3. Asiatic also referred to as Semites (including Israelites, Canaanites, Amorites, Arameans, etc.).
4. Indo-Europeans (Hittites and Philistines).[33]

Most of the people that made ethnic Israel using the aforementioned markers would be considered Black and brown primarily. Additionally, Genesis 10 primarily mentions people of color as the ancient peoples.[34]

Adam and Eve

The Garden of Eden was described in Genesis as having four rivers: Pishon, Gihon, Tigris, and Euphrates (Genesis 2:11-14). Today, these rivers would be near the borders of Eastern Sudan, Ethiopia, and Eritrea. When we think about geography and how it's used to denote historic ethnicity, it's vital to understand that the historic birthplace of humanity would be between Iraq and Africa, not Europe as presented. While we don't have a smoking gun to definitively make them Black, the biblical evidence leans more towards them as people of color, and this shouldn't be ignored.

Abraham

Abraham didn't only have children with Sarah; he also had children with Hagar and Keturah (Genesis 25:1), both from African (Hamitic) tribes. This means that Abraham would not have had European lineage, but a Jewish and African lineage, and this should be celebrated.

Moses

Moses was mistaken for an Egyptian in Scripture (Exodus 2:19). This means that he looked like an Egyptian and most likely spoke their language, being that he was raised in an Egyptian household and taught Egyptian customs. It's amazing that scholars would think that a white man would easily blend in with Egyptians

---

[33] Russell Moore, *The Gospel Life: The Gospel & Racial Reconciliation*, (B&H Nashville, TN 2016), 11.
[34] ibid.

without Pharaoh or any of his men noticing a distinction between him and the rest of the Egyptians.

Jewish historian Flavius Josephus, makes it clear that the Egyptians saw Moses as one of their own, based on how he looked and he recounts how Moses was divinely protected:

> When he was three years old as for his beauty there was nobody so unpolite as when they saw Moses were not greatly surprised at the beauty of his countenance [face]. For the beauty of the child was so remarkable and natural to him on many accounts it detained spectators, and made them stay longer to look upon him. Thermuthis, therefore, perceiving him to be so remarkable a child, adopted him for her own son, having no child of her own. And when one time she carried Moses to her father, she showed him to him; and said she thought to make him her father's successor, and said unto him, "I have brought up a child who is of a divine form, and a generous mind; and as I received him from the bounty of the river, in a wonderful manner, I thought it proper to adopt him for my own son and the heir of thy kingdom. And when she had said this she put the infant into her father's hands; so he took him, and hugged him close to his breast; and on his daughter's account, in a pleasant way, put his diadem [crown] upon his head; but Moses threw it down to the ground, and in a puerile mood he wreathed it round, and trod [stomped] upon it with his feet; Then the sacred scribe saw this he, the same scribe who foretold that his nativity would bring the dominion of that kingdom low, made a violent attempt to kill him; and crying out in a frightful manner, he said, "This O, king! This child is he of who God foretold, that if we kill him we shall be in no danger; he himself affords an attestation to the prediction of the same thing, by his trampling upon thy government, and treading upon the diadem, but Thermuthis prevented him, and snatched the child away. And the king was not hasty to slay him, God himself, whose providence protected Moses, inclining the king to spare him. He was then educated with great care. [35]

---

35   Flavius Josephus, *The Works of Josephus Complete and Unabridged*, book 2 chapter 10, 251-253.

Moses blended in and was assumed to be one of them because he looked like an Egyptian and because of his adopted mother. If Moses and the original Jews were white, wouldn't Moses have been killed based on the decree Pharaoh made (Exodus 1:16, 22) because it would have been evident that he was not one of them? Yet, facts like this are ignored because remember, whitewashing is deliberate in painting the Bible with one broad, white stroke.

Moses' Melanin Mrs.

Moses married a Cushite woman (Numbers 12:1). Many have used this verse to imply that because Moses married a dark-skinned Black woman, that infers that Moses was white. For instance, in an article printed in 2010 titled, Did Moses Marry a Black Woman? John Piper says,

> "Consider this possibility. In God's anger at Miriam, Moses' sister, God says in effect, 'You like being light-skinned Miriam? I'll make you light-skinned.' So we read, 'When the cloud removed from over the tent, behold, Miriam was leprous, like snow' (Numbers 12:10)."

Notice how Piper infers that Miriam is light-skinned and her punishment is to become more light-skinned.[36] If an assumption of white or lighter skin is made based on the darkness of his wife, why isn't the same assumption applied to the overwhelming biblical evidence that suggests most of the presence in Scripture is people of color from Africa and the Middle East? What's missed here is the reality of colorism. *Colorism* is discrimination based on skin color, also known as shadeism, and is a form of prejudice or discrimination in which people are treated differently based on the social meanings attached to skin color.[37] This differs from racism, which is typically Black and white, because Black people come in different shades and there's a historic precedent of Black people distancing themselves from other Black people that are darker than them. Colorism was also referred to as the "light versus dark skin issue." Colorism within a specific race has always been

---

36 John Piper, *Did Moses Marry a Black Woman?* 9 Marks https://www.9marks.org/article/didmoses-marry-black-woman/, February 2010.

37 Dictionary, *Colorism* https://www.dictionary.com/browse/colorism, accessed October 2020.

associated with slavery in America, where the skin color of slaves was used as the basis of work responsibilities assigned. Dark-skinned slaves, who were likely of pure African ancestry, were given the more physically taxing tasks like working in the fields, while lighter-skinned slaves who were the product of both nonconsensual rape and consensual sexual relationships with their slave masters, were given more desirable (still enslaved) and valued positions inside the house.[38] Colorism actually predates chattel slavery, as Scripture denotes people of African descent enslaving and discriminating against people based on class, and the Hebrews themselves discriminating against people based on skin tone, as seen in how they responded to Moses' dark-skinned wife. What Miriam and Aaron did to Moses' Cushite wife could be the first account of colorism and another situation in which people complained against God's plan. Miriam's issue wasn't just Moses' wife's beautiful dark skin, Miriam was jealous as she thought that God made a mistake making Moses their leader (Numbers 12:2). Ignoring the possibility of colorism within the Bible makes it easier to paint all light-skinned people with one broad, white stroke, and whitewashing biblical figures becomes the acceptable scholarly norm.

Ruth

Ruth was a Moabite woman who would give birth to Obed, who would father Jesse, who would father King David. Moab originated from an incestuous relationship between Lot and his daughter. As a result, Moab was excluded from "the assembly of the LORD"—that is, from the communal life of God's people—for "ten generations" (Deuteronomy 23:3). Moab was a morally corrupt place where Elimelech, Ruth's father-in-law, as one of God's people was not supposed to dwell. Thus, God had warned the Israelites not to "promote the welfare and prosperity of the Ammonites or Moabites" (Deuteronomy 23:6). Ruth, a non-Jewish woman, was instrumental in continuing Christ's lineage, and of the five women mentioned in Matthew's genealogy of Christ, four are of **Hamitic descent**: Tamar, Rahab, Bathsheba, and Ruth. The Hamites are connected to Ham. Ham had four sons: Canaan, Put, Mizraim, and Cush. Cush is the earthly originator of the Ethiopian people, and this is substantiated by the reality that Cush and Ethiopia are interchangeable in Scripture (Genesis 2:13; 10:6). Dr. Tony Evans points this out in his book, *Oneness Embraced: Through the Eyes of Tony Evans* by

---

38 ibid.

highlighting Mizraim as the originator of the Egyptian people who are biblically understood to be Hamitic people and therefore, African (Psalms 78:51; 105:23 and 106:21-22).[39] We can clearly see African people of color are an integral part of Jesus' earthly lineage.

David

Matthew's Gospel traces Jesus' lineage to Abraham and David (Matthew 1:1). David historically has been presented as a white man resembling Matt Damon as a nude adolescent. Scripture lets us know that David's great-grandmother was a Canaanite woman named Rahab who was heralded as a great person of faith by the author of Hebrews (Hebrews 11:31). His grandmother was Ruth, a Moabite woman who married Boaz and gave birth to Obed (Luke 3:32). This means that David had Jewish and Hamitic ancestry through Rahab and Tamar, which would mean that making David white is both biblically and historically inaccurate. How so? The Hamites are biblically associated as African, not European. This means that David had African ancestry, and so does Jesus (in His earthly lineage, since Jesus is both human and divine. This is commonly referred to as the hypostatic union), but this is ignored in much of our literature and art. Making Abraham and David white made way for making Jesus white.

Jesus Was Ethnically Jewish

Jesus was Jewish ethnically as well as religiously. Jesus undoubtedly identified with the Jews of His day; He considered them His physical people and tribe. In God's providence, Jesus was sent to Judah: "He came to His own [Judah], and His own [Judah] people did not receive Him. But to all who did receive Him, who believed in His name, He gave the right to become children of God" (John 1:11-12). And He clearly said, "You [Gentiles] worship what you do not know; we [Jews] worship what we [Jews] know, for salvation is from the Jews" (John 4:22). We can clearly see in Scripture that Jesus did not deny his Jewish ethnicity. In fact, the very first verse of the New Testament clearly proclaims the Jewish ethnicity of Jesus when it states, "The book of the genealogy of Jesus Christ, the son of David, the son of Abraham" (Matthew 1:1). The author of Hebrews declares that Christ

---

39 Tony Evans, *Oneness Embraced*, (Moody Publishers, 2011), 116.

descended from Judah (Hebrews 7:14).[40] Jesus descending from Judah is where we get the name "Jew." Jesus' mother Mary's Jewish heritage is also recorded in Scripture, which lets us know that His mom was Jewish ethnically, too (Luke 3:23-38). When you examine His genealogy, you'll find a vast array of ethnicities, which suggest that the idea of Jesus being white would be inconsistent with His earthly lineage, but this is ignored in how He's portrayed in Bibles, children's Bibles, art, print, and film. This isn't accidental or amoral. Whitewashing Jesus was used as a tool for white supremacy, Black inferiority, and institutional control. Dr. Tabatha L. Jones Jolivet, a professor of higher education, and one of the authors of *White Jesus: The Architecture of Racism in Religion and Education*, says that there has been a whitewashing process over time, and that white Jesus is a function of white supremacy. In the book, she asserts that, "White Jesus is so much more than an icon. It's not neutral because it has been proliferated and it's expanded in terms of its presence over centuries and it has been largely tied to what we call an imperial project. The agenda of a nation state."[41] Depending on your theological camp, any statement confronting the reality of the role that white supremacy played in the formation and propagation of white Jesus is immediately dismissed because it's presented as a liberal agenda meant to divide. The historical evidence proving such is ignored and, thus, whitewashing is preserved.

Where Did White Jesus Come From?

Certainly not the Bible, but why is he such a widely accepted fallacy? Many people are guilty of thinking anachronistically, meaning, they assume that the past was largely like the present. This is seen in medieval art, as paintings present Jesus as a European male, often wearing medieval-European garb, as opposed to first-century Jewish attire. This image of Jesus, I affectionately call Patene Pro V Jesus, he has an immaculate beard and straight hair, but is historically inaccurate. The fallacy of white Jesus starts early because when you pick up a children's Bible, most of the artwork depicts the men and women of the Bible as white. Consequently, many Westerners adopt the notion that the central figures of the Christian faith

---

40   Got Questions, *"Was Jesus a Jew?"* https://www.gotquestions.org/was-Jesus-a-Jew.html 2018.

41   Tabatha L. Jones Jolivet *White Jesus: The Architecture of Racism in Religion and Education*, (Peter Lang Publishing 2018).

The Whitewashing of Christianity

were white Europeans. The reality is that most of the central characters of the Bible were African and Middle Eastern. When we examine history, one can quickly identify the non-biblical origins of white Jesus. Physical depictions of Jesus aren't contained in the Synoptic Gospels nor John's Gospel. The book of Acts presents Yeshua as the "light from heaven" that temporarily blinded Paul the Apostle (Acts 9:3), but physical descriptions of Him aren't provided in that text. John, the author of the Gospel of John and the Epistle of John, gives some physical descriptions in the book of Revelation, but they are primarily symbolic. John describes Jesus as follows: "The hairs of his head were white, like white wool, like snow. His eyes were like a flame of fire, his feet were like burnished bronze, refined in a furnace, and his voice was like the roar of many waters. In his right hand he held seven stars, from his mouth came a sharp two-edged sword, and his face was like the sun shining in full strength" (Revelation 1:14-16). Again, the Revelation text isn't making Jesus Black, but He's certainly not white based on that description, either. The Revelation passage is symbolic because it refers to His head and hair being like wool, and bronze burned in a furnace is orange and yellow, so if we were to take John's text literally, Jesus would resemble candy corn: white on top, yellow in the middle, and then orange. Ethnic images of Jesus didn't really appear until around the fourth century. The early church fathers disagreed about his attractiveness, but not necessarily his ethnicity. The African Church father Tertullian (220 AD), didn't think that Jesus would have been that appealing based on Isaiah 53:2, which says, "For he grew up before him like a young plant, and like a root out of dry ground; he had no form or majesty that we should look at him, and no beauty that we should desire him." The African theologian Origen (248 AD) and Augustine of Hippo (430 AD) argued that He must have been beautiful based on Psalm 45:3 which says, "Gird your sword on your thigh, O mighty one, in your splendor and majesty!" While images of Christ preceded the Roman Empire, an influx of artistic images of Christ occurred during the reign of Constantine. Emperor Constantine legalized Christianity (meaning it was already in existence, so he didn't create Christianity at the Council of Nicea as some opponents to the Christian faith purport) with the sanctioning of the Edict of Milan to end Christian persecution in 313 AD. This move was not one necessarily done in sincerity. While it's reported that Constantine converted to Christianity, it seems to be a move of expedience due to the exponential growth of the Christian faith. While in power, depictions of Jesus reflected the Romans, not the brown-skinned Jews. From then on, images portrayed a brown-skinned Middle Eastern Jew as a White man.

Jerome Gay Jr.

The walls of Santa Sabina in Rome (430-32 AD) portray Jesus as a white man turning water into wine and multiplying a Hebrew Happy Meal (2 fish, 5 loaves of bread) to feed thousands.[42] There was then a back and forth between beardless and bearded Jesus primarily in the third and fourth centuries. It was around the sixth century that a long-haired, bearded Jesus became the acceptable image by many. By the late Middle Ages, the beard became almost universal when Michelangelo created a clean-shaven, Apollo-like Christ in the Sistine Chapel (1534–41).[43] This painting depicts God as a white man reaching for Adam (who is also white), which helped to normalize European images of a Judeo-Christian God. By the 1500s, slavery was in full effect, and ethnic images of Christ were almost erased because the people in power were also in control of the printing and the narrative. Edward J. Blum and Paul Harvey explore the history of white Jesus in their book, *The Color of Christ: The Son of God and the Saga of Race in America*. They argue that whiteness was not made hallowed in Jesus, but this changed soon. They say, "Whiteness was not made sacred in the form of Jesus, in part, because whiteness itself as a marker of racial identity and power did not yet exist."[44] But this began to change in the years following the American Revolution. By the early 1800s, new printing technologies and advances in transportation combined with the rise of multiple missionary societies, changed everything. During the 1800s the American Bible Society, the American Sunday School Union, and the American Tract Society all used the printing press wanting to flood the nation with a Jesus-centered national identity. The American Tract Society used tracts in order to connect Jesus to white American identity. They mass-produced, mass-marketed, and mass-distributed images of Jesus, who was always depicted as a white man. This was done in order to entice Protestants to see American identity in white Jesus.[45] Soon the "white Christ" was everywhere, and the remains of the gospel-

---

42 Cartlidge and Elliott, 53–55. See also The Two Faces of Jesus by Robin M. Jensen, *Bible Review*, 17.8, October 2002, *and Understanding Early Christian Art* by Robin M. Jensen, Routledge, 2000.

43 Esperancy Camara, Khan *Academy Blunt Anthony Artistic Theory in Italy, 1450–1600*, 112-114, 118-119.

44 Edward J. Blum and Paul Harvey, *The Color of Christ: The Son of God and the Saga of Race in America*, (University of North Carolina Press 2014), 29.

45 Ibram Kendi, *Stamped from the Beginning: The Definitive History of Racist Ideas in America* (New York Nation Books, 2016), 153.

centered Puritans who actively opposed oppression failed to temper the spread of His portrait. In fact, some of them even contributed to the spread of white Jesus.

White Jesus is now an acceptable image of Christianity in the West, and He's not a symbol of hope, redemption, and renewal, but, rather one of hierarchy, degradation, and domination. Why? A Savior that resembled the enslaved would undermine the mission of unregenerate slave owners who misused Scripture to enact oppression on people of color.

White Jesus on the Big Screen

White Jesus has been popularized in every form of media, whether in print, or on the big screen. Jim Caviezel played Jesus in the 2004 film, *The Passion of the Christ*. Mel Gibson chose to cast an actor with European features to play the role of Jesus, not to mention almost every other character in the movie was played by white people. However, Gibson wasn't the first to whitewash the Bible by presenting almost every person in both Jewish and Christian history as white. *The Bible*, which debuted on the History Channel, deployed the same playbook. In *Touched by an Angel*, Roma Downey and Mark Burnett presented a whitewashed narrative of Christian history to more than 70 million viewers who were seeing the Bible in white. By 2020, you would think historical accuracy in the portrayal of biblical figures would have made some progress, but Pureflix, which is essentially a family friendly Christian version of Netflix, displays Ruth and Esther as white women. Countless white actors have been chosen to work in various biblical roles. Ann Baxter played the African Nefertari, Russell Crowe played Noah, and who could forget Charlton Heston as Moses? Or Yvonne De Carlo as Zipporah? Or John Derek as Joshua? Almost every one of these African and Middle Eastern people have most often been played by white people. All of this makes it possible and acceptable to make Jesus (who is God in the flesh) white. What's even more disheartening is the response of some evangelicals, who see pointing out this glaring disparity in imagery as being divisive, yet they don't see (or rather refuse to see) the theological and historical malpractice of portraying almost everyone in the Bible as white as divisive. Through this strategic process of whitewashing, whiteness is now sacred. It's no wonder that Megyn inaccurately, yet comfortably assumed that Jesus was a "white man too" and Florida Evans pointed to a picture of a white Jesus as "the only Jesus I know."

In the next chapter we will look at what makes white Jesus so dangerous.

Discussion Questions

1. What did the first image of Jesus presented to you look like? How did it impact you?
2. Does how we present Jesus matter socially? Why?
3. Why is it important to not present almost everyone in Scripture as white?
4. How will you actively communicate a diverse narrative of Christian history?

3

The Danger of *White Jesus*

> *That white Jesus picture is one of the greatest weapons of mass destruction in the Black community.*
> – Dr. Umar Johnson

"CHRISTIANITY, I DON'T THINK SO. White people used Christianity to justify slavery and segregation. A Black Christian is a Black person with no f@*#$^% memory."[46] This statement was made by the famous comedian, producer, and actor Chris Rock. He's not alone in this sentiment. In an interview with BET, rapper, activist, and entrepreneur Killer Mike had this to say about the white savior complex that whitewashed Christianity perpetuates. When asked about the religion episode of his Netflix special *Trigger Warning*, he had this to say:

> I wanted to free Black people of the image of white Jesus and the bondage of Christianity. What I ended up discovering is that not only

---

[46] Freedom from Religion Foundation, *Chris Rock*, https://ffrf.org/news/day/dayitems/item/22283-chris-rock, accessed February 2021.

is that image oppressive because it denies the identity of myself—all of it hurts the followers.[47]

Notice that both Chris Rock and Killer Mike associate Christianity with bondage. Many within the Black community have not only started to embrace this view, but to spread it as well. Therefore, this begs the question. Is Christianity a white man's religion? Of course not; why is that even the question? says the average Christian, aloof to the reason why this question must be broached. When one is willing to acknowledge that white supremacy didn't just have anthropological implications, but social and theological effects as well, they will soon see why many still see Christianity as a religion by white people and primarily for the benefit of white people, at the expense of Black and brown people. Of course, this isn't Jesus' fault, nor does it accurately represent the historic Jesus whose mission was the Father's glory seen in the redemption of humanity (Colossians 2:14). As Reverend Walter Arthur McCray accurately asserts in his book *The Black Presence in the Bible*, "people from every race and ethnic group... have sinned and have fallen short of God's glory... [and] it is revealed in the Bible that every group of people are included in God's redemption circle."[48] The issue is not and has never been Jesus, but, rather, those who claimed to be his followers, and the use of false imagery enacted to enslave people physically, mentally and spiritually.

In 2016, *The Breakfast Club* had Dr. Umar Johnson on their show. Dr. Umar Johnson is a psychologist, historian and self-proclaimed P.O.P.A. (Prince of Pan-Africanism).[49] Pan-Africanism is the notion that people of African descent have common interests and should be unified. It's an intellectual movement that aims to encourage and strengthen the bonds of solidarity amongst people of African descent with the core values being personal value based on being made in God's image, economic empowerment for people of color, and repatriation. Historically, Pan-Africanism has often taken the shape of a political or cultural movement,

---

47 Marjua Estevez, *Killer Mike Thinks Christianity Does Black People More Harm than Good* https://www.bet.com/music/2019/02/08/netflix-trigger-warning-killer-mike-christianity-interview.html, February 2019.

48 Walter Arhtur McCray, *The Black Presence in the Bible: Discovering the Black and African Identity of Biblical Persons and Nations*, (Chicago, IL: Black Light Fellowship, 1990), 30.

49 Dr. Umar Johnson, https://www.drumarjohnson.com/#bio, accessed February 2021.

The Whitewashing of Christianity

but Pan-Africanism was started by a Christian man by the name of Alexander Crummell who saw the need to affirm *the imago dei* (Latin phrase that means the image of God) in Black and brown people based on the lack of dignity given to them by white people. If Dr. Umar Johnson is the prince of Pan-Africanism, Alexander Crummell is the king of Pan-Africanism. On this particular episode of *The Breakfast Club*, the topic of religion came up and Dr. Johnson took full aim at white Jesus, who has permeated American churches, houses, books, screens, and art. I remember vividly as the hosts hung on his words as if to concur that white Jesus will actually never empower or free Black people.

Johnson said, "which is why for me that white Jesus picture is the greatest weapon of mass destruction in the Black community, when a Black boy or girl goes to Sunday school and sees a white Jesus from birth until they are five-years-old they see God as white… and if God is white than the devil must be Black by contra-indication, which is why Black folks gotta stop worshipping a white Jesus… no one worships a deity in the image of their enemy or oppressor, except slaves… you can take the slave out of slavery, but until the slave takes the slavery out of himself, he will never be free."[50] As I listened and watched, I saw people hanging on every word, and concurring with his sentiments. I remember thinking this is why the whitewashing of the Bible and Christian history is so dangerous, because it creates an unnecessary barrier to a faith that historically flourished in Africa long before Europe. Some of you are reading this and thinking Black people are already free and why would they need to look to a white Jesus for help? Or you're thinking that Dr. Johnson's statements are misguided. Therein lies the issue; the false depiction of a blond-haired blue-eyed Jesus has not only been championed, but presented as authentic at the expense of history and authentic scholarship. Worse, when confronted, many claim that race doesn't matter, while still printing, painting and presenting white Jesus as factual. This has caused many to shun the Christian faith based on erroneous information that is propagated as fact: white Jesus, white disciples, white prophets, white Mary, white Apostle Paul and white missionaries. All of these whitewashed images eclipse the Gospel for a false gospel, one that benefits people of European descent. The Gospel is colorless, but the message presented to unbelievers with the flood of white imagery is that God will save you, but He didn't use anyone that looked like you in His redemptive plan,

---

50 The Breakfast Club Umar Johnson Interview, https://www.youtube.com/watch?v=SaUMQDjsAt0 July 2016, Time stamp: 36:31—37:51.

nor are you included in Scripture. The issue at hand here is how the propagation of white Jesus has impacted people of color historically, and how the residue of this fallacy impacts us all today, because white Jesus is the foundation of European historical whitewashing. Tom Skinner addresses the danger of white Jesus in his book *How Black is the Gospel*:

> "Black America is not about to follow a white Christ. The image of Christ patterned after Sallman's portrait is more than suspect. It has become a contemptuous symbol to the Black man all the fakery and chicanery endorsed by so many white Christians. If Christ takes on the image of an Anglo-Saxon Protestant suburbanite, he's obviously not for Black men. It is inconceivable that this kind of Christ would die for Black people."[51]

Tom Skinner wrote this in 1970, and Black Christian leaders are still dealing with this today. Tom Skinner wasn't conceding that Jesus was white or that Jesus' ethnicity determines the veracity of his message, but he had to deal with the danger and difficulty that white Jesus and a whitewashed Bible creates; a barrier to the Gospel that contributes to lostness. This barrier causes many cults, individuals, and other faiths to point to whitewashing as a reason to deny Christ. The way in which white Jesus was deployed was to enact inferiority on Black and brown people while promoting white supremacy, which was a diabolical impediment to Black advancement, as noted by pastors during the Harlem Renaissance:

> To many African American Christians, pastors in Harlem, and intellectuals of the Harlem Renaissance movement, the white Christ was a problem. He represented a type of Christianity that served only to instigate Black suffering. The God represented by the white Christ could be described as sadistic; he was a transcendent pedagogue who stood at a distance, coming near only to chastise the sinner with misery… Black Christians identify Black suffering with Jesus' suffering.[52]

---

51 Tom Skinner, *How Black is the Gospel*, (Fourth Printing 1970), 13.
52 Reggie L. Williams, *Bonhoeffer's Black Jesus: Harlem Renaissance Theology and an Ethic of Resistance*, (Waco, TX: Baylor University Press, 2014), 41.

The Whitewashing of Christianity

Many white evangelicals don't understand the evangelistic and apologetic issues that whitewashing Christ and the Bible creates for those ministering to urban communities. This is why understanding the church's complicity in the subjugation and silencing of Black people is so pivotal. To understand this, it's vital that we understand the attack on Black and brown value was never just political or social, but it was theological as well. Understanding racial inequality is essential in engaging it in a restorative way, as Bryan Stevenson, the director of the Equal Justice Initiative, says:

> You can't understand many of the most destructive issues or policies in our country without understanding our history of racial inequality. And I actually think it begins with our interaction with native people, because we took land, we killed people, we disrupted a culture. We were brutal. And we justified and rationalized that land grab, that genocide, by characterizing native people as different. It was the first way in which this narrative of racial difference was employed to justify behaviors that would otherwise be unjustifiable. When you are allowed to demonize another community and call them savages, and treat them brutally and cruelly, it changes your psyche. We abused and mistreated the communities and cultures that existed on this land before Europeans arrived, and then that narrative of racial difference was used to develop slavery.... I genuinely believe that, despite all of that victimization, the worst part of slavery was this narrative that we created about Black people—this idea that Black people aren't fully human, that they are three-fifths human, that they are not capable, that they are not evolved. That ideology, which set up white supremacy in America, was the most poisonous and destructive consequence of two centuries of slavery. And I do believe that we never addressed it.[53]

---

53   James McWilliams, *"Bryan Stevenson on What Well-Meaning White People Need to Know About Race,"* Pacific Standard, updated February 18, 2019, https://psmag.com/magazine/bryan-stevenson-ps-interview.

Jerome Gay Jr.

The War on Black Identity

There were three sectors that were intentional in conspiring against the value of Black and brown people. While the identity of Black people is rooted in Genesis 1:26, being image bearers of God and for God, Black people's collective American experience did not affirm this reality. The three sectors intentional on devaluing Black and brown bodies were:

- Social
- Judicial
- Religious

It was Calvin Lockhart who said, "One of the major psychological problems of the Black man outside the parent continent of Africa is that while he can always say, I have a country, he cannot really say, I have a home."[54] One of the reasons Black people historically and presently don't feel at home in the United States is because we weren't welcome to the dinner table as equals, just to the field as workers. One of the main reasons for this reality is that the people in power didn't see Black people as people. The myth of white superiority was/is drenched in pseudo-science, mischaracterization, and innuendo. The social attack against Black people was presented as scientific, when in actuality it was just horrific. From the purity of Anglo-Saxon blood to the climate, nothing stopped white supremacist from presenting themselves as just that, supreme.

Social

While race may be a social construct, it's clearly one that we can't ignore. Some scholars have even asserted that race and racism did not exist in antiquity, but there's considerable evidence that refutes this claim.[55] Race is a fifteenth century concept. Ancient Greeks did not think in terms of race, but rather in terms of geography. For them, African meant Egypt and Libya, Asia meant Persia and as far as India and Europe meant Greece and neighboring lands like Sicily. Many of the

---

54 P. Olisanwuche Esedebe *Pan-Africanism The Idea and Movement 1776-1991,* (Howard University Press, 1991), 227.

55 Denise Kimber Buell, *"Rethinking the Relevance of Race for Early Christian Self-definition,* (The Harvard Theological Review, 2001), 449-476.

Greek scholars relied on climate to explain visual human differences, and while there wasn't a concept of race, there was still the myth of superiority.[56] Where their season shifted dramatically, their thought was that revealed levels of incivility. Hippocrates describes this in his writing *Airs, Waters, and Places* when he says, "wildness, unsociability and spirit. For frequent shocks to the mind impart wildness, destroying tameness and gentleness."[57] The Greeks, Romans, Vikings, and yes, Africans, were all active in the enslavement of others, but it wasn't about race; this is why I wanted to connect the idea of superiority and oppression to sin and what Pharaoh said about the Jewish people in Exodus because oppression doesn't come from racism, oppression leads to racism based on presumed superiority.

Anglo-Saxon Superiority

As stated earlier, Publius Cornelius Tacitus attributed white superiority to their blood, but that wasn't the only pseudo-science used to falsely present whites as superior and Blacks as inferior. Aristotle, Johann Friedrich Blumenbach, and Gomes Eanes de Zurara are names to know when examining the history of oppression and racism.

Climate Theory

Aristotle (384—322 BCE) believed that Greeks were superior and came up with a climate theory which stated that extreme cold or hot climates produced intellectually, physically, and morally inferior people. He labeled Africans "burnt faces," and based on this absurd theory, he concluded that hot climates created ugly people (Blacks) who lacked the capacity for freedom and self-government. Aristotle said, "Humanity is divided into two: the master and the slave, or, if one prefers it, Greeks and the Barbarians, those who have the right to command, and those who are born to obey." Sadly, many Puritans bought into this sinful theory rooted in the oppressive views of Pharaoh and the sin of partiality.[58]

---

56   Nell Painter, *The History of White People*, (W.W. New York Norton & Company, 2010 Kindle Edition), 174.

57   Hippocrates, *Airs, Water, Places, part 23 in Hippocrates*, with an English Translation by W.H.S. Jones, vol. 1, (Cambridge: Harvard University Press, 1923), 24.

58   Ibram Kendi, *Stamped from the Beginning: The Definitive History of Racist Ideas in America* (New York Nation Books, 2016), 17.

Jerome Gay Jr.

Teleological Argument Against Black Value

Teleology is the philosophical attempt to describe things in terms of their apparent purpose, directive principle, or goal. During the 18th and 19th centuries, there was a revival of the argument for the oppression of Black and brown people. It was rooted in a philosophy that devalues Black and brown intelligence, purpose and value. This was known as the *Teleological Argument*. The Teleological Argument purported that the Creator intentionally made men unequal. To whites, he gave intelligence to enable them to wisely direct the activities of others. To nonwhites, he gave strong backs fortified with weak minds and an obedient temperament, so that they might labor effectively under the supervision of white masters. This type of barbaric thinking in many ways mirrors Tacitus, who wrote *Germania* in 98 C.E.

The Degenerative Hypothesis

Johann Friedrich Blumenbach (1752-1840) was a German physician, naturalist, physiologist and anthropologist, born into a well-connected family in the region of Thuringia. Much of Blumenbach's scientific work was based on skull size, which he used to determine beauty and value. In fact, by the end of his life he owned Europe's greatest collection, which he called his Golgotha, which consisted of 245 skulls and fragments and two mummies.[59] He's credited with creating racially-based categories: Caucasian = White, Mongolian = Yellow, Malayan = Brown, Ethiopian = Black, and American = Red. His studies were based on the *Degenerative Hypothesis*, which sought to avert social decline by using pre-scientific methods to find the lowest contributors to society. These ideas derived from pre-scientific concepts of heredity and were used to justify the dehumanization of Black and brown bodies.

Racist Ideas

Gomes Eanes de Zurara was commissioned by Prince Henry's nephew, King Afonso V, in 1452. Zurara was a commander in Prince Henry's Military Order of Christ, and his mission was to create reasons to affirm the monetary decision to exclusively trade African slaves. In 1453, just a year later, Zurara finished the first

---

59   Nell Painter, *The History of White People*, (W.W. New York Norton & Company, 2010 Kindle Edition), 1250.

The Whitewashing of Christianity

book on Africans written by a European in the modern era called *The Chronicle of the Discovery and Conquest of Guinea*. This would be one of the first recorded documents of anti-Black racist ideas, this was more than class hierarchy, but race-based oppression.[60] This would be the document Prince Henry needed in order to focus his slave-trading on African people and Zurara distinguished the Portguese by framing their African slave trades as missionary expeditions.[61] His grouping of darker-skinned people as Black was the foundation of seeing African people as uneducated degenerates. While Zurara didn't create whiteness, he certainly attempted to define Blackness. For those in favor of oppression, this was needed in order to demean Black people and make others superior.

This is some of the pseudo-science and theory, most of which preceded the Trans-Atlantic slave trade. By the fifteenth century, race-based oppression was in full effect in the East, and would soon be brought to the West. Socially, Blacks were devalued even before 'Black was a thing,' but the war against Black value didn't stop with social hierarchy; it also permeated our system of government.

The Black Experience in America—Judicial

The global Black experience doesn't begin with slavery, but the Black experience in America does. In 1619 a ship landed in Jamestown, Virginia. This ship would shape the Black experience in America just one year before the *Mayflower*. This ship, called *The White Lion*, contained Black people who weren't labeled slaves, but weren't exactly free, either. This was when indentured servitude was primarily based on class, not race, but this would soon change. By 1660, the growth of tobacco and cotton plantations required more labor, but indentured servitude was too expensive and somehow the people who called Black people barbarians saw the cost of business as a reason to enslave people, Black people. While whites were indentured servants, too, when they escaped, it was much harder to recapture and re-enslave whites. White indentured servants were allowed to be Christians, and white Christians couldn't easily justify enslaving other Christians, white servants also had the privilege of appealing to European governments that their Black counterparts weren't afforded. In fact, Virginia and Maryland lawmakers passed

---

60 Ibram Kendi, *Stamped from the Beginning: The Definitive History of Racist Ideas in America* (New York Nation Books, 2016), 23.

61 ibid.

laws to make Blacks slaves for life.[62] In 1667, the issue of whether baptism would render Black slaves free and the Virginia Assembly decided that "it is enacted and declared by the Grand Assembly, and the authority thereof, that the conferring of baptism does not alter the condition of the person as to his bondage or freedom."[63] Our judicial system wasn't one that was for Black people, and this was evident in how legislation was used against Black people. Clearly, this was systemic injustice where the government literally conspired and enacted unjust, inhumane, unbiblical, and debilitating laws against Black people. The reality is that chattel slavery preceded American democracy and the structure and content of the original constitution was largely based on an effort to preserve slavery while affording political and economic rights to whites.[64] The Southern slaveholding colonies formed a union on the condition that the federal government would not interfere with the right to own slaves. Federalism (a type of government in which the power is divided between the national government and other governmental units) was used to support the institution of slavery and the political power of slaveholding states. This is why Thomas Jefferson could write that *all men are created equal* while owning slaves, and not feel an ounce of hypocrisy; because Black and brown people were seen as beasts, not people. What's interesting is that the first man to die in the American Revolution was a Black man by the name of Crispus Attucks.[65] Black men, many of them slaves, signed the Declaration of Independence with their lives, so that white men could be free, because Jefferson didn't have Black people in mind when he wrote all men were created equal, he had only white men in mind. The same was true of President Abraham Lincoln and the Emancipation Proclamation, which changed the law of his day, but not the hearts of white supremacists. As Tom Skinner notes, "the Emancipation Proclamation merely said the Black man is not a slave; it never defined him as a man."[66] I know what some of you are thinking: laws aren't supposed to define people; God is. The problem was that being Black in America from the seventeenth to twentieth centuries meant that you were told your earthly master— a white man— defined you. He had jurisdiction to beat you, change your name, sell your children, and even

---

62   Tom Skinner, *How Black is the Gospel*, (Fourth Printing, 1970), 19.
63   ibid.
64   Michelle Alexander, *The New Jim Crow*, (The New Press New York, 2012), 25.
65   Tom Skinner, *How Black is the Gospel*, (Fourth Printing, 1970), 19.
66   ibid.

kill you without consequence. How was all of this justified? Here is where we make our way back to white Jesus and the whitewashing of Scripture, and where we see how religion was one of the biggest culprits in the subjugation of Black and brown bodies.

Religious

The most damning as well as disheartening aspect of whitewashing is the church's complicity in the devaluing of Black and brown lives. This is in part why Chris Rock can make the claim that serving Jesus while Black is stupid, and Killer Mike says that following Jesus does Black people more harm than good. White pastors throughout American history preached a false gospel of anthropocentric servitude and racial hierarchy. The most intentionally misinterpreted text was from Genesis 9, where Noah went to bed drunk and naked. His son Ham, the father of Canaan, mocked him and the following morning, once his hangover wore off, he cursed Canaan. It was then believed that Canaan, being a descendent of Ham (Ham meant Black), meant that Black people were cursed by God and sentenced to perpetual servitude. These unregenerate slave masters would tell their slaves the gospel in its original purity and simplicity is Ephesians 6:5, "slaves, obey your masters..."[67] They were told that Africans and their descendants were destined to be servants and should therefore accept their status as slaves in fulfillment of biblical prophecy.[68] There are several problems with this assertion, as Dr. Tony Evans points out in his 2010 article, Are Black People Cursed:

1. The Bible says, cursed be Canaan (Genesis 9:25), which means only one of Ham's sons was cursed.
2. Curses have expiration dates, typically 3-4 generations, based on Exodus 20:5. This means even if Black people were cursed— which we're not, nor was this verse asserting a permanent curse on Black people— that Black people would not be cursed forever.
3. Canaan's curse was fulfilled by the subjugation of Canaan by Israel (1 Kings 9:20-21).

---

67   Tom Skinner, *How Black is the Gospel*, (Fourth Printing, 1970), 24.
68   C.F. Keil and F. Delitzsch *The Pentateuch" in Commentary on the Old Testament*, (Grand Rapids: Wm. B. Eerdmans, 1987), vol. 1, 178.

4. God's word says that disobedience-based curses can be reversed when people repent in Exodus 20:6.

The chronic eisegesis displayed by slave-owning people who claimed to be Christians, but clearly were not, because Scripture teaches you can't love God and willfully hate others (1 John 4:20), is glaring. They didn't stop there; as mentioned earlier, making Jesus white was essential for their power dynamics. A brown-skinned Savior doesn't go well with a false gospel of white superiority, those who were enslaved were told that their earthly master and Heavenly Savior were both white, which again was a lie. This is why White Jesus is historically and presently dangerous: He affirms a gospel that opposes what Jesus Himself proclaimed. Jesus declared a gospel that tears down walls of hostility. Ignoring the white Jesus myth doesn't tear it down: it adds bricks to the walls of division. Some even pointed to Origen, an African church father, who concluded that the Egyptians were Ham's descendants and cursed to slavery and servanthood. What they failed to mention is that Origen, whose African-ness is often hidden, did not comment on skin color in association with Ham, nor did he connect servanthood to skin color.[69] The church's complicity is something that can't be ignored, because we're reminded of this stain when the reality that those presented as Christian heroes were in favor of owning Black and brown people.

This is why Dr. Umar Johnson's words resonate with so many people. While I reject his conclusion that we should reject Christianity, I understand how he arrived at his premise. Whitewashing contributes to Black and brown lostness, and to ignore it is to devalue souls that Christ died to redeem. Whitewashing often has to be addressed before the gospel can be presented in urban areas, because an urban apologist has to deconstruct the false narrative that white Jesus died for your soul after laws were changed, but He doesn't care about your person. This is why whitewashing is so dangerous, and why white Jesus is indeed a social, theological and anthropological weapon of mass destruction, not just for the Black community, but the Christian faith.

Next, we'll see how this plays out presently in the form of cultural imperialism, mainly among those that herald reformed theology.

---

69 David M. Whitford, *The Curse of Ham in the Early Modern Era: The Bible and the Justification of Slavery*, (Farnham: Ashgate Pub. Ltd., 2012), 104.

Discussion Questions

1. How have Christians contributed to the white Jesus myth?
2. What are some things you've heard about Jesus' race from believers and non-believers?
3. Do you understand how whitewashing misrepresents the Christian faith? How so? If not, why not?
4. Do you see how whitewashing contributes to lostness? Explain.

4

Reformed Theology vs Reformed Culture

*If I quoted the great reformer Martin Luther...
never did I get an email about his blatant anti-Semitism*
— Matt Chandler

TYPICALLY, when the topic of Reformed Theology is raised, the discussion usually focuses on 5-Point Calvinism or aspects of it like limited atonement and efficacious grace. The Reformed Tradition has played a huge role in whitewashing because it tends to start Christian history with The Protestant Reformation of the sixteenth century, while African church fathers like Augustine and Cyprian are mentioned, their African-ness is often omitted or rarely acknowledged. Rich African Christianity is ignored in favor of the European-led Protestant Reformation. This oversight seems to be intentional in a lot of cases, and it has led to the assumption that Blacks don't want much to do with reformed theology, when the reality is Blacks shaped Reformed Theology being that orthodoxy is found and influenced by Africans who gave us the concept of sovereignty, the Trinity and the like. Reformed Theology is often presented in culturally imperialistic ways, which is why many people of color reject the presenters of RT, not all of its tenets. Many in the reformed community verbally express a desire for diversity and multi-ethnic ministry, but functionally, they communicate they are happy with homogeneity, or that one would need to acquiesce to their way of doing things in order to be embraced. Additionally, many within the reformed community perpetuate white imagery in their churches and only refer people to white authors, missionaries, and theologians and functionally contribute to whitewashing by rarely if ever referencing other races that have contributed to the Christian faith. This may or may not be intentional, but it's a reality that widens the gap between white reformed evangelicals and Blacks and stifles the testimony of grace that we proclaim destroys the walls of hostility. Less than 14 percent of US churches are multi-ethnic.[70] This gap isn't entirely due to doctrinal differences, but, rather, cultural mores that are more exclusive than many are willing to admit. It seems that walls exist between majority and minority groups, not necessarily in theology, but in the culture of the reformed community. Many minorities have trouble embracing the culture, not the theology of reformed evangelicalism, because in many ways, it's historically synonymous with racism, and it contributes to a whitewashed narrative of Christian history. Being that the Protestant Reformation is emphasized more than the African martyrs that made it possible. Remember, Christianity was in Africa 300 years before it reached Europe.

What is Reformed Theology?

Depending on who you ask, you'll get a lot of responses to this question. The guys at CARM.org define it for us. **Reformed Theology** is the theology of the Protestant movement that "reformed" the theological perspective held by the Roman Catholic Church. This movement began in the sixteenth century with Martin Luther and John Calvin, and has continued on since then. It has since come to be known as Calvinism, and is a biblically-centered theological perspective focusing on the sovereignty of Scripture, the sovereignty of God, election, redemption, and our securing in Christ's work. Reformed theology holds to the five *solas*:

1. *Sola Scriptura*—Scripture alone
2. *Sola Christus*—Christ alone

---

70 Bob Smietana, *Research: Racial Diversity at Church More Dream Than Reality* https://lifewayresearch.com/2014/01/17/research-racial-diversity-at-church-more-dream-than-reality/, January 2014.

3. *Sola Gratia*—Grace alone
4. *Sola Fide*—Faith alone
5. *Soli Deo Gloria*—the Glory of God alone

It is also known by the Five Points of Calvinism, that not everyone embraces, but they are:

1. Total Depravity
2. Unconditional Election
3. Limited Atonement
4. Irresistible Grace
5. Perseverance of the Saints

What's interesting is that many proponents of Calvinism don't know that John Calvin didn't coin the phrase. The description "Calvinist" was coined in 1552 by a Lutheran polemicist by the name of Joachim Westphal, not by John Calvin. In fact, Calvin didn't like the term, nor did he see it as a term of endearment.[71]

While Calvinists respect John Calvin, Calvinism actually preceded him, and aspects of it can be seen throughout church history in the lives of Aquinas, Anselm, and most notably, the African theologian Augustine. For much of history, the focus is on the white German reformer instead of the African theologian that precedes him and in many ways shaped his theology. It's important to note that Calvinism is a view of the Bible and is not on par with Scripture itself— and here is where the problem begins. Many proponents of Calvinism present their views of Scripture and history as the only way to approach Scripture, theology, history and liturgy.

I agree with most of the tenets of Reformed Theology, but I think it's important to note that Reformed Theology is not the gospel because the gospel doesn't need reform, we do. RT is a view of Scripture, not Scripture itself. This is vital because RT is often presented as if it is the only way to practice hermeneutics, liturgy, and mission, when only whites are referenced and celebrated as theological heroes, although many of them owned and championed slavery. Blacks are often

---

[71] David Qaoud, 3 *Common Misconceptions of Calvinism* https://www.gospelrelevance.com/2015/12/06/3-commonmisconceptions-calvinism-theology/ December 2015.

The Whitewashing of Christianity

turned away from RT because we're presented with a choice of losing our culture if we embrace the theology, and this, for many of us, is simply unacceptable. We don't mind losing a pre-Christian identity in order to follow Yeshua, but we reject the idea that acceptance in white circles validates our calling, theological knowledge, and ministry effectiveness. In many cases, the theology isn't the only thing presented to Black and brown people who join churches where RT is the theological position and they are the racial minority. It's also accompanied by an ignorant vitriol for the Black church and criticism of predominantly Black churches. The criticism assumes a lack of theological potency along with an assumption of biblical illiteracy without actually ever attending a Black church, reading Black authors or being under Black leadership. The rebuttal is I don't need to attend to spot bad doctrine, but rarely are cultural blind spots considered in the assumption of bad doctrine without actually knowing an individual or using the testimony of a few Blacks to paint the entire historic Black church as lacking doctrinal astuteness. Oftentimes, because whitewashing isn't confronted (or in worst cases ignored), white culture is seen as normative and the universal standard for the universal church to follow. Additionally, Reformed Theology rarely acknowledges the African Christians alive in Europe during the Reformation. Vicente Lustitano, an African-Portuguese Roman Catholic Priest, gives us a glimpse of the sub-Saharan African Christians who lived in Europe during the Reformation. He was one of the first Roman Catholic clergy to convert to Protestantism during the sixteenth century Reformation. So, even Blacks that responded positively to the Protestant Reformation are often ignored.[72] This oversight is beginning to be addressed, as Dr. David Daniels says:

> Studying Afro-Europeans and African Christians in Reformation Europe as a topic within the academic discipline of World Christianity challenges the dominant historiography of the Reformations in which the Reformations are basically interpreted as a European phenomenon, focusing solely on the activities of "white" European Christians while being silent on the presence and activities of the African

---

72   Maria Augusta Alves Barbosa, *Vincentius Lusitanus: Ein portugiesischer Komponist und Musiktheoretiker des*, (Lisbon: Estado da Cultura 1977).

Christians in the Reformation Europe. World Christianity pursues other historiographic directions.[73]

This historical oversight is indicative of both the whitewashing and imperialism that many in the reformed community are guilty of, which is often what's rejected by people of color, not theology.

One of the biggest proponents of RT and writers is theologian and author John Frame.

John Frame, in his book, *The Doctrine of the Christian Life*, gives five reasons for minorities not embracing reformed churches. Frame's reasons provide a starting point from which I'll make several observations about the Reformed Theology v. Reformed Culture line of reasoning:

1. The Reformation has been a movement of scholars.

He says, "This approach appeals to the well-educated, who are also often relatively wealthy members of society. It tends to turn away others, in the present case the relatively poor minorities."[74] "The poor minorities?" And by poor, his conclusion doesn't seem to be just economic, intellectually poor as well. I'm not saying that Frame believes that all minorities are unintellectual, or that he's a racist, since he says, "the church of Jesus Christ is to embrace all nations,"[75] but this statement would certainly fall under the *racially insensitive* category. Statements like this need to be explained and not said in passing. I wonder if Frame knows how many ethnic minorities would respond to this? It appears that he's implying that minorities aren't intellectuals, nor wealthy, and that those factors keep us from embracing Reformed Theology, but if we examine history, he'd have a more compassionate and informed response. Africans were enslaved, oppressed, dehumanized, and tortured. Additionally, the systemic oppression that they endured went beyond physical abuse; it included mental abuse as well. At one point in America, it was illegal for Black people to read and write. Fast-forward to Jim Crow (enacted in 1876 and 1965) during which, the phrase 'separate but

---

73 Vethanayagamony Peter, *Essays in Christian Scholarship in Honor of Kurt Karl Hendel*, (Lutheran University Press Minneapolis, MN 2016), 102.
74 John Frame, *Doctrine of the Christian Life*, (P&R Publishing Company 2008), 679.
75 ibid.

equal' was coined, but the truth is it was only separate. Blacks were given dilapidated schools, incomplete books, endured social oppression, etc. and while many would say we're passed that, many white evangelicals are either unaware of or ignore the fact that Reformed seminaries did not allow minority students at their schools. He ignores the cultural climate and racism of those that held and hold a reformed position in his conclusion about Black and brown people. Yet, somehow, this is considered a level playing field. Some will be quick to say that discrimination is outlawed, but suspend their theology when it comes to inequity when theologically, we know that the heart can't be legislated. Changing laws didn't change the hearts of white evangelicals who didn't want to be in schools with Black and brown people. The 1954 Brown vs. The Board of Education case not only opened access for minorities to public schools; sadly, it was needed for many of our seminaries that celebrated the good doctrines of grace, mercy and the gospel, yet ostracized believers of different races. They celebrated grace conceptually, but did not extend that grace to Blacks practically. They comfortably and consistently separated their theology from the ethics that should match it.

Blacks aren't unintellectual; the reality is that we've had to fight not only for social but also for access to theological equality in America. Whites were extended theological white privilege in which their skin color gave them access to truth shaped by African men and women whose African-ness was omitted, but African Americans weren't given this luxury. Blacks were rejected by reformed institutions based on the color of their skin. This disparity needs to be discussed because for decades Blacks were denied access to Reformed institutions while Oral Roberts welcomed many. To be clear, I'm not giving anyone a pass for bad doctrine, but to my original point, statements like Frame's that aren't explained by white reformed proponents come across as insensitive to the historical struggle of Blacks and displays blatant ignorance of the role racists who claimed to be "Christians" played in attempting to oppress the social and theological progress of Black and brown people. African Americans have historically embraced and believed in the sovereignty of God, salvation by grace through faith alone (Ephesians 2:8-9), and the deity of Christ. Belief in a "Big God" (as John Piper said in an interview with Reformed African Americans Network, now The Witness) is nothing new for us, nor are we returning to it because we've abandoned it. The reality is the reformed community in many ways is just now taking notice and seeing the need for diversity and new voices as the landscape of America changes. White reformed men in particular need to engulf themselves in the rich history of Blacks and consider serving under theologically sound non-whites to gain experience as practitioners and not just as idealists of the rich theological, intellectual and social history of minorities in particular of Africans and African Americans. The reality that Christianity was in Africa long before Europe must be taught verbally and written about extensively to change this broken narrative that only Europeans shaped the Christian faith while ignoring the first five centuries of African Christianity. The Christian faith and sound doctrine didn't start in Wittenberg and the African men and women who preceded the reformers were clearly intellectual enough to give us concepts like the Trinity.

2. Being an intellectual movement, the Reformation in some circles disparaged feelings, in my judgment to an unscriptural extent.

I agree that the disparagement of emotions is unscriptural, but I think that this is a present problem that we're not past. In some places, it seems that removing emotions in favor of a more subdued response to salvation by grace and internal celebration during a worship gathering are eisgeted into Scripture in order to make our response to the gospel exclusively cognitive. This is primarily seen in liturgy (worship) and preaching. Many white evangelicals have not had many experiences of being the minority in a worship service and many stay in circles of agreement as mentioned earlier and studied in the book *Divided by Faith*. Consequently, the delusion about minorities being unintellectual and overly emotional is nurtured instead of shunned and they allow stories of bad experiences heard from others and assumptions to drive their understanding of minorities as it relates to worship and preaching, thus resulting in a xenophobic view of the Black church. For instance, when one doesn't allow themselves to hear others, one could hear the same sermon and when the white guy gets loud, he's passionate, but when the Black guy gets loud, he's angry, overly emotional and lacks substance. Why the disparity? I think it has a lot to do with elevating the Reformation to a point of cultural imperialism. This causes reformed churches, which historically are predominantly white, to see "their" way as "the way," and again minorities feel rejected and not embraced because if we express ourselves, we're viewed as overly emotional, unintellectual, or even theologically and socially liberal. From a liturgical and homiletical perspective, it seems that the worship needs to be predictable when the regulative principle is wrongly applied and the preaching needs

The Whitewashing of Christianity

to be monotone to be spirit-led in many reformed circles, which leads to many associating reformed theology with racial and cultural oppression. Again, I know that not everyone feels this way, but it's still prevalent and needs to be addressed. Keller affirms this notion in his book *Center Church*. He notes how Shoki Coe, a Taiwanese-born man who challenged Western Christians' presentation to him of how to reach his people with the gospel. "He observed that the missionaries still gave national leaders forms of church ministry ways of expressing and formulating the gospel and structuring churches that were unalterably Western. National Christians were not being encouraged to think creatively about how to communicate the gospel to *their own culture*."[76] In other words, they were being presented with a way that spoke to white culture without taking other cultures into consideration, but a lot of times white reformed evangelicals don't see themselves as having a culture because they assume their way is right. This is the heart of whitewashing, making white the universal standard for all to follow. The results Keller acknowledges for minorities is that "this is the issue non-white culture faces in America they are given a model that often doesn't fit their culture, or they'll deny their culture altogether."[77] I'll address how minorities that internalize whitewashing are guilty of self-hatred and denial of their culture; they develop a disdain for it. In context, this chapter was addressing contextualization, but my aforementioned points apply because contextualization isn't limited to mission and evangelism. The results of denying their (Blacks and brown people) own culture is being embraced by many minorities because they want acceptance in reformed circles, but the fact that this is a trend is really an indictment if we have to lose ourselves culturally to be embraced theologically. If cultural expressions aren't denying any aspect of Scripture, then they should be embraced. The 1978 publication *Christianity in Culture* points out the same reality of whiteness being the standard for Christian life. They say, "Western logic was considered to be proper logic and those who do not think in our way were said to be pre-logical, prescientific, or possessed of a primitive mentality" (Levy-Bruhl 1923). "Western Christians often saw such divergence from normality as the result of unchecked sin in these other cultures. If such peoples were to be won to Christ, **they would first need to be civilized in order to be evangelized** (Anderson 1838 in Beaver 1967)."

---

76 Tim Keller, *Center Church: Doing Balanced, Gospel-Centered Ministry in Your City*, (Zondervan 2012), 91.

77 ibid.

Whatever our race, we should allow our citizenship to be in heaven (Philippians 3:20) and we should be embracing of the differences in approach as a display of the creative genius of God. Obviously, we shouldn't compromise the gospel for anyone, but if one culture is louder, volitional in their expression while another is more reserved should that really separate us or be labeled as heretical? It shouldn't, but it does when Blacks are functionally given two options: **1)** Be you and be on your own or; **2)** Join us just tone down the passionate and responsive preaching and movement during worship, because if it makes white people uncomfortable then it must not be right, but Blacks aren't given this same consideration when it comes to comfort. When these are our options minorities reject the culture of RT and not necessarily theology. The lines are blurred because it appears that those that have the doctrines of grace don't extend that grace to those that are culturally different in many cases.

3. The minimalist aesthetic of Reformed worship

This point is somewhat obscure because artistic expression is subjective, so I won't belabor his point here. As stated earlier, when it comes to worship from songs to expression, passion is interpreted and labeled as uncontrolled emotion. If I were to label worship gatherings void of emotion as lifeless, would I be heralded or confronted? A refusal by many in the reformed tradition to allow room for nuance in expression causes many Black and brown people to simply walk away, which is why The New York Times wrote an article attempting to understand the Black exodus from predominantly white churches called *A Quiet Exodus: Why Black Worshipers Are Leaving White Evangelical Churches*. In it Michael Emerson, author of *Divided by Faith* says, "Everything we tried is not working, a seminal work on race relations within the evangelical church. The 2016 election itself was the single most harmful event to the whole movement of reconciliation in at least the past 30 years, it's about to completely break apart." The election wasn't the only thing; the article chronicles how Blacks were essentially told that assimilation was a key component of racial integration, but Blacks were the only ones asked to assimilate in many cases and told to subject their Blackness to the gospel, but whites didn't see the need to do the same and subject their whiteness to the gospel.

4. Some Reformed theologians, particularly R.L. Dabney, have made statements deemed racist.

Historically the patriarchs of reformed theology were white men, many of which were either anti-Semitic like Martin Luther—who's heralded as a great reformer—owned slaves, or were in favor of slavery. I'm not saying everyone historically shared these views, but the fact that some of these guys are heralded does speak to minorities and the concern of minorities are either ignored or labeled as being "overly sensitive." Here are two quotes from Dabney, who Frame says can be "deemed" racist:

"It is well known that, as a general rule, [Negroes] are a graceless vagabondish set, and contribute very little to the support of the State by which they are protected. They are not citizens, never can become citizens, and wherever found in large numbers they are an expense and a source of trouble."

"The Black race is an alien one on our soil; and nothing except his amalgamation with ours, or his subordination to ours, can prevent the rise of that instinctive antipathy of race, which, history shows, always arises between opposite races in proximity."

If these statements are only "deemed racist," I wonder what qualifies as overt racism? When the racist history of many within the reformed tradition is broached, it seems that many of the heroes are given a pass because of their perceived theological prowess, and this is the biggest indictment against Reformed culture. If a willful racist gets a pass because he was a "product of his culture," then functionally one is saying that ethics don't matter if your theology is right. This is textbook antinomianism, which is a heresy. It's interesting that many come to the defense of a blatant racist without disavowing his racism in many cases. While none of our earthly heroes are perfect outside of Christ, when you couple the immense Anglo influence with racist history and the cultural ignorance about minorities, you're essentially telling minorities to "do your thing" and we'll do ours. I want to reiterate that I have tons of brothers in the faith of all racial backgrounds, but as stated earlier, reconciliation is impossible without confrontation and if this continues to be ignored and books are printed with broad statements about Black people that lack sources, we will continue to regress. My hope is to point out the holes within the culture and how we can close them to grow together, but as long as whitewashing and overt racism is ignored, this won't happen.

5. The Reformed emphasis on objective, absolute truth has sometimes been misused.

I covered this point in my response to his first reason for minorities not being in reformed churches. The issue isn't truth, but rather it's the culturally imperialistic way worship, preaching and hermeneutics are presented to minorities in many cases and a whitewashed narrative of Christianity that leaves Blacks out, even Blacks that were active during the Reformation.

The reality is any movement led by a predominant race is going to have some form of culture and not all forms of culture are welcoming to others. I won't deny this reality, but it's vital to own this reality and not try to present it as exclusively theological when it's drenched in culture, which some aspects are optional to embrace. Keller says in *Center Church* "they (white evangelicals) don't see any part of how they express or live the gospel to be 'anglo'—it is just the way things are. They feel that any change in how they preach, worship, or minister is somehow a compromise of the gospel. In this they may be doing what Jesus warns against— elevating the "traditions of men" to the same level as biblical truth (Mark 7:8). This happens when one's cultural approach to time or emotional expressiveness or way to communicate become enshrined as the Christian way to act and live."[78]

The reformed community has a culture that many view as exclusive in both culture and ideals and my hope is to start a conversation and seek reconciliation. I've witnessed this when the president of Acts 29 Network, Matt Chandler, met with all the minorities at a yearly retreat and apologized and asked how "we" can move forward. He owned it as our issue and not just the minorities' issue. I've seen the president of Southeastern Baptist Theological Seminary continue to push this issue as our issue and not a minority issue and that's encouraging and a step in the right direction, but there's obviously more work to be done. A29 and SEBTS have a long way to go, as does the Body of Christ in general, but let's not lose sight of this because there are non-believing witnesses that need us.

In order to get past this, we need to be intentional about making it clear that a person doesn't have to be reformed to be embraced (received by proponents of RT), especially if reformed is a smokescreen for cultural assimilation and imperialism. Reformed Theology is not the gospel and we should lead with being

---

78   Tim Keller, *Center Church: Doing Balanced, Gospel-Centered Ministry in Your City*, (Zondervan 2012), 96.

gospel-centered over being Reformed Calvinist. Blacks quite frankly aren't interested in being associated with anti-Semitic or slave-owning figures as paragons of the faith. I am acutely aware that Martin Luther and John Calvin are more than that, but I want to help many understand that leading with a frail man instead of Christ will not go well and ignoring their frailty doesn't help understanding, either. Lead and end with the gospel and be sure to not leave out the Black influence in Scripture and Christian history.

I think the African church father Augustine said it best: "unity in things necessary, liberty in things doubtful, charity in all things."

Discussion Questions

1. How was Reformed Theology presented to you?
2. What are some ways cultural differences can be appreciated?
3. Has any of the issues addressed in this chapter convicted you? If so, what steps toward change will you take?
4. What aspects of worship are essential vs. cultural? How do you make the proper distinction between the two?

5

Whitewashing Africa

> *Decisive intellectual achievements of Christianity were explored and understood first in Africa before they were recognized in Europe.*
> – THOMAS ODEN

IT'D BE IMPOSSIBLE to ignore the effects of whitewashing on the academic sector once one readily admits that whitewashing is a thing. Since Jesus has been inaccurately presented as a white man and this narrative has been widely accepted, it's vital that we examine how this has impacted institutions of higher education, in particular seminaries that purport the myth.

Most of those that work in these institutions will acknowledge that racism is wrong, yet they fail to see how racial bias has infected the way that they approach Scripture, history and academia. Most scholars will call out the blatant racist things said and written, but many ignore the subconscious effects of whitewashing that are sometimes unintentional, but no less factual, especially when it comes to the overwhelming Black presence in Scripture that is either ignored or wrongly represented. Scholarship that is racially biased is uncritically accepted as authentic without the same level of scrutiny. How can we acknowledge racism, yet limit its affects when it comes to how history and scholarship are presented? J. Daniel Hays points this out by addressing the fact that several of the twentieth-century giants of Old Testament studies, for example, were located in pre-WWII Germany, where racism was not only frequent, but widely accepted and extremely influential on the thinking of intellectuals. Additionally, the colonial outlook of many pre-WWII British intellectuals had a strong influence on biblical scholars and archaeologists in Britain as well. Because of the veneration of these white scholars by white scholars, their racial prejudice was overlooked, and many white scholars continue to be influenced by their views.[79] Remember, whitewashing is deliberate and Thomas Oden confronts the attempts to eradicate and demean African contributions to faith, philosophy and intellectualism in the hopes of whitewashing Africa in his book *How Africa Shaped the Christian Mind*, Oden says:

> It has seemed to leave Africa as if without a sense of distinguished literary and intellectual history. But this history that Africa already owns but which has remained buried and ignored. European intellectual history has gone on to proceed as if the great Christian intellectual and literary textual traditions of the Nile Valley and the Maghreb did not even exist. Its vast effects on Europe have not been grasped. Much of its history has been dismissed as heretical, as argued by German scholars like Adolf von Harnack and Walter Bauer, based on criteria that prevailed centuries later in Europe, interpretations which now are increasingly regarded as unpersuasive.[80]

Despite these attempts, Africa's mark on the world is indelible.

Ethiopia

Dr. David Daniels has done extensive research to refute the false narrative that Christianity spread to African nations through slavery. He points out that the church of Ethiopia was firmly established during the first century, Ethiopia was the first kingdom to accept Christianity as its state religion, that's right, a country in Africa, not Europe, embraced the Christian faith long before chattel slavery and the during The Protestant Reformation, and Ethiopia was commended by Martin Luther for not wavering in their faith during times of persecution.[81] While Rome added unbib-

---

79   J. Daniel Hays, *Racial Bias in the Academy Still?*, (Ouachita Baptist University), 316.
80   Thomas Oden, *How Africa Shaped the Christian Mind*, (IVP Books, 2007), 30.
81   Lisa Fields, *Through the Eyes of Color*, (Jude 3 Project 2019), 29.

lical practices that were antithetical to the gospel, Ethiopia was faithful.[82] The entire Ethiopian Kingdom was reached with the gospel and other countries in Africa as well; the first 100 years of Christianity reveals churches established in Egypt. By the fifth century, churches were established in Nubia and by 543, Nubia experienced Christianization that wasn't influenced by colonization.[83]

Library of Alexandria

The library of Alexandria of the third century provided the standard of the European university used in practically all of medieval Europe, but Africa and Africans aren't given credit or acknowledged for their scholarship and influence which impacted European theologians.[84] African Christians like Tertullian, who came up with the concept of the Trinity, the African philosopher Origen, who is considered by many to be one of Africa's greatest scientific investigators of sacred text, and African scholars like Didymus the Blind and Tyconius as stated earlier have all contributed heavily to the way people approach and interpret Scripture. These African men are presented as white men on almost every piece of literature in seminaries and institutions of higher education when you look on the cover of most textbooks. This goes back to a whitewashing of the continent of Africa in order to preserve the false narrative, which sadly, many seminaries and college support through inaccurate imagery.

Whitewashing Africa

As I stated earlier, whoever controls the printing controls the narrative. Time and time again, European scholars have depicted African church fathers in their image. In fact, early European archaeologists and anthropologists were aggressive in attempting to connect Egypt ethnically and culturally to Western Civilization. Their xenophobia had them denying the intellectual and technological prowess of Africans because they viewed Africans as primitive and intellectually inferior. The

---

82 David Daniels, *The African Roots of the Reformation* [audio podcast]. retrieved from https://podcast.apple.com/us/podcast/african-roots-reformation-special-guest-dr-dadiddaniels/id978012810?i=1000394480912. The Jude 3 Project (November 2017).

83 Everett Ferguson, *Church History, Volume One: From Christ to the Pre-Reformation*, (Grand Rapids, Michigan: Zondervan, 2013), 8.

84 Thomas Oden, *How Africa Shaped the Christian Mind*, (IVP Books, 2007), 38-39.

The Whitewashing of Christianity

preponderant theory among European Egyptologists throughout the latter half of the nineteenth century and up into the twentieth was that practically *all* significant cultural achievement in *all* African empires (including Egypt) was brought about by a small group of white elite rulers. Many of these scholars argued that the Africans were utterly unable to achieve anything significant in the area of culture or government even though they had it prior to whites learning about them. This is another example of whitewashing because we'll see how this has impacted the way the African Church Fathers who are innumerable are presented as white. If many of the early scholars were racist and viewed Blacks as primitive, how can their scholarship be trusted? Why would they continue to be used? Hays points out how racist scholars' works are repackaged, but not necessarily rebuked.

Many of Wallis Budge's works on Egypt have been reprinted and repackaged with flashy, attractive, contemporary covers. Waldenbooks, Borders, and Books-A-Million display his works prominently, and it takes a rather discerning reader to realize that his books are out-of-date by 100 years. Reflecting commonly held views of his time, Budge is frequently blatantly racist. For example, in one work he acknowledges that the archaeological data points to an African element in the early origins of "primitive" Egypt. However, he then assumes that some type of advanced outside civilization *must* have invaded in order to produce the early dynasties of Egypt, even though there was no archaeological evidence of this. He writes, "The facts related in it [the following chapter] illustrate the manner in which the civilization of the dynastic Egyptians developed out of the primitive culture of the indigenous predynastic peoples of Egypt, after it had been modified and improved by the superior intelligence of a race of men, presumably of Asiatic origin, who invaded and conquered Egypt."[85] Likewise, H. Hall, in the prestigious *Cambridge Ancient History*, in discussing intermarriage that occurred later in Egyptian history after the development of this "superior race," writes, "This cannot have been any but a degenerate component in the new Egyptian race, to which the Ethiopian and the Negro elements contributed nothing good except a certain amount of energy."[86] Hall continues by describing the results of this intermarriage as a "particularly villainous cast of countenance," and as a "contamination."

---

85 J. Daniel Hays, *Racial Bias in the Academy Still?*, (Ouachita Baptist University), 316.
86 ibid.

Although Hall wrote this back in 1927, it continued to be reprinted as part of the *Cambridge Ancient History* until just a few years ago.[87]

Are you starting to notice a pattern? If it's of significance, it must be white and if it's Black, it must be inferior. Racism in scholarship didn't limit itself to painting Africa with one broad white stroke; it did the same thing to how Scripture was interpreted. Cush, a Black African kingdom south of Egypt, has been wrongly presented as slaves by these "scholars" and their contributions essentially ignored even though the term Cush or Cushite appears 54 times in the Hebrew Scriptures, revealing that the Africans played a significant role in redemptive history, especially in the Old Testament.

Tainted Translation

Scholars, and I use that term loosely, didn't stop with whitewashing Africa; this continued with how they treated Africans in Scripture. Most notably the Cushites are undeniably Black Africans mentioned in Scripture. The word Cush itself means "Black," and, historically, the people of Cush have been dark-skinned people. Jeremiah mentions the Cushites' skin color when he rhetorically asks, "Can the Cushite change his skin?" (Jeremiah 13:23). The Cushites were soldiers and mercenaries in the army of Egypt, the primary ally of Judah in her rebellion against the Babylonians.[88] Ethiopians have a tradition that after the flood Ham traveled up the Nile River to the Atbara plain. From there, they could see the Ethiopian tableland. Ham's family settled there and also in the nearby lowland. This tradition, supported by the biblical account, makes the Cushites among the most ancient people-groups in existence. Scholars, however, took the liberty to use several terms when referring to them which makes them hard to place or acknowledge. They've been labeled Nubia, Wawat, Cush, Meroe and Ethiopia, and while these terms were accurate throughout history, the problem arises with how the Greeks called all Black people south of Egypt Ethiopian (the burnt faces). While the Hebrew Bible used the term Cush for the region as well as the inhabitants, scholars elected to be inconsistent as it related

---

87   ibid.

88   R. Deutsch and M. Heltzer, *Forty New Ancient West Semitic Inscriptions* (Tel Aviv, 1994); J. D. Hays, "The Cushites: A Black Nation in the Bible," (BSac 153 (996), 396-409.

to the terms Cush or Cushi (Cushite).[89] The King James Version translates Cush as Ethiopia two thirds of the time in Scripture, The English Standard Version Cush two thirds of the time and make it Ethiopia one third of the time; most notably the ESV uses Cush in Jeremiah 38-39, but Ethiopia in Jeremiah 46:9. The 1988 Jewish Publication Society's English translation of the Tanakh (the Hebrew Bible) uses all three terms—Ethiopia, Cush and Nubia—and doesn't provide any legitimate or scholarly reason for the change. The issue here is that the use of the term Ethiopia is misleading because modern day Ethiopia is a different location than Cush. Why is this significant? The use of several different terms to describe Cush is an attempt to diffuse the significance these Black Africans play in redemptive history. As stated earlier, whitewashing is deliberate and while they didn't paint the Cushites as white, whitewashing degrades their contributions. Additionally, the liberty that was taken on Africans in Scripture is emblematic of the indifference of some white translators as it relates to the terms and the people it represents, which is why scholarly effort wasn't deemed necessary to present them in Scripture consistently.

Black Erasure from Scripture

As stated earlier, the Cushites are one of the most ancient people groups and appear 54 times in the Hebrew Scriptures, with more variation than any other group. While the Hittites (indo-European group) are mentioned 61 times, 10 of the 61 refers to the same person: Uriah the Hittite. Arab or Arabia appears less than 20 times and the Sumerians and Hurrians aren't mentioned directly in undisputed biblical text. Guess who scholars choose to focus on? You guessed it, everyone but the Black African Cushites, who are mentioned more times and with greater variation than any other group. Donald J Wiseman's *People of the Old Testament* focuses on the Hurrians, Hittites and his updated work *People of the Old Testament World* dropped the chapter on Arabs and Ethiopians and added a chapter on the Sumerians, who aren't even mentioned in Scripture. Both books address the Old Testament world, but neither 'world' includes the Black African Cushites, yet this is considered scholarly and credible. Do scholars envision or desire a world void of Blacks? If so, this world is an unbiblical one. It gets worse; the Anchor Bible Dictionary devotes two pages to what they write as Kush and fourteen pages to the Hittites. The Hurrians, who aren't mentioned in Scripture, get three pages, one more than the Black Africans

---

89   ibid.

mentioned 54 times in Scripture. Whitewashing in biblical translation and historic engagement has consistently completely ignored Blacks or demeaned their contributions, and this is something that should be shunned and corrected. If practically ignoring the Cushites wasn't enough, 'scholars' literally removed Cush from the map. The Cushite empire is omitted from maps and if included, it's wrongly placed. The book *People of the Old Testament World* locates the Hittites and Sumerians, but, you guessed it, they leave out Cush. The omission is also common in popular Old Testament Surveys and Introductions. Cush is removed in *The Old Testament: An Introduction to the Hebrew Bible* by Stephen L. Harris and Robert L. Platzner, *The Old Testament Story* by John H. Tullock and Mark McEntire, and *An Introduction to the Hebrew Bible* by Barry Bandstra.[90] Consistently scholars exhibit laziness and carelessness when it comes to Cush as a people and a geographic location, but don't show this lethargy when it comes to other groups. Again, whitewashing is deliberate and has infected scholarship to a point where what's written about Africans almost can't be trusted if anything is written at all. These intentional omissions contribute to many Black millennials questioning the reliability of the Bible when people who are supposed to be committed to truth and history ignore certain sects of Africans in Scripture. They may not view this as important, but people serving in urban areas have to deal with these barriers created by people who highlight one group over another. To be clear, these omissions aren't in the Bible itself; I must say this for hoteps. "Hotep" is an Egyptian word that means "at peace." Over the past several decades, the word has also been utilized primarily by Black Americans who happen to be more Afrocentric. Hoteps and other Afrocentric faiths will point to the mishandling of white scholars as it relates to Blacks in Scripture and history as a reason for Black people to leave Christianity alone. They don't realize they are acquiescing to white supremacy when they give whites credit for a faith that thrived in Africa before Europe. Scripture reveals that people of color are on essentially every page of Scripture and loved and used by God in his plan of redemption.

Careless Commentaries

We've established that the Cushites were an African group of people with high visibility and contribution to biblical history, yet have been largely ignored and misrepresented by scholars. While scholars have chosen to ignore them, the

---

90   ibid.

prophet Isaiah did not. The first 39 chapters of the book of Isaiah mentions them. The truth about the Cushites is that they conquered southern Egypt and established a dynasty in 715 B.C.E., after their conquest in 728 B.C.E. The Cushites also opposed the Assyrians during the reign of King Hezekiah, which is one of the main reasons that Isaiah mentions them so extensively.[91] It's disheartening that many commentaries on the book of Isaiah fail to mention the Cushites in their introductions when providing historical background information about the book of Isaiah even when the prophet himself mentions them.

Slaves, Not Soldiers?

Whitewashing is intentional about Black erasure and rewriting a less favorable story of what Africans have contributed to the Christian faith. After practically ignoring the Cushites, wrongly placing Cush and not giving them scholarly mentions, lastly, scholars have been intentional about painting the Cushites as inferior and as slaves. When they are mentioned, they are primarily referenced in a place of subservience. While there's no biblical support to label the Cushites as slaves, scholars have taken the liberty to fill in white spaces of history with a white narrative on this great group of people. During the Old Testament era, the Cushites were known as soldiers, archers to be more specific. Biblically speaking, we see that Cushite soldiers in David's army (2 Samuel 18:19-33), and it was a Cushite who shared the news of Absalom's death with David. The text points to the Cushites being soldiers, not slaves. Commentaries have wrongly labeled them slaves, while conquered nations would make slaves of their conquest, this is true of all nationalities during that time—Hittites, Israelites, Amorites, Canaanites and Arameans, etc, but other nations aren't painted with the same broad slavery stroke. Hays points out how Henry Smith assumes that Blacks during the biblical times must have been slaves when he writes, "Joab then calls a Negro (naturally, a slave) and commands him…" Naturally a slave? This is what makes people question the veracity of the Christian faith when its 'followers' ignore commands of love and dignity especially as it relates to Black and brown people. Henry Smith isn't alone in his assumption of the Cushites being slaves, Keil and Delitzsch, Alexander Kirkpatrick, Robert Bergen and Mary Evans all make

---

91 ibid.

the same inaccurate assumption.[92] They don't do this with Uriah the Hittite, but they make this assumption with African people. White scholars repeatedly start with the assumptions that Black people in Scripture must be slaves and work from that presupposition. What they don't provide by in large is evidence, history or footnotes, because Black inferiority is widely accepted in many white Christian scholarly circles, and this is something that must be addressed and must cease because assumptions don't constitute as textual support. The scholars J. Daniel Hays mentions, show themselves to be guilty of confirmation bias, motivated reasoning and lacking proper hermeneutics when it comes to Africans and approach the text looking for confirmation of Black inferiority instead of accurate depictions of biblical history.

While not all white scholars are guilty of the aforementioned, a concerted effort is needed to stop the whitewashing of Africa and Africans in Scripture. Unless this is confronted and repaired, this will only continue to widen the gap of understanding, racial harmony and Black and brown lostness. In order to capture a comprehensive narrative of the richness of Christian history, there must be a rejection of any narrative that ignores Africa or paints the continent and its inhabitants in an exclusively negative light. When you whitewash the contribution of Africa to the Christian faith, you not only have an incomplete presentation of biblical history, you have a dishonest one. Thankfully, while efforts to ignore and, in many cases, remove Africa from the hearts and minds of many, God's use of African people in redemptive history is indelible.

Discussion Questions

1. Why is celebrating Africans essential to our understanding of biblical history?
2. How has omitting the Black and brown presence in Scripture negatively affected people socially, theologically and culturally?
3. Were you aware of the overwhelming presence of Africans in Scripture? If not, why not?
4. How does understanding the African influence on Christianity change your own understanding?

---

92   ibid.

6

Product of his Culture
The Whitewashing of Slavery

We have been trained in slaveholder exegesis, where the limits on sin have transformed into the ideal and the stories have been sapped of their strength.
– Dr. ESAU MCCAULEY

ON JULY 15TH, 1787, two women made it to Paris. One was named Polly; the other was named Sally Hemings. She (Sally) was only fourteen-years-old. She was described as "very handsome, with long straight hair down her back." Sally was introduced to a 44-year-old man who was very influential and powerful, and unfortunately, this much older man forced himself on her. This older man only wanted her for his sexual exploits and didn't care about her as a person or anyone that looked like her. Two years later Sally would become pregnant with his first child at the age of sixteen, and this young lady would lead a revolt against her abuser because she refused to return to slavery and she had to fight for her freedom and for the freedom of her children against their own father.

What's both heartbreaking and interesting is the man who didn't want the freedom of his own children wrote these words just eleven-years prior to forcing himself on a fourteen-year-old girl:

"We hold these truths to be self-evident, that all men are created equal, that they are endowed by their Creator with certain unalienable Rights, that among these are Life, Liberty and the pursuit of Happiness."[93]

Thomas Jefferson penned the preamble of the Declaration of Independence in 1776, yet "liberty" didn't apply to everyone, because Jefferson was a staunch proponent of slavery of people of color largely based on pseudo-science and the myth of racial superiority, and while he verbally bemoaned the existence of slavery and attempted abolition in some ways, he continually profited off of owning people and thought that emancipation should be gradual. At the time he co-wrote the Declaration of Independence, Jefferson owned an estimated 600 slaves. Freedom for people of color wouldn't be realized until 1865 in Galveston, TX by what is known as Juneteenth, which is recognized and celebrated primarily by people of color. It was in 1865, not 1776 when at least on paper all of God's image bearers were free, but there were people fighting for freedom for generations that would come after them and one of the many catalysts for the fight for freedom was a girl named Sally Hemings. Thomas Jefferson comfortably wrote a document he didn't actually believe or practice, and this aspect of his legacy is often overlooked in hopes to preserve one aspect of this story; slavery is something that should be vehemently opposed, but it becomes subjective when evangelical heroes participated in this heinous institution. Slavery has consistently been an area of duplicity in the heart of the United States and the American church and the Civil War highlighted this contradiction, as Jemar Tisby says, "the nation emphasized liberty as a natural right, made repeated concessions to allow for slavery."[94] Religious institutions consistently dropped the ball intentionally when it came to the subject of slavery; Tisby highlights how Methodists split over slave-owning bishops, Baptists split over slave-owning missionaries, and Presbyterians split over "Christ of Caesar." When it came to the Bible and slavery, Southern white Christians didn't view slavery as wrong or sinful and affirmed that God sanctioned the institution of slavery and that bondage under white people was a natural state for people of African descent.[95] They argued that the Bible never repudiated slavery. I guess they

---

93   National Archives, *Declaration of Independence: A Transcription* https://www.archives.gov/founding-docs/declaration-transcript accessed February 2021.

94   Jemar Tisby, *The Color of Compromise*, (Grand Rapids, MI, Zondervan 2019), 72.

95   ibid., 80

missed Exodus 21:16, which states that man stealing was a crime that deserved death. Despite the epic failure of many, there were abolitionists who constantly challenged proslavery advocates, asking "where is the sentence [of Scripture] in which God ever appointed you, the Anglo-Saxon race [over another people], you, the mixture of all races under heaven, you who cannot tell whether the blood of Shem, Ham, or Japheth mingles in your veins?"[96] This mindset still exists in the form of a phrase to excuse the heinous acts of slave owners by simply saying they were products of their culture.

I remember a good friend of mine shared a story with me that was disheartening, but not surprising. He was in his seminary class and they were discussing the topic of slavery. As the only Black person in the room, he explains, he felt the tension in the room, but this wasn't anything new, being that this was his third year at this seminary. Each student was tasked to give a biblical explanation of slavery and what alarmed him was how classmate after classmate defended the institution and those who owned slaves. In fact, one student championed the institution of slavery by saying that "America had no choice, either we enslave the Africans, or we would've gone bankrupt as a country, we had to do it and God sovereignly allowed it, so it can't be too bad." Sitting in his chair furious with the willful ignorance and lack of compassion of his classmates and the silence of his teacher, he asked about Christians who owned slaves and how it could align with Christian ethics and to his surprise, he was told, we have to remember that slavery was acceptable during those times and that's just the way it was back then. Additionally, so we don't judge these men who were excellent communicators of the gospel too harshly, we must extend grace, they were just "products of their culture." My friend sat there speechless. This wasn't in the early 1900s; this was 2014, and this sanctioning of sin continues. Whitewashing will present the most heinous acts as noble or necessary in order to give a pass to white men who embraced white supremacist anthropological ethics at the expense of the faith they claimed to hold. The phrase 'product of his culture' applies to white slave owning homiletical heroes like George Whitefield and Jonathan Edwards, but not Blacks who weren't allowed into reformed institutions. They are quickly labeled liberal heretics while slave masters are imperfect, but orthodox. This is the diabolical nature of whitewashing; it defends sinful institutions while disparaging others.

---

96   Stephen R. Haynes, *Noah's Curse: The Biblical Justification of American Slavery* (New York: Oxford University Press, 2002), loc. 2737, Kindle.

Whitefield was a product of his culture, but Martin Luther King Jr. was an adulterous heretic. The Bible says to love your neighbor as yourself, but if the majority of white people during a certain era didn't love their Black neighbors or reject the idea that they were neighbors, then apparently that Scripture no longer applies.

One of the reasons many people see Christianity as oppressive is because of the mishandling of the topic of slavery. Scripture never has and never would affirm chattel slavery and the heinous acts of the Trans-Atlantic Slave Trade. God never sanctioned the rape, murder, or disbanding of families committed by white supremacists, nor would He affirm people who continue these acts as His children. Sadly, the mishandling of the subject has caused many to associate slavery with Christianity, as if God affirmed the degradation of Black and brown bodies. This is most notably seen in how Lena Waithe, director of the critically acclaimed movie *Queen & Slim*, responded in an interview with Elle. Waithe says, "I'm a person who is constantly marinating on religion, because I was raised religious. [It's] very much a residue left behind from slavery, in terms of Sunday being the only day they got off. It was the one thing that was sort of honored, yet it was the thing that [made] them say, 'Oh, this is why we're slaves, because the Bible says so.' It was [what] they needed to give them joy, but it was the thing that kept them in captivity. There's still a lack of freedom, because of religion, in the Black community."[97] Waithe is not alone in her sentiments. Many have wrongly embraced an incomplete version of history, one that presents white supremacists as beating Christianity into slaves when in actuality, they attempted to beat inferiority and slavery into them, but were unsuccessful; this is why Harriet Tubman was also known as Grandma Moses. Free Black people and slaves who could read knew that God didn't condone their degradation and knew that "massa" had something to hide by making it illegal for them to read or wrongly presenting verses on slavery. History reveals that Caribbean slave owners published what they called the "Slave Bible" in 1807. This was three years after the Haitian revolution (Toussaint L'Overture, the leader of that revolution was a literate Christian). A successful uprising of African slaves in North America sent shockwaves of panic throughout the slaveholding European nations. In response to the uprising, slavery proponents commissioned a "Slave Bible" which removed 90% of the Old Testament,

---

97   Anita Little, *The Women of Queen & Slim Survive at All Cost* https://www.elle.com/culture/a29339190/lenawaithe-jodie-turner-smith-melina-matsoukas-queen-and-slim-interview-2019/ October 2019.

The Whitewashing of Christianity

and 50% of the New Testament and was meant to be read by slaves. Why would slave masters remove specific sections of Scripture? It's because they didn't want slaves reading verses of Scripture like:

Exodus 3:7-9 (CSB)

7 Then the Lord said, "I have observed the misery of my people in Egypt, and have heard them crying out because of their oppressors. I know about their sufferings, 8 and I have come down to rescue them from the power of the Egyptians and to bring them from that land to a good and spacious land, a land flowing with milk and honey — the territory of the Canaanites, Hethites, Amorites, Perizzites, Hivites, and Jebusites. 9 So because the Israelites' cry for help has come to me, and I have also seen the way the Egyptians are oppressing them.

What Waithe and others may not know is that many Blacks who were forced into slavery, were Christians prior to getting to America and had strong beliefs about Yeshua and His plan for their lives, yet this isn't known and is often ignored because proponents of whitewashing and opponents of Christianity benefit from an inaccurate interpretation of Scripture and an incomplete view of history.

The Trans-Atlantic Slave Trade involved stealing humans in addition to some of them being forcefully sold. Biblically, this act was punishable by death, and verses that opposed the acts of slave owners obviously weren't referenced by slave owners. When this isn't explained, many walk away thinking that because God allowed the slave trade that God affirmed the slave trade, white supremacists, and their actions. We must make a distinction between what God allows and what God affirms. God never affirmed rape, abuse and hatred, and not explaining this has many thinking that only Black and brown people were on the short end of the stick as it relates to who God accepts and favors historically and presently. The Old and New Testaments condemn the practice of "man-stealing," which is what happened in Africa in the sixteenth to nineteenth centuries through primarily a race-based form of oppression. Africans were gathered by slave-hunters, then sold to slave-traders, who forcefully brought them to the New World to work on plantations and farms for their own economic and social gain. This practice was and is reprehensible to God. As the book of Exodus teaches us, the penalty for such a crime in the Mosaic Law was death, not a "product of his culture" pass, but death: "Whoever steals a man and sells him, and anyone found in possession of him, shall be put to death." (Exodus 21:16) The New Testament speaks against abusive slavery and man-stealing, too; slave-traders are listed among those who are "ungodly and sinful" and are in the same category as those who kill their fathers or mothers, murderers, adulterers and perverts, and liars and perjurers:

> 1 Timothy 1:8-10
>
> 8 Now we know that the law is good, if one uses it lawfully, 9 understanding this, that the law is not laid down for the just but for the lawless and disobedient, for the ungodly and sinners, for the unholy and profane, for those who strike their fathers and mothers, for murderers, 10 the sexually immoral, men who practice homosexuality, enslavers, liars, perjurers, and whatever else is contrary to sound doctrine,

It's important to notice that enslavers in this context are mentioned as ungodly, why? Because of their willful hatred of others. The Apostle John also makes it clear that no willfully hateful person is a child of God nor loves God, so, the Bible is clear that the acts of unrepentant white supremacists that profited, benefited and propagated a race-based hierarchy were not and are not of God:

> 1 John 4:20-21
>
> 20 If anyone says, "I love God," and hates his brother, he is a liar; for he who does not love his brother whom he has seen cannot love God whom he has not seen. 21 And this commandment we have from him: whoever loves God must also love his brother.

So if you're reading this and thinking that God affirmed the acts of oppression against people of color, you're wrong. It's important not to blame God for the actions of men or assign to Scripture the wrong interpretation based on how people intentionally misused Scripture. A person can use a hammer to build a beautiful home or they can use a hammer to batter someone to death. That doesn't make all hammers bad; we wouldn't blame that hammer, we'd look at what a person did with the hammer and judge the person. This principle must apply to Scripture. We can't blame God and the Bible for how people intentionally misused it in order to paint the Bible with one broad stroke of oppression. I'm sure

The Whitewashing of Christianity

some of you are reading this and thinking what about Ephesians? Let's examine what Paul meant when he said "slaves, obey your masters":

Ephesians 6:5-6

5 Slaves, obey your earthly masters with fear and trembling, with a sincere heart, as you would Christ, 6 not by the way of eye-service, as people-pleasers, but as bondservants of Christ, doing the will of God from the heart,

Many use Ephesians 6 as the "gotcha" verse against Christianity and see this verse as the reason Black and brown people should never be Christians. They see this verse as the Bible condoning all forms of slavery, including the Trans-Atlantic Slave Trade. What many fail to understand is that slavery in biblical times was very different from the slavery that was practiced in the past few centuries in many parts of the world. To understand Paul's words and view of slavery, we must look at the Old Testament. What causes the confusion for contemporary readers is the assumption that the word "slave," as it is found in Old Testament legal passages, meant the same thing in ancient Israel as it does for us today or that it mirrors the slavery of the antebellum South in all cases. The Old Testament was written in Hebrew, and so it is not surprising that certain words do not have perfect equivalents in modern English. The Old Testament does not call an individual bound to the service of another a "slave"; it calls him an 'ebed (pronounced eved), and a woman in such a role is called an 'āmâ and in most cases the term refers to class.[98] Additionally, hoteps and the like don't take into account that the book of Ephesians was written around A.D. 60, long before the Trans-Atlantic Slave Trade, which makes reading something that happened over a thousand years after something that was written over a thousand years before both historically and culturally irresponsible. Some think the word slave holds the same meaning and that all slavery is the same, which simply isn't true. The slavery in the Bible was not based exclusively on race. People were not enslaved because of their nationality or the color of their skin during biblical times. In Bible times, slavery was based primarily on economics; it was a matter of social status, not skin color. Believe it or not, people sold themselves as slaves when they could not pay their debts

---

98 Doug Becker, *Does the Bible Condone Slavery* https://emergencenj.org/blog/2019/01/04/does-the-bible-condoneslavery January 2019.

or provide for their families. Slavery was primarily indentured servitude, which at times was voluntary and never intended to be abusive, nor was a person to be a slave forever. We see the concept of indentured servitude which at times was voluntary in Deuteronomy 15:12-18 which says,

> "If your brother, a Hebrew man or a Hebrew woman, is sold to you, he shall serve you six years, and in the seventh year you shall let him go free from you. 13 And when you let him go free from you, you shall not let him go empty-handed. 14 You shall furnish him liberally out of your flock, out of your threshing floor, and out of your winepress. As the Lord your God has blessed you, you shall give to him. 15 You shall remember that you were a slave in the land of Egypt, and the Lord your God redeemed you; therefore I command you this today. 16 But if he says to you, 'I will not go out from you,' because he loves you and your household, since he is well-off with you, 17 then you shall take an awl, and put it through his ear into the door, and he shall be your slave forever. And to your female slave you shall do the same. 18 It shall not seem hard to you when you let him go free from you, for at half the cost of a hired worker he has served you six years. So the Lord your God will bless you in all that you do."

Notice that the person was promised to be released, that the person was to be released furnished and not empty handed and that the person had the option to stay. Remember, the term slavery means servant in this context not being someone's personal property for dehumanization. Another scriptural passage that should inform one's understanding of what was legal in ancient Israel as it pertains to slavery is Deuteronomy 23:15–16, which says, "You shall not give up to his master a slave who has escaped from his master to you. He shall dwell with you, in your midst, in the place that he shall choose within one of your towns, wherever it suits him. You shall not wrong him."[99] Notice the passage says, "you shall not wrong him." The Trans-Atlantic Slave Trade thrived on wronging and dehumanizing Black lives. It is simply historically inaccurate to import chattel slavery into the biblical reality of the Old Testament institution of indentured servitude.

---

99 Moshe Weinfeld, *Deuteronomy and the Deuteronomic School*, (Winona Lake, IN: Eisenbrauns, 1992), 272.

Additionally, according to the law of Moses, it was actually illegal to return a fugitive slave. In fact, this passage commands his fellow Israelites to allow him to dwell wherever he pleases. Effectively, Israelite slaves could break their service contracts simply by leaving. Slavery in Israelite law was entered into voluntarily and could be ended voluntarily.[100] There was nothing voluntary about being stolen from your native land and forced into manual labor.

When we read the New Testament, what we'll find is that sometimes lawyers, doctors, and even politicians were slaves of someone else. Some people actually chose to be slaves as a means to have all their needs provided for by their masters.[101] When Paul wrote this (Ephesians 6:5-6), he didn't have rape, breaking up families, racial hierarchy or any of the terrible acts against people of color in mind; he had the cultural norms of slavery during his day in mind, which was working, not being dehumanized. This is why slaves are exhorted to obey their earthly masters. There is a deliberate wordplay on the Greek kyrios ('master, lord'), which is usually rendered 'Lord' with reference to Christ (Ephesians 6:4) or God. The adjective earthly is not to be understood negatively or disparagingly; rather, it shows that these masters are lords within an earthly realm and aren't better or have more value than the person that works for them within the sphere of human relations, in contrast to the Lord, who is in heaven. Ultimately, Christian slaves in Paul's mind belong to the one Lord, Jesus Christ (read Ephesians 6:6), and their obedience to their earthly masters is all of a piece with their serving Him: Yeshua (Ephesians 6:7-8). Some of you may be wondering, what about the fear and trembling, that doesn't sound voluntary to me? The word for fear in the Greek here is the word phobos and it means fear in some cases, but in this text it's the idea of reverence/respect/honor, not fear for your life. Paul is addressing the idea of motivation, saying to work unto God, not man. Paul is the only New Testament writer to use this expression (1 Corinthians 2:3; 2 Corinthians 7:15; Philippians 2:12), and on each of these occasions, consistent with what is known as the LXX.[102] The LXX is the Greek Old Testament, or Septuagint (from the

---

100 Doug Becker, *Does the Bible Condone Slavery* https://emergencenj.org/blog/2019/01/04/does-the-bible-condoneslavery, January 2019.

101 Got Questions? *Does the Bible condone slavery?* https://www.gotquestions.org/Bible-slavery.html, accessed October 2019.

102 Peter Thomas O'Brien, *The Letter to the Ephesians*, The Pillar New Testament Commentary (Grand Rapids, MI: W.B. Eerdmans Publishing Co., 1999), 450.

Latin: septuāgintā literally "seventy," often abbreviated as 70 in Roman numerals, i.e., LXX), is the earliest extant Koine Greek. The phrase has to do with an attitude of due reverence and awe in the presence of God, a godly fear of the believer in view of the final day when Yeshua returns. When Paul encourages slaves to obey their masters, that obedience should be rendered with reverence and awe in the presence of God. What people miss about Ephesians 6 is that it has a command for the slave master, too, which is another case against assigning oppression to God, Scripture and Christianity. This verse wasn't read by slave masters, but it's in Scripture to remind us of God's care for all people. Verse nine says to stop threats, why? Paul is addressing that not every boss will honor God in how they treat people, but God's standard never changed. Paul essentially rejects all forms of manipulating, demeaning, or terrifying slaves by threats, which opposes what the slave trades of the sixteenth through the nineteenth centuries were all about. In the immediate context, slaves have already been instructed to show respect, sincerity of heart, and goodwill; now masters are urged to treat them in a similar manner. The command God gave to masters was always omitted by slave masters because Scripture undermined their unbiblical practices.[103]

Any good theologian would immediately reject the idea that embracing chattel slavery was submitting to Scripture. They would know that embracing degradation would be submitting Scripture to culture, when in fact Scripture should transcend culture, but nevertheless the 'product of his culture' phrase is used when people realize that their heroes weren't really that heroic after all. For instance, Cotton Mather ensured that slaves were included in his compensation package when he became the pastor of a church. He used the biblical name Onesimus for one of his slaves and referred to him as an "it."[104] Additionally, the Puritans were complicit in crafting a hostile culture toward people of color by seeing them as less than people, whitewashing slavery is done by ignoring the duplicity of its proponents which are highlighted for their robust soteriology, while ignoring their flawed, unbiblical and unloving anthropology.[105] Two of the most heralded men given a pass for their views on slavery are George Whitefield and Jonathan Edwards.

---

103   Peter Thomas O'Brien, *The Letter to the Ephesians*, The Pillar New Testament Commentary (Grand Rapids, MI: W.B. Eerdmans Publishing Co., 1999), 454.
104   Ibram X. Kendi, *Stamped from the Beginning: The Definitive History of Racist Ideas in America* (New York: Nation Books, 2016), 69.
105   Bryan Loritts, *Inside Outsider* (Grand Rapids, MI, Zondervan 2018), 20.

The Whitewashing of Christianity

George Whitefield

George Whitefield grew up in Gloucester, England, and has been presented as one who confronted slavery when he began to visit America in the late 1730s. By 1740, he reportedly indicted Southern slave masters for their abuses of slaves. In his writing, Letter to the Inhabitants of Maryland, Virginia, North and South Carolina, he says "Your dogs are caressed and fondled at your tables; but your slaves who are frequently styled dogs or beasts, have not an equal privilege. They are scarce permitted to pick up the crumbs which fall from their masters' tables.... Although I pray to God the slaves may never be permitted to get the upper hand, yet should such a thing be permitted by Providence, all good men must acknowledge the judgment would be just." From a distance, one would think that Whitefield demonstrated compassion for Blacks who responded to his proselytization, believing that they could become educated Christians, while simultaneously ignoring the system structured against them being 'educated.' A few years later, Whitefield would become connected with slave masters who had converted under his ministry and complied with their offers to give him slaves and a South Carolina plantation. It was at this point that Whitefield became convinced that he needed slaves to work at a Georgia plantation to fund the operations of his Bethesda orphanage. He convinced himself that slavery was good for slaves and imagined that slaves could work the Bethesda farms, which in turn would fund operations at the orphanage. Whitefield is presented as not seeing the contradiction between Christian altruism and the development of chattel slavery, but the reality is he saw it, but chose to ignore it. Even though Georgia banned slavery from the colony, Whitefield became a staunch proponent of the legalization of slavery and he even had slaves working prior to the ban being lifted. This doesn't sound like a man who was a **product of his culture** when slavery was banned, and he fought for its legalization. When we make excuses for social injustices like slavery, we ignore the deplorable acts committed by slave owners against their victims: men, women and children. Are we to apply the same logic to what's culturally acceptable today? If a man is in a polyamorous relationship yet holds to justification by faith and memorizes tons of Scripture, are we to give him a pass? The phrase "product of his culture" is a way to ignore the sin of men who preached against sin and, while I don't expect perfection from any man, whenever the topic of slavery is addressed and those that participated in this injustice are given excuses, it communicates that you can sin against Black and brown people and not be held accountable. It says that theology can be separate from ethics. Secondly, the idea that Whitefield was a product of his culture isn't true; he strongly opposed it in his younger years and as he got older there were still white Quakers opposing it (slavery). How could they know it was wrong, but culture caused him to forget? Whitewashing uses phrases like the product of his culture in order to avoid the reality of their past indiscretions as well as to present them (slave owners like Whitefield) as noble. The reality is that Whitefield wasn't a product of his culture; he saw Black people as products so much so that Whitefield did not even free his Bethesda slaves in his will.

Jonathan Edwards

Jonathan Edwards was born on October 5, 1703 and was the son of Timothy Edwards (1668–1759), a minister in the state of Connecticut. His mother, Esther Stoddard, was the daughter of Reverend Solomon Stoddard. Jonathan, their only son, was the fifth of 11 children. He was trained for college by his father and elder sisters, all of whom received an excellent education and one of whom, Esther, the eldest, wrote a semi-humorous tract on the immateriality of the soul, often mistakenly attributed to Jonathan. Edwards was an influential American theologian, philosopher, revivalist, missionary, and chancellor. He's regarded as one of the most prolific preachers and writers of his day, and while he had the ability to break down a text of Scripture and the eloquence of a poetic preacher, Edwards owned slaves like his father Timothy Edwards, and personally purchased slaves himself. He, like Whitefield, defended slavery. Edwards defended the institution of slavery against abolitionists, and according to George Marsden, Edwards defended slavery by arguing that "the Bible expressly allowed slavery and it would not contradict itself."[106] Not only is Edwards given a pass, but his eisegesis on the topic of slavery is often ignored as well.

Whitefield and Edwards aren't the only two who justified their acts against people of color. There are a myriad of examples of 'heroes' who were in favor of owning people and it was justified by proponents of the institution and admirers of their teachings. The product of his culture phrase is another way of giving a pass to people who want to merge Christianity and an unbiblical form of slavery, but this is a smack in the face of orthodoxy. This is what Katherine Gerbner calls

---

106   George Marsden, *Jonathan Edwards: A Life*, (Yale Publishers 2003), 257.

The Whitewashing of Christianity

Protestant Supremacy in her book *Christian Slavery*. Gerbner's argument traces three historical steps in the transition from the belief in "Protestant supremacy" to an all-out defense of "Christian slavery." Gerbner shows how the construction of racialized slavery in the Atlantic world was closely tied with unbalanced definitions of what it meant to be a Christian. Gerbner focuses on Anglican, Quaker, and Moravian missionaries, while demonstrating how their formulation of Christian slavery shaped and anticipated the thinking of key Great Awakening leaders like the aforementioned George Whitefield. The three-step process and the first step was to create an identity around the idea of "Protestant supremacy." They tied their belief in the superiority of Protestantism to their belief in the superiority of white ethnicity and culture. Second, as an increasing number of enslaved and free Blacks in the New World did convert, get baptized, and join a church, their conversions destabilized the fundamentals of Protestant supremacy by mystifying the assumed bond between Christianity and white ethnicity. In response, the white plantocracy, which is a population of planters regarded as the dominant class, especially in the West Indies, altered the definition of Christianity to include a wider ethnic diversity. However, they also altered the relationship between Christian identity and freedom, basing free status and social hierarchy no longer in religion but in race—i.e., no longer in their exclusive Protestant identity but in exclusive whiteness. Third, they had missionaries to purport this egregious view of Scripture and humanity by attempting to convince slaves that conversion didn't alter their social or eternal status. Facing resistance from the plantocracy to evangelize slaves for spiritual regeneration, but perpetual servitude, missionaries of various Protestant backgrounds cast a vision for what Gerbner calls "Christian slavery," hence the title of her book. They tried to appease the fears of the plantocracy by arguing that Christianity and slavery were compatible, and that conversion wouldn't grant slaves freedom or social equality.[107] Many even promoted legislation that ensured baptism wouldn't lead to manumission. They argued that while Christian conversion made slave and master spiritual equals, it had no bearing on social equality on this side of heaven, which was determined by racial difference.[108] In essence, since Christianity and chattel slavery could never mix biblically, 'Christian' (I don't believe any unrepentant slave-owning

---

107   Ryan Hoselton, "*A Tragic Chapter in Christian Missions*" https://www.thegospelcoalition.org/reviews/christian-slavery/, February 2019.
108   ibid.

person was an authentic Christian if they were proponents of chattel slavery and the dehumanization of image bearers) slave owners had to manipulate Scripture in order to justify their heinous inhuman barbaric acts. So the phrase "product of his culture" is one that aligns itself with white supremacy and whitewashing, especially when that phrase is used almost exclusively for slave-owning white men who claimed to be Christ followers.

While Scripture was used to justify chattel slavery, Black people knew the difference between slave-holding religion which was void of an authentic Christian ethic and how the Bible saw Black and brown people. Frederick Douglass, one of slavery's most vocal opponents, was an escaped slave who became a protuberant activist, author and public speaker. He became a leader in the abolitionist movement, which sought to end the practice and propagation of slavery, before and during the Civil War. After that conflict and the Emancipation Proclamation of 1863, he continued to push for equality and human rights until his death in 1895. While active and influential in getting President Abraham Lincoln to sign the Emancipation Proclamation, Douglass was intentional about calling out slave-owners who claimed to adhere to the Christian faith. Frederick Douglass speaks of this dichotomy as he points out the difference between slaveholding religion and Scripture:

> What I have said respecting and against religion, I mean strictly to apply to the slaveholding religion of this land, and with no possible reference to Christianity proper; for, between the Christianity of this land, and the Christianity of Christ, I recognize the widest possible difference—so wide, that to receive the one as good, pure, and holy, is of necessity to reject the other as bad, corrupt, and wicked. To be the friend of the one, is of necessity to be the enemy of the other. I love the pure, peaceable, and impartial Christianity of Christ: I therefore hate the corrupt, slaveholding, women-whipping, cradle-plundering, partial and hypocritical Christianity of this land. Indeed, I can see no reason, but the most deceitful one, for calling the religion of this land Christianity. I look upon it as the climax of all misnomers, the boldest of all frauds, and the grossest of all libels. Never was there a clearer case of "stealing the livery of the court of heaven to serve the devil in." I am filled with unutterable loathing when I contemplate the religious pomp and show, together with the horrible inconsistencies,

which everywhere surround me. We have men-stealers for ministers, women-whippers for missionaries, and cradle-plunderers for church members. The man who wields the blood-clotted cowskin during the week fills the pulpit on Sunday, and claims to be a minister of the meek and lowly Jesus. The man who robs me of my earnings at the end of each week meets me as a class-leader on Sunday morning, to show me the way of life, and the path of salvation. He who sells my sister, for purposes of prostitution, stands forth as the pious advocate of purity. He who proclaims it a religious duty to read the Bible denies me the right of learning to read the name of the God who made me. He who is the religious advocate of marriage robs whole millions of its sacred influence, and leaves them to the ravages of wholesale pollution. The warm defender of the sacredness of the family relation is the same that scatters whole families—sundering husbands and wives, parents and children, sisters and brothers,—leaving the hut vacant, and the hearth desolate. We see the thief preaching against theft, and the adulterer against adultery. We have men sold to build churches, women sold to support the gospel, and babes sold to purchase Bibles for the POOR HEATHEN! ALL FOR THE GLORY OF GOD AND THE GOOD OF SOULS![109]

It's interesting that people who were enslaved themselves knew the difference, but others were products of their culture. While Edwards and Whitefield were staunch proponents of the heinous institution of slavery, Charles Spurgeon was an unfaltering opponent who understood what Scripture said about all people being made in the image of God. Born on June 19th, 1834, in Kelvedon, Essex, to John and Eliza Spurgeon, he was the firstborn of seventeen children, although unfortunately only eight survived adolescence. Considered the "Prince of Preachers," Spurgeon is known for his hermeneutic and homiletic prowess that led thousands of people to Christ, trained hundreds of people for ministry and spoke out against the injustice of slavery. Spurgeon exchanged correspondences with Frederick Douglass, received former slaves into his Pastors' College and pulpit, and condemned slavery in his sermons and media articles. Spurgeon says, "I

---

109 A Public Domain Book Narrative of the Life of Frederick Douglas, (Anti-Slavery Office 1845), 105.

do from my inmost soul detest slavery ... and although I commune at the Lord's table with men of all creeds, yet with a slave-holder I have no fellowship of any sort or kind. Whenever one has called upon me, I have considered it my duty to express my detestation of his wickedness, and I would as soon think of receiving a murderer into my church ... as a man stealer."[110] If Spurgeon knew the difference, how come the others are giving a pass for this grave sin against humanity, namely, Black and brown people? Spurgeon was willing to have his character assassinated throughout the Confederacy, have his sermons, which in 1862-1863 sold one million copies annually, censured and his books, which sold 1,000 copies per minute at trade shows, publicly destroyed in order to live out his faith.[111]

Proponents of chattel slavery weren't products of their culture, but rather products of white supremacy, which some whites were willing to oppose, even to their own social detriment, like Spurgeon. Thankfully, while Jonathan Edwards Sr. dropped the ball both theologically and socially as it pertained to seeing the image of God in Black and brown people, Jonathan Edwards Jr. didn't continue the tainted legacy of his father, but rather fought for the equality of the marginalized. Jonathan Edwards Jr. was said to possess a deep, abiding, and all-too-rare compassion for the most marginalized people of society in the eighteenth century. During Edwards's time, slavery was legal in every British North American colony. Jonathan Edwards Sr., his dad, owned at least four slaves during his childhood. Inspired by his faith and revolutionary principles, however, Edwards Jr. was a leader in the first wave of American abolitionism—and one of the few abolitionists Princeton (with its long history of conservatism on the issue of slavery) ever produced.[112] In 1773 while serving as pastor of the White Haven Church near Yale, Edwards Jr. published a series of antislavery articles in a local newspaper.[113]

---

110 Godfrey Holden Pike, *The Life and Work of Charles Haddon Spurgeon*, (Nabu Press, 2012), 331.

111 Spurgeon Center Staff, The Reason Why America Burned Spurgeon's Sermons and Sought to Kill Him, https://www.spurgeon.org/resource-library/blog-entries/the-reason-why-america-burned-spurgeons-sermons-and-sought-to-kill-him/, 2016.

112 R. Isabela Morales, *"Some Observations upon the Slavery of Negroes," "An Address to Americans, Upon Slave-Keeping,"* https://slavery.princ eton.edu/stories/jonathan-edwards-jr, October.

113 ibid.

The Whitewashing of Christianity

He was 28 years old, a relatively new minister who had been ordained only four years prior.[114] Edwards Jr. was intentional about challenging the biblical arguments often used to defend slavery. While he acknowledged that Old Testament patriarchs such as Abraham "had servants born in his house and bought with his money," he rightfully questioned whether these servants were subject to the same form of "perpetual bondage" that enslaved people in his day suffered.[115] But even if they were, Edwards continued, that didn't mean the Father of Israel had been right to enslave them: For, however good a man he was, he had not arrived at sinless perfection.[116] "Why," he asked, "are the slave-holders exempt from attending to the golden rule of our Saviour? 'Whatsoever ye would that men should do to you, do ye even so unto them.'"[117]

Pastor James Pennington David, who was also an abolitionist and prominent thinker of his day during the 1840-1850s, eloquently addressed the fact that Scripture isn't silent on the issue of slavery. He said, "Is the word of God silent on this... greatest of... curses? I, for one, desire to know... If the word of God does sanction slavery, I want another book, another repentance, another faith, and another hope! Slavery is condemned by the general tenor and scope of the New Testament, which did not sanction cruelty or the imprisonment, starvation, or torture of other human beings."[118]

When slavery is presented as noble or necessary, it ignores the plight of the enslaved and provides those that oppose the Christian faith with social ammunition to fire shots at us. We must address the topic of slavery with biblical fidelity and social consciousness in order to address the concerns of those that think God affirmed an insitituion of oppression that he clearly opposed.

---

114 Jonathan Edwards Jr., 1765; Undergraduate Alumni Records, 18th Century, Box 14; Princeton University Archives, Department of Rare Books and Special Collections, (Princeton University Library).

115 "Some Observations upon the Slavery of Negroes," The Connecticut Journal and New-Haven Post-Boy (New Haven, CT), 1.

116 ibid.

117 [Untitled], 12 November 1773, The Connecticut Journal and New-Haven Post-Boy (New Haven, CT), 1, 4.

118 David Swift, *Black Prophets of Justice: Activist Clergy Before the Civil War* (Baton Rouge Louisiana State University Press, 1989), 236.

Discussion Questions

1. Why must the topic of slavery in the Bible be addressed?
2. How should biblical slavery be explained?
3. What are some differences between slavery in Scripture and chattel slavery?
4. How should we treat theologians of the past who have clear contradictions between their theology and their ethics?

7

Hidden Heroes

> *It's not a gripe against Christianity; it's a gripe against Christianity as given by Western society.*
> – Killer Mike

IN 1961, mathematician Katherine Goble worked as a human computer. This phenomenal woman was literally a math wizard, and her intelligence was incalculable, unlike the math she was so astute at performing. She worked in a division separated by race and gender at West Area Computers of the Langley Research Center in Hampton, Virginia, alongside her colleagues, aspiring engineer Mary Jackson and their unofficial acting-supervisor Dorothy Vaughan. This inspiring story was captured in the 2016 movie Hidden Figures. I remember watching this movie with my daughter and letting her know how this was history, but something else struck me deeply as my family left the movie theater. I wondered why I had never heard about them? I realize that not every aspect of history can be taught in school, but there was not one mention of the amazing accomplishment of these women. Christianity has its own hidden figures or hidden heroes that have been intentionally ignored or presented as white. This has been most prevalent in how church fathers and martyrs are displayed. Dr. Tony Evans points out this revisionist history in his book *Oneness Embraced*:

> For centuries church fathers, anointed men of erudition, have sculpted the development of the Christian faith and have postulated

ways to articulate the deep and intricate truths of Christian theology. A great disservice has been done to people of African descent in the failure of church historians to identify the African, Hamitic descent of many of the most noted church fathers. By looking at the strategic place Black African people have played in the history and development of the Christian faith, both through their piety and intellectual prowess exercised for the glory of God, we authenticate God's continual activity in the Black race. We also encourage Christians of African descent to see ourselves as the continuation of a divine legacy. Our opulent heritage should serve to motivate us to continue dispensing God's truth by means of the talents He has deposited in our community; not only for the benefit of the Black community in particular but also for the Christian community at large.[119]

This willful omission has led to what I call a hidden past which in part is the goal of whitewashing: erasure. Erasure of the Black influence on history, philosophy, theology and education and Christianity, but thank God that He has used countless Blacks in history and Scripture to accomplish His plan.

Christianity in Africa

There are two great kingdoms that get ignored from the scope of Christian history, and they are Ethiopia and Nubia. There were African Christian churches that spread the gospel, were committed to orthodoxy and discipleship centuries before the Christian faith entered England, Ireland, Sweden or Russia. In fact, Ethiopia was a Christian nation three centuries after Christ during A.D. 300s. Around the year A.D. 100 Ethiopia was a major Christian nation that held to biblical tradition and established monasteries in honor of Christ. Ethiopia holds a significant place in Christian history. Christianity became the religion of Ethiopia around the same time that Christianity became the state religion of Rome. It accepted the same doctrines of North Africa while formally recognizing the Councils of Nicea (325 A.D.), Constantinople (381 A.D.), and Ephesus (431 A.D.). Ethiopia may have been the most open and ready nation

---

119 Tony Evans, *Oneness Embraced* (Moody Publishers, 2011), 122.

The Whitewashing of Christianity

in which Christianity has ever taken root.[120] When Islam began to spread, it was Ethiopia that fought for the rights of oppressed Christians in foreign lands, and it's the first Sub-Saharan nation to accept Christianity. By the fourth century, Ethiopian believers were making pilgrimages to the holy city of Jerusalem and by the sixth century, Ethiopia established military protectors of Christian communities in surrounding areas.[121] Ethiopian Christians had exuberant worship and incorporated African cultural expressions of dance and drums in worship of Yahweh (God). There were even Ethiopian monasteries that focused on prayer, purity, fasting and self-denial as ways for one to devote themselves to God in fulfillment of the Scripture to love God with all your heart, mind and strength (Matthew 22:37). Ethiopia was home to tons of art that depicted Adam and Eve, Abraham, Mary the mother of Jesus, and Jesus Himself with brown complexions and afro-hair, yet, while these images predate European imagery, these images don't find their way in most of seminary, scholarly and historical literature written about early Christianity. Questioning this intentional omission isn't divisive; it's necessary. Centuries of rich Christian faith is skipped and what's mentioned is the Arab conquest, but for 660 years prior to Arab conquest, Christian believers experienced life and safety on African soil. It should be noted that while Western Christianity is guilty of often starting church history with the Protestant Reformation, many fail to acknowledge that one of the leaders of the Protestant Reformation, Martin Luther, was obsessed with Ethiopian Christianity. Luther developed a fascination with the history and theology of Ethiopian Christianity. Ethiopia, in Luther's estimation, provided a glimpse into what was in Christianity's past and what ought to be in her future. In 1534, Luther met a representative of the Ethiopian Church, Michael the Deacon, and the details of this encounter reinforced Luther's positive assessment of the Ethiopian church.[122] African cultures for many generations thrived

---

120 Ernest Grant, *Whitewashed Christianity* https://thewitnessbcc.com/whitewashed-christianity/, The Witness October 2016.

121 David Daniel, *Christian Witness of African People through the Ages in Africa, Europe and the Americas*, 60.

122 Martin Brecht, *Martin Luther, Volume 3: The Preservation of the Church, 1532-1546* (Minneapolis: Fortress Press, 1993), 59.

between 42 and 692 A.D. and were staunch believers in Christ, whose theology shaped that of many European theologians that are heralded today.[123]

Nubia

Nubia received the Christian message about five centuries after Christ, and they were intentional about testifying about God's power and had many murals of Black African Christian families in Nubia. Black Africans also lived in areas occupied by Rome in Europe and West Asia. One pivotal event that's been immortalized by African Christians is the witness of St. Maurice and what was known as His Theban Legion, a Roman militia. During the third century, these African Christian soldiers were captured in what is now known as Switzerland, and they were demanded to deny their faith in Christ. They refused and were consequently executed for their faith.[124] This means it was safer for Christians in African nations than it was in European nations for the first three centuries after Yeshua's (Christ) death and Africans were willing to die for Christ because they knew him long before the Trans-Atlantic Slave Trade and didn't find Christ through white missionaries as the story is often presented. The artwork found in these African countries is omitted from most of what's presented in the West, because Black imagery threatens proponents of a whitewashed version of Christianity which thrives on false imagery and historical omissions. The omissions aren't the only issue that must be addressed; the reimaging of early African Christians is something that must be vehemently opposed as well. Almost all of the African Christian fathers and martyrs are presented as white in literature; for instance, *The Select Works of Saint Athanasius* has a white man on the cover of the book while mentioning that Athanasius was African. This false narrative must be opposed as there are a myriad of African believers whom we can celebrate as instrumental in God's plan.

Blacks in Christian History

One of the many hurtful aspects of whitewashing is how it presents the Christian faith and history inaccurately. Many Black and brown people have

---

123 Thomas Oden, *How Africa Shaped the Christian Mind* (IVP Books, 2007), 125.
124 David Daniel, *Christian Witness of African People through the Ages in Africa, Europe and the Americas*, 61.

The Whitewashing of Christianity

responded to this by assuming that Christianity was only received by Black people during slavery; therefore they've drawn the conclusion that Christianity was not a faith that Africans embraced prior to the Trans-Atlantic Slave Trade. Additionally, many reject Christianity as a viable faith for them because they associate it exclusively with oppression. While this is historically inaccurate, because many of the images of African church fathers has made them white, they are unaware of the countless Black African men and women who lived and died for Yeshua long before the slave trade. Below is a list of some of the influential thinkers, philosophers and theologians who not only embraced the Christian faith thousands of years before the slave trade, but also have given us theological terms, monasteries, books, and hermeneutical brilliance that are still in use today.

Jerome Gay Jr.

Tertullian (160-220)

Tertullian was a prolific writer and author from Carthage and another influential Black African man to impact the Christian faith and the world for over a millenia after his death. Tertullian was the first Christian author to produce an extensive quantity of Christian literature in Latin. An avid apologist for the Christian faith and a debater against heresy, Tertullian consistently engaged and confounded those that wanted to propagate a false gospel. He was instrumental in verbalizing and creating new theological concepts and was integral to the development of early Church doctrine. He's perhaps most celebrated for being the first writer in Latin known to use the term trinity to describe the fact that God is one (Deuteronomy 6:4) and exists in three persons: Father, Son and Spirit. Black and brown Christians can celebrate that not only was Christianity embraced by Africans long before the slave trade, but that Black people have shaped how we engage and understand God, His nature and faith in general.

The Whitewashing of Christianity

Jerome Gay Jr.

Origen of Alexandria (184-254)

Origen of Alexandria, also known as **Origen Adamantius**, was one of the many early African Christian scholars to merge faith and reason. He was born and spent the first half of his career in Alexandria. While he influenced and served the Greek Church, Origen was indeed an African man. He was a prolific writer who wrote many treatises in multiple branches of theology, including textual criticism, which is the branch of textual scholarship concerned with the identification of textual variants in either manuscripts or printed books. He also gave us the concepts of structure of biblical exegesis and biblical hermeneutics, which is the art and science of Scripture interpretation and homiletics, which focuses on preaching and sermon structure. He was one of the most influential figures in early Christian theology and apologetics, which addresses how to defend the Christian faith. One of his greatest apologetic works is *Against Celsus*, where he defends orthodoxy against pagans, Jews and heretics. His knowledge of Trinitarian thought influenced other scholars like Athanasius, Jerome and the Cappadocians. While he defended the faith against heresy, he died as a result of Decian persecution and was labeled a heretic by many based on how he spoke of the Son and the Spirit being subject to the Father. This view led others to something known as subordinationism. Origen should primarily be remembered for his defense of Scripture and orthodoxy. He is an example that Black people and all people can be elated about God using the early Christian church.[125]

---

125   Walter Elwell, *Evangelical Dictionary of Theology* (Baker Publishing Grand Rapids, MI, 2001), 870.

The Whitewashing of Christianity

Cyprian of Carthage (200-258)

Saint Cyprian was one of the many African bishops of Carthage. He was a prolific writer of Berber descent. Born around the beginning of the 3rd century in North Africa, Cyprian was considered a provocative figure during his lifetime. He exhibited great oratory skills and was a proficient apologist that defended the church against Novatianism, and it was in 248 that he became the bishop of Carthage. His oratorical skills didn't limit him from being a prolific writer. He also shared his strict views on the church that shaped many ecclesiologically as he had a deep appreciation for the church. As he famously said, "He is not a Christian who is not in Christ's church," and "He cannot have God for his father who has not the church for his mother." Cyprian's love for the church led to views that many would not completely embrace today.[126]

---

126   ibid., 314

The Whitewashing of Christianity

Jerome Gay Jr.

Perpetua and Felicity (died 203 AD)

Perpetua and Felicity (both believed to have died in 203 AD) were Christian martyrs of the 3rd century. Perpetua was a married noblewoman, said to have been 22 years old at the time of her death for Yeshua (Christ), and mother of an infant she was nursing and stood for faith in the midst of crisis. Felicity, who stood with her and was pregnant at the time, was martyred with her. They were put to death along with others at Carthage in Africa. These two women are a true testament to the phrase "Black girls rock" and an example of how God has consistently used women throughout history.

The Whitewashing of Christianity

Jerome Gay Jr.

Lactantius (ca. 240-320)

Lactantius was an African teacher who converted to Christianity and deeply impacted the Christian faith with his gift of rhetoric, philosophy and apologetics. His writing infused philosophy and his personal literary training in order to confound opponents of the faith that he converted to. *The Anger of God* addressed both crime and punishment. His work *On the Workmanship of God* addressed the pinnacle of God's creation—humanity—and he used creation to point to God's infinite wisdom and goodness. Lactantius taught that the Christian faith combined religion and true wisdom, his views on the Trinity would be rejected by many and viewed as deficient. We can thank this African Christian for his ability to engage opposing views with literary precision and passion.[127]

---

127   ibid., 668

The Whitewashing of Christianity

Jerome Gay Jr.

Pachomius the Great (ca. 292-348)

Saint Pachomius was born in 292 in Thebes (Luxor, Egypt) to parents who were not Christians. Pachomius is of Egyptian origin and encountered Coptic, or Egyptian, Christianity among his cohorts in the Roman emperor Constantine's North African army and, on leaving the military about 314, he withdrew alone into the wilderness at Chenoboskion, near his Theban home. Soon after, he joined the hermit Palemon. Pachomius is credited for building the first monastic enclosure, replacing the scattered hermits' shelters, and he drew up a common daily program providing for proportioned periods of work and prayer patterned about a cooperative economic and disciplinary regimen. He instituted rules in order to address the individualistic trends he saw Christians falling victim to through the use of a cenobitic, or uniform communal, existence as the norm, the first departure from the individualistic, exclusively contemplative nature that had previously characterized religious life. Pachomius instituted a monarchic monastic structure that viewed the relationship of the religious superior's centralized authority over the community as the symbolic image of God evoking obedient response from man striving to overcome his egocentrism by self-denial and charity. By the time he died, Pachomius had founded 11 monasteries, numbering more than 7,000 monks and nuns.[128] We can thank this African man for teaching the importance of quiet and solitude with God and establishing places for people to honor God through meditation.

---

128   Encyclopedia Britannica, *Saint Pachomius* https://www.britannica.com/biography/Saint-Pachomius, accessed November 2019.

The Whitewashing of Christianity

Jerome Gay Jr.

Athanasius (ca. 296-373)

Athanasius, arguably the most historically significant thinker, theologian and writer of all time in the church, was a Bishop of Alexandria and is most notably known for his defense of the faith at the Council of Nicea in 325 AD. Athanius fought for the essence of Yeshua based on Scripture and not culture. One of the primary opponents to the deity of Yeshua was a man named Arius who was instrumental in spreading the teaching that Jesus was a created being. Many attribute his education as Greek, but that doesn't change his African heritage and nationality. He was known as the Black dwarf because of his dark skin and short stature.[129] As a young man he was chosen to serve as secretary to Alexander Bishop of Alexandria and upon the death of Alexander, he was notified that he had been selected to succeed Alexander as bishop of Alexandria. Once Alexander died, Athanasius was elected to the bishopric of Alexandria on May 9th, 328, three years after the Council of Nicea. His election was controversial, mostly because he was below the canonical age to take this office. He also faced opposition from those that rejected the Nicene Creed. They worked to eliminate its conclusions that the Father and Son were the same being. The opposition he faced didn't stop there; he also came up against Constantine's son, who was ruling the eastern half of the Empire. Athanasius was constantly accused by his enemies as being divisive, angry and sowing division. He was banished on five occasions from the city of Alexandria. He nevertheless remained unwavering in his commitment to the divinity of the Son. His most famous work today is *On the Incarnation*—a book more on the divinity of the Son before he took on flesh than on the incarnation itself. The legacy of Athanasius reveals a man committed to defending the deity of Yeshua by a plain reading of the Scriptures.[130] When people attempted to strip Yeshua of his deity, Athanasius passionately argued:

> For the Word (Yeshua), realizing that in no other way would the corruption of human beings be undone except, simply, by dying, yet being immortal and the Son of the Father the Word was not able to die for this reason he takes to himself a body capable of death, in order that it, participating in the Word who is above all, might be sufficient for death on behalf of all, and through

---

129 Justo Gonzalez, *The Story of Christianity*, vol. 1 (San Francisco: Harper San Francisco, 1984), 173.
130 Ryan Reeves, *Who was Athanasius and Why was He Important* https://www.thegospelcoalition.org/article/whowas-athanasius-and-why-was-he-important/, May 2016.

ATHANASIUS

the indwelling Word would remain incorruptible, and so corruption might henceforth cease from all by the grace of the resurrection. Whence, by offering to death the body he had taken to Himself, as an offering holy and free of all spot, he immediately abolished death from all like Him… For being above all, the Word of God consequently, by offering His own temple and His bodily instrument as a substitute for all, fulfilled in death that which was required. And now the very corruption of death no longer holds ground against human beings because of the Word that became flesh.[131]

An avid writer, *Contra Gentiles* is one of his most notable works where he discusses how God can be known, highlighting Yeshua's imminence while rejecting the idea of deism, which asserts that God created the world and left humanity on our own. Athanasius exhibited theological prowess that was beyond his years and still impacts minds today.[132]

---

131   Athanasius & C.S. Lewis, *On the Incarnation: The Treatise De Incarnatione Verbi Dei* (Crestwood, NY: St. Vladimirs Seminary Press, 2003), 58.
132   Walter Elwell, *Evangelical Dictionary of Theology* (Baker Publishing Grand Rapids, MI, 2001), 110.

Jerome Gay Jr.

Shenoute of Atripe (347-465)

Shenoute the Great, also known as Shenoute of Atripe, was an African church father and saint in the 4th and 5th centuries. He was committed to orthodoxy, confronted the heresy of his day, a prolific writer, led the White Monastery (white because of the walls, the monks were primarily people with melanin as Shenoute was himself) and was fluent in Coptic and Greek. He's an example of the rich Christian history in Africa and how Africa and Africans influenced orthodoxy and shaped the Christian faith.

The Whitewashing of Christianity

Jerome Gay Jr.

Augustine of Hippo (354-430)

He was born in Thagaste, North Africa, in present day Algeria. Augustine has an unparalleled influence on Western Christianity, both Catholic and Protestant. His writings were huge in shaping people theologically during his time and even now. His mother was named Monica and is historically assumed to be a Berber, and some have even heralded her as a Black saint. Augustine was a master in rhetoric and to use modern vernacular he had what many in urban communities and fans of hip hop call "bars"; he's given us quotes like "unity in things necessary, liberty in things doubtful, charity in all things; with love for mankind and hatred of sin" (this is where we get the phrase "love the sinner, hate the sin" from); "Jesus Christ will be the Lord of all, or he will not be Lord at all," and many others. There is a story about Saint Augustine following his conversion where he passed by one of his former mistresses on the street. Seeing him walk by she yelled after him, "Augustine, it is I!" without turning back or stopping his stride, Augustine replied, "Yes, but it is no longer I!" Augustine is another example of the myriad of Blacks used to form theology and philosophy.[133] As Jonathan Hill observes, "His [Augustine's] influence over Western thought—religious and otherwise—is total; he remains inescapable even over fifteen centuries after his death."[134]

---

133 Walter Elwell, *Evangelical Dictionary of Theology* (Baker Publishing Grand Rapids, MI, 2001), 122.

134 Jonathan Hill, *The History of Christian Thought*, (Downers Grove, IL: InterVarsity Press, 2003), 79.

The Whitewashing of Christianity

Jerome Gay Jr.

Cyril of Alexandria (376-444)

Cyril was born in the small town of Didouseya, Egypt and was a Patriarch of Alexandria from 412-444. During his tenure, he encountered immense controversy and opposition from Nestorius. One of the major factors that contributed to this disagreement was that there were theological differences between Antioch and Alexandria. The sharpest disagreement took place in 428 when Cyril went as far as to label Nestorious a heretic based on his view of the Virgin Mary and thinking that she should be called Christotokos (the Greek title of Mary used historically by non-Ephesian followers of the Church in the East). Its literal English translations include Christ-bearer and the one who gives birth to Christ. Less literal translations include Mother of Christ. Theotokos was another term of disagreement, which means Mother of God. The council of Ephesus, which Cyril presided over, would elect to send Nestorious into exile.[135] Cyril was committed to a deep understanding of the nature of Christ and affirmed the hypostatic union which asserts that the humanity and divinity of Christ are two distinct natures that don't conflict with each other. Cyril is another example of the many Blacks who loved Christ, affirmed his deity, and fought for orthodoxy and should be recognized globally for his contributions.

The Black men and women who fought for, shaped and influenced Christianity for thousands of years should be accurately represented in every form of communication. The revisionist history as it relates to their race must be reversed to reveal the beautiful tapestry of people used by God. This doesn't mean every act and ideology of the aforementioned people is to be embraced, but their contributions to the faith shouldn't be ignored or denied.

As stated earlier, four of the five women mentioned in Matthew's account of the genealogy of Christ (Matthew 1:1-16), were of Hamitic descent. Tamar, Rahab, Bathsheba and Ruth, but these are not the only Blacks that are not only in Scripture but wrote Scripture. A contributing factor to this misconception is how we present people in Scripture on film and literature. One of the glaring ways this has played out is by how we present the disciples; for instance, Jesus did not call the disciples "Peter" or "Matthew." Rather, he referred to them by their Hebrew or Aramaic names, which was consistent with their heritage.

---

135   Walter Elwell, *Evangelical Dictionary of Theology*, (Baker Publishing Grand Rapids, MI), 315.

- Matthew was *Mattityahu,* meaning "gift from God."
- Thomas was *Tau'ma,* an Aramaic name.
- Andrew was *Andreas.*
- Simon was *Shimon.*
- James was *Yakov* (that is, Jacob).
- John was *Yochanan.*
- Bartholomew was *Bar-Talmai* (son of Ptolemy, which is Greek).
- Phillip was *Filippos.*
- Thaddaeus was a variant of Theudas, which was a Grecian version of Judas or *Yehuda.*
- Judas Iscariot was *Yehuda.*

There aren't Hebrew equivalents for Andrew and Philip because those are Greek names that translate as *Andreas* and *Filippos.* We can assume that Andrew and Philip were either Grecian-Jews or Grecian-Gentiles. Many are unaware of the Black heroes and sheroes in Scripture. While none compare to Yeshua, who was sinless, God has used countless Black and brown people in His redemptive plan.

The Black and Brown Presence in the Bible

Noah

Noah's son Ham had four sons: Cush, Mizraim, Put and Canaan. Cush was the progenitor of the Ethiopian people (Genesis 2:13; 10:6). Mizraim was the progenitor of the Egyptian people, who are understood in Scripture to have been Hamitic people (Psalms 78:51; 105:23, 26-27; 106:21-22). God repopulated the world through Noah and his sons; the table of nations in Genesis 10 affirms this reality and associates each son with nations of peoples. Black people, as all other races, can celebrate the reality that it's God's intention that we exist, survive, thrive and function under his divine rule.

Joseph

Joseph's wife was an Egyptian woman (Genesis 41:45, 50-52) and was the mother of Manasseh and Ephraim, who became leaders of Jewish tribes. This means that the Jewish people included people of color and not all white as presented in film and literature—which brings us to Moses, who has been included in the whitewashed narrative of both Jewish and Christian history.

Moses

Contrary to the Charlton Heston version of Moses America has erroneously presented as fact, Moses was a man of color. He was born in Africa, raised by Africans, trained in African wisdom, and was mistaken for an Egyptian, yet he's still depicted as a bearded white man in most Jewish and Christian literature. The current portrayal of Moses and the Hebrews would have us believe that Moses led a million white people out of Egypt. The argument against the fact that Moses was a person of color is that he was mistaken for an Egyptian based on his clothes or that it's an isolated incident; the reality is that Hebrews and Egyptians could tell the difference, but others are not as easily fooled. In Exodus 2:19 it's clear that he was mistaken for an Egyptian:

The Whitewashing of Christianity

And they said, an Egyptian delivered us out of the hand of the shepherds, and also drew water enough for us, and watered the flock, again, they were referring to Moses (Exodus 2:17). The Midianite girls believed Moses to be an Egyptian. This isn't the only example of a Hebrew being mistaken for an Egyptian:

- The Canaanites mistook them for Egyptians when they buried Jacob (Genesis 50:11).
- The king of Moab believed the Hebrews originated in Egypt (Numbers 22:5).
- Paul was mistaken for an Egyptian by a Roman soldier (Acts 21:38).

In order to whitewash Christianity, you must whitewash the Jews, which is why white Moses is almost as significant as white Jesus. There is overwhelming biblical evidence that Moses and the original Jews were not a group of white people, but rather African and Middle Eastern people of color who were used in God's plan of redemption.

The Tribes

- Kedar means dark, the Kedarites are dark-skinned people (Genesis 25:13; Psalms 120:5 Isaiah 42:11; 60:7).
- Phinehas means negro or Nubian were dark-skinned people (Exodus 6:25 1 Chronicles 9:20).
- Jeremiah speaks of Tahpanhes, which means palace of the negro (Jeremiah 43:7).
- Simeon was called Niger meaning he was dark-skinned (Acts 13:1).
- Cushites were an African group (Numbers 12:1).

David

David's great-grandmother was a Canaanite woman, Rahab, David's grandmother was Ruth, a Moabite woman. David had Hamitic ancestry and therefore David was a man of color, contrary to the statue deemed a masterpiece of the Renaissance period. The sculpture created in marble between 1501 and 1504 by the Italian artist Michelangelo is another example of whitewashing biblical figures who aren't white.

Paul

The writer of thirteen letters of the New Testament was mistaken for an Egyptian for how he looked. Luke records this about Paul in his letter to Theophilis, in Acts 21:38: "Are you not the Egyptian, then, who recently stirred up a revolt and led the four thousand men of the Assassins out into the wilderness?" Again, they were talking about Paul and, while the text doesn't outright say he's Black, it begs the question why authors and artists freely portray Paul as a white man despite this passage of Scripture and others that present the Hebrew people as being people of color.

John Mark

Many are aloof to the fact that one of the gospel writers was an African man. John Mark, who wrote the Gospel of Mark, was the son of Aristopolus and Mary his mother. In fact, his Gospel was written first based on a theory known as Markan Priority (the hypothesis that the Gospel of Mark was written first of the three Synoptic Gospels and was used as a source by the other two Matthew and Luke). He was a Cyrenian Jew.[136] Many Jews fled to Africa for safety, and the two primary places they fled to were Cyrene and Alexandria. They blended well in Africa because like the African people, many of the original Jews had melanin; they were people of color.

There are many that I'm leaving out, but you get the point. The reality is there are more people of African descent in Scripture than there are of European descent. This isn't to remove all white people, but rather to accentuate the fact that most of the people mentioned and used by Yahweh were people of color, which isn't functionally acknowledged in print or film in many cases. Whitewashing purports a false narrative that the Bible and its figures are Europeans who evangelized the surrounding nations, when the opposite is true. While the myriad of white characters representing the Hebrews and Egyptians is both historically and biblically

---

136 Thomas Oden, *The African Memory of Mark: Reassessing Early Church Tradition*, (IVP Academic 2011), 18.

inaccurate, the negative effects are undeniable. Next, we'll look at some responses to historic whitewashing, both positive and negative.

Discussion Questions

1. Why is it important to highlight Black and brown people as it relates to Christian history?
2. What are some of the residual effects of presenting biblical figures and African people as white?
3. How can accurate imagery help change the way people view Christianity?
4. Which of the people listed in this chapter have you imagined as white? Why?

8

Responses to Whitewashing: *Liberation*

> *One of the major psychological problems of the Black man outside the parent continent of Africa is that while he can always say, I have a country, he cannot really say, I have a home.*
> —CALVIN LOCKHART

THE LANDSCAPE OF THEOLOGY IS VAST, and when one thinks about the various nuances of theological thought, there are many things to consider. Typically, we consider hermeneutics, ecclesiology, eschatology, pneumatology and the like, but how often is culture and race taken into account? So far, we've established the fact that many scholars and authors of commentaries have allowed their cultural blind spots and presuppositions of inferiority as it relates to Blacks to cloud their interpretation of Scripture and history. Theologian, author, and minister James Cone addressed both the culturally oppressive, culturally imperialistic and theologically inconsistent practices of Protestant Christians during the Civil Rights Movement. His critique and concerns were more cultural than they were theological; he pushed back against a whitewashed narrative of Christian history and application. Cone was intentional about revealing how the practices of many white Christians during the Civil Rights Movement seemed to separate ethics from theology and presented white culture as normal at the expense and neglect of considering the plight of African Americans in America primarily during the Civil Rights Movement.

In order to understand James Cone's perspective and the millions of African Americans who lived through the Jim Crow South, it is important to establish a working definition of racism. Again, racism is the oppression of one race for the preservation of another primarily based on race, but can include class; biblically it's the sin of partiality. As stated earlier, this is clearly seen in the book Moses pens in the book of Exodus. Exodus 1:9-10 says, "And he said to his people, "Behold, the people of Israel are too many and too mighty for us. Come, let us deal shrewdly with them, lest they multiply, and, if war breaks out, they join our enemies and fight against us and escape from the land." While race may be inferred, Pharaoh clearly reveals the tactic of oppression. In the Exodus text, Pharaoh used the Hebrews' growth rate and faith as the impetus to enslave the Israelites for the preservation of his people, which he deemed to be the dominant and superior race, and he viewed the Israelites as inferior. Thousands of years later, it would not be Egyptians enslaving Israelites, but rather Europeans enslaving Africans through the Trans-Atlantic Slave Trade.[137] During these times, millions of Africans were abducted, abused, dehumanized and displaced and forced into slave labor in the name of enterprise and religion. The religion of the white oppressors often was Christianity in name, but certainly not in its practice. Whites saw Blacks as less human or more wicked than whites, as Gregory Wills points out in his book *Democratic Religion* that Baptist Christians view of Blacks reveals an intellectual and moral inferiority when he says, "all are strangers to intellectuals, and a large portion of them to moral culture. Blacks were more wicked than whites, in this view, because passion ruled them."[138] It is interesting that being ruled by passions was a label freely placed on Blacks, but the sin of slavery and oppression was not seen as wicked because the imago dei (image of God) was not affirmed in people of color and proponents of racial oppression did not see anything wrong with racial injustice because Blacks were an inferior cursed race in their minds. White supremacists were the true barbarians in need of salvation and civility, but they refused to repent. Pharaoh's oppressive practices would continue at the hands of white supremacists as the pillaging of life, liberty, labor and

---

137   Albert J. Raboteau, *Canaan Land*, (New York, NY: Oxford University Press, 2001), 6-7.
138   Wills A. Gregory, *Democratic Religion*, (New York, NY: Oxford University Press, 1997), 61.

land; through the flaying of backs; the chaining of limbs; the strangling of dissidents; the destruction of families; the rape of mothers; the sale of children; and a myriad of other heinous acts were done to African Americans in the name of religion.[139] This is the cultural climate in which James Cone was born. A world where the Black race, while emancipated, was still not free from oppression, systematic racism and a culturally imperialistic society that presented the white race as pure and any other races or cultures as deficient. James Cone would be a witness and victim of racism and whitewashing, and this informed his theological and cultural critique of white Protestants during this time.

From the Emancipation Proclamation to the Civil Rights Movement

In 1863, President Abraham Lincoln signed the Emancipation Proclamation. The stroke of his pen changed the legal status of millions of enslaved Blacks from slave to free. The Emancipation Proclamation would be ratified two years later in 1865 at the conclusion of the Civil War. While millions were legally free, they certainly were not practically free from the tyranny and dehumanization of disgruntled slave owners.[140] Lincoln's pen changed the law, but it did not change the hearts of slave masters that saw African Americans as commodities void of humanity, because you can't legislate the heart, and their hearts remained diabolical as they joyfully saw Blacks as no more than cheap labor rather than as image bearers worth dignity, respect and honor. While many present President Lincoln as a hero, Cone points out that this move was not one of compassion for African Americans, but rather a move to save the Union. Cone quotes Lincoln saying:

> I will say then that I am not, not ever have been in favor of bringing about in any way the social and political equality of the Black and white races—that I am not nor ever have been in favor of making voters or jurors of Negroes, nor qualifying them to hold office, nor to intermarry with white people; and I will say in addition to this that

---

139 Ta-Nehisi Coates, *Between the World and Me*, (Melbourne, Australia: The Text Publishing Company, 2015), 8.
140 Albert J. Raboteau, *Canaan Land*, (New York, NY: Oxford University Press, 2001), 63.

The Whitewashing of Christianity

> there is a physical difference between the white and Black races which I believe will forbid the two races living together on terms of social and political equality. And inasmuch as they cannot so live, while they do remain together, there must be the position of superior and inferior, and I as much as any other man am in favor of having the superior position assigned to the white race.[141]

Lincoln's statement represents the social climate and the view of Black people that was not intercepted by signing of the Emancipation Proclamation and extended decades beyond its signing. Lincoln made it clear that prior to signing the Emancipation Proclamation that his goal was to save the Union, not the equality of Black people, he said, "if I could save the Union without freeing any slave I would do it, and if I could save it by freeing all the slaves would do that. What I do about slavery, and the colored race, I do because I believe it helps to save the Union." [142] America would soon enter the Reconstruction Era, which lasted from 1863 to 1877. This is a time when after the Civil War, Presidents Abraham Lincoln and Andrew Johnson took positions to restore the South since the issue of slavery was hotly contested as the majority of the South was in favor of dehumanizing, enslaving and abusing Black and brown people. Legislation cannot go beyond the paper on which the ink is written, since one cannot legislate a person's heart. The heart of the South and much of America still did not value the Black life and vehemently defended a view of hatred toward African Americans.[143] Johnson's elucidation of Lincoln's policies proved successful until the elections that took place three years after the Emancipation Proclamation. In 1866 the North was able to successfully remove the Confederates from control; contrary to popular belief popular in the South that the Confederacy is heritage, not hatred, the reality is that the Confederacy is a heritage of hatred and slavery was the primary issue of the Civil War. Confederate leaders like Alexander Stephens who served as the vice president of the Confederacy in the 1860s said the Confederate government

---

141 James H. Cone, *Black Theology and Black Power*, (Maryknoll, NY: Orbi Books, 1997), 10.

142 Abraham Lincoln, *"A Letter from the President,"* (National Intelligencer, August 23 1862).

143 Albert J. Raboteau, *Canaan Land*, (New York, NY: Oxford University Press, 2001), 71.

rested "upon the great truth that the negro is not equal to the white man, that slavery subordination to the superior race is his natural and normal condition. This, our new government, is the first, in the history of the world, based upon this great physical, philosophical, and moral truth." In fact, Stephens said that this "great... truth," was the "corner-stone" of the Confederacy.[144] A free labor economy was instituted, the Freedmen's Bureau established, which protected the rights of freedmen and set up schools and churches for them. This was a form of progress, because this began Black institutional development. Schools like Storer College were established in 1865 in Harpers Ferry, West Virginia. Storer was among the first to educate freed slaves and teach them reading and writing. Bishop College was established in 1881 by the Baptist Home Mission Society to build colleges for African American Baptists.[145] A noble move looking from the outside in, but the underpinnings of the devaluation of African Americans still existed even amongst those who would claim to be saved by grace and through faith as these institutions were established to keep whites from having to share a classroom with Black people.[146] Again, the heart cannot be legislated, because it needs emancipation from itself; only the gospel can change someone's inner being to see all of God's created people as precious and worthy of respect. By 1915 the effects of systematic racism on African Americans that lived in the South continued. Pulitzer Prize winning author Isabel Wilkerson chronicles The Great Migration of 1915-1970 in which over six million Black Southerners left the South and moved primarily to the North. In her book *The Warmth of Other Suns*, Wilkerson says:

> From the early years of the twentieth century to well past its middle age, nearly every Black family in the American South, which meant nearly every Black family in America had a decision to make. There were sharecroppers losing at the settlement. Typists want to work in an office. Yard boys scared that a single gesture near a planter's wife would leave them hanging from an oak tree. They were all stuck in a

---

144   Alexander H. Stephens, *"Cornerstone Speech,"* Teaching American History, http://teachingamericanhistory.org/library/document/cornerstone-speech, accessed October 2020.

145   Albert J. Raboteau, *Canaan Land*, (New York, NY: Oxford University Press, 2001), 65.

146   ibid.

caste system as hard and unyielding as the red Georgia clay, and they each had a decision before them.[147]

Why would they move north in a "free" country? The proclamation of freedom was not applied to them nor was their value affirmed, because Blacks did not have any value beyond making America more profitable and comfortable for their white counterparts. The Declaration of Independence only had white people in mind when it said "all men are created equal"; since African Americans were not seen as people it clearly did not apply to them and in the South it was clear that Black people were not esteemed and were not wanted. The Great Migration was a response to the reality that the proclamation of free and equal does not lead to the application of free and fair treatment of all people.[148] During the migration, The Civil Rights Movement would emerge because of the systematic oppression directed toward African Americans and by this time millions of African Americans had spread all over America. The Civil Rights Movement spanned from the 1950s to the 1960s, and this would highlight the reality that while African Americans were emancipated one hundred years prior, they still were not free. Two Supreme Court decisions were highlighted for their hypocrisy during this time. Plessy v. Ferguson passed in 1896, which upheld and coined the phrase "separate but equal" in order to keep schools segregated constitutionally, and Brown v. Board of Education which would overturn Plessy v. Ferguson in 1954. Prior to Brown v. Board of Education, several events took place highlighting the plight of African Americans in their quest to be treated like human beings made in God's image. The murder of Emmet Till, Rosa Parks and the Montgomery Bus Boycott, Dr. Martin Luther King Jr's leadership, and President Lyndon B. Johnson passing the Voting Rights Act were pivotal events during the Civil Rights Movement that helped move African Americans toward actual freedom. The aforementioned highlights how a tragic murder can spark a transformative movement. In 1955 an African American teenager named Emmet Till who was from Chicago, Illinois was in Mississippi visiting relatives. In August of 1955 Till allegedly flirted with a white woman. A few nights later, Till was abducted and lynched by Roy Bryant and J.W. Milam for allegedly flirting with 21-year-old Carolyn Bryant, Roy

---

147   Isabel Wilkerson, *The Warmth of Other Suns*, (New York: Random House, 2011), kindle. 252.
148   ibid.

Bryant's wife. Decades later, she (Carolyn Bryant) admitted to lying about young Emmet Till flirting with her. Till was beaten, mutilated, shot and thrown into the Tallahatchie River. Till's body was returned to Chicago and his mother Mamie Till Bradley insisted on an open casket to highlight America's hypocrisy and her (America's) treatment of African Americans. Bryant and Milam were acquitted for Till's murder, which was a common occurrence when African Americans died at the hands of racist white men.[149] Cone remarks that "Till's lynching would provide the spark that lit the fire of resistance in the Negro masses, inspiring them, as King said, to rock the nation and to demand their freedom now."[150] While there is nothing to celebrate about the brutal murder of a teenager at the hands of white racists, the militant response that it evoked was remarkable. This for many African Americans would be the final straw and a revolution against America's hypocrisy would ensue and move America closer to fulfilling her claim of all men being created equal. That same year, a woman by the name of Rosa Parks was riding the bus and refused to give up her seat for a white passenger. Her story has been whitewashed and presented as if Parks was an accidental activist. Parks wasn't physically tired and refused to move because of fatigue or because she was old and frail. Parks was only 42 years old at the time she was asked to move to the back of the bus, and she had worked a 6-hour shift as a seamstress, meaning she wasn't on her feet all day. It was December 1, 1955, just months after the heinous murder of Emmet Till. In fact, Parks was like the thousands of other African Americans who were outraged by the acquittal of Bryant and Milam and was still thinking about the brutal murder of young Till. This fueled her defiance against an unjust, unfair, and unequal America that she finally refused to accept any longer, Parks was not the first Black woman to refuse to give up her seat; Claudette Colvin did it nine months before Parks on March 2, 1955, and was arrested at the age of 15 in Montgomery, Alabama for refusing to give up her seat to a white woman on a crowded, segregated bus. While she wasn't the first, Parks' actions led to the Montgomery Bus Boycott, which spanned from December 5, 1955 to December 20, 1956. It was in 1956 that the federal ruling Browder v. Gayle resulted in segregated buses being declared unconstitutional. Many crucial figures took part in this movement and one of the most vocal was Dr. Martin Luther King, Jr., who

---

149   James H. Cone, *The Cross and the Lynching Tree*, (Maryknoll, NY: Orbis Books, 2011), 10.

150   ibid.

The Whitewashing of Christianity

was born on January 15, 1929 in Atlanta, Georgia. King's legal name was Michael King, but his dad made a trip to Germany and learned of the reformer Martin Luther. It is captivating that Martin Luther, who led the Protestant Reformation with John Calvin, would influence the elder King to change his son's name. Like Luther, Dr. King would lead a civil Reformation, challenging Christians to live out their faith and not be silent about the injustice aimed toward African Americans. While Martin Luther was anti-Semitic, King saw the image of God in all people, unlike the German Reformer. King saw the blatant silence and affirmation of the treatment of African Americans as an indictment against the faith they claimed. It was on April 16, 1963 that King wrote a Letter from a Birmingham Jail as he sat in a jail cell for leading the Birmingham campaign; this included marches, protest and non-violent disobedience aimed at getting equal, fair and just treatment for African Americans. King was criticized primarily by white Christians as he placed their hypocrisy on display as their main response to racial injustice was to tell African Americans to simply to wait for things to get better.[151] King responded with a letter highlighting the urgency and reality of African Americans during this time. King writes in a jail cell:

> When you take a cross-country drive and find it necessary to sleep night after night in the uncomfortable corner of your automobile because no motel will accept you; when you are humiliated day in and day out by nagging signs reading white and colored; when your first name becomes nigger, your middle name becomes boy (however old you are) and your last name becomes John, and your wife and mother are never given the respected title Mrs.; when you are harried by day and haunted by night by the fact that you are a Negro, living constantly at the tiptoe stance, never quite knowing what to expect next, and are plagued with inner fears and outer resentments; when you go forever fighting a degenerating sense of nobodiness—then you will understand why we find it difficult to wait.[152]

---

151 Bryan Loritts, *Letters to a Birmingham Jail*, (Chicago, IL: Moody Publishers), 23.
152 James Washington, *The Essential Writings and Speeches of Martin Luther King Jr.*, (New York, New York: HarperCollins Publishers), 293.

Jerome Gay Jr.

The response of the majority of Protestant Christians was not "Christianly" at all. While some did join the movement in order to change the laws and climate of America, many were silent and even complicit. This is why legislative changes were a pivotal part of the Civil Rights Movement and why many fight for justice reform today. By and large, African Americans could not count on their white Christian counterparts to aid them in their efforts. Sadly, not much has changed, as many white evangelicals see justice issues that disproportionately affect Black people as Black issues and not human issues that God cares about. In fact, during the Civil Rights Movement, African Americans and whites did not worship together, and African Americans in most cases were either not allowed into predominantly white churches or forced to sit in the back if they were allowed to attend the service. Rejection, oppression, and abuse by the hands of white "Christians" is what led Richard Allen and Absolam Jones to create the African Methodist Episcopal (A.M.E.) in 1787. Cone was a member of an AME church in Arkansas. In order for change to take place, the Black church would have to align itself with people that saw racism as sinful and who were willing to put their lives on the line because of their faith in Christ and not at the expense of it. The Civil Rights Movement was not exclusively Black, though the focus was a fair America for people of color. Many white evangelicals did join the Civil Rights Movement, but of those that did, a lot of them were disowned, called "nigger lovers" and some even disfellowshipped from their churches.[153] Many white American Christians were blinded by their hatred and allowed the gospel to be eclipsed by pseudo-patriotism and their allegiance to their racist Southern "heritage."[154] The treatment of African Americans is why King was a dreamer, because the African American experience in America was a nightmare. King's dream was rooted in a healthy understanding of the gospel and the fact that it is a message that joins and not excludes, the gospel is a message of God redeeming and reconciling the outcast to himself. Five months after writing his prolific, insightful and sociologically rich letter from a Birmingham jail, King would deliver his I Have a Dream speech on the steps of the Lincoln Memorial in August of 1963.[155] While Lincoln did not have the true

---

153　Charles Marsh, *God's Long Summer: Stories of Faith and Civil Rights*, (Princeton, New Jersey: Princeton University Press), 69.
154　Ibid., 232
155　James Washington, *The Essential Writings and Speeches of Martin Luther King Jr.*, (New York, New York: HarperCollins Publishers), 217.

The Whitewashing of Christianity

freedom of African Americans in his heart when he signed the Emancipation Proclamation, his statue would figuratively watch an African American theologian deliver a speech rooted in the gospel to over 250,000 people. Lincoln did not want African Americans to have political rights or hold office, but he would figuratively witness his plan thwarted. King would reference the Emancipation Proclamation in his speech. King's first words of his speech were, "One hundred years later, the Negro is still not free."[156] This would finally change two years later when President Lyndon B. Johnson would sign the Voting Rights Act of 1965, which prohibited voting discrimination based on race and guaranteed the rights meant by the Fourteenth and Fifteenth Amendments of the United States Constitution. This act secured voting rights for all racial minorities and aspects of King's dream were realized. African Americans could ride on buses freely, African Americans could now vote, and play an active role in American democracy at least on paper, but the residue of the sin of racism still remained. The institution which actually has the answer for not the unjust evils of America, but of all humanity were still separated by the thing we should celebrate, race. Racial indifference, racial insensitivity and racism were still active, and James Cone was a witness and victim of it all. The racist and culturally oppressive tactics of Jim Crow laws would impact Cone's critique of the theological hypocrisy and culturally dominant practices of many white Protestants during this time; before I would write about it, Cone functionally said the whitewashing must stop.

The Rise of Liberation Thought

The idea of liberation and the critique of the culturally oppressive practices of white Protestants in history did not begin with Cone, but was expounded upon by Cone. While Cone is the most prolific and well-known Liberation scholar, the idea and movement toward liberation did not start with him. There were several African American leaders that played a pivotal role in the rise of Liberation thought amongst African Americans. Each of them had a faulty unbiblical version of Christianity presented to them by white oppressors. At the forefront of their response was not only social, but religious freedom as well. The fight for freedom is difficult to pinpoint with certainty, but one could not deny the revolutionary **Nat Turner** (1800-1831). Turner is considered one of the most notorious slave

---

156   Ibid., 217

preachers who ever lived on American soil. Turner's hatred of slavery drove him to seek freedom by violent means; he was a real-life *Django Unchained* (a little more from this movie will be addressed later). Turner killed nearly sixty white people before being captured and hanged in September 1831.[157] White slave owners responded to his revolt by prohibiting education and further restricting free Blacks and requiring that white ministers be present during Black worship services; in other words, a whitewashed version of Christianity was presented to them that kept whites in the position of power and favor and Blacks in the subservient position. The presence of white ministers was designed to keep Black Christians at arm's length and to further eisegete racial inferiority into Scripture and the perpetual "Curse of Ham" over the Black race.[158] This was one of the first acts of ecclesiological imperialism and whitewashing, as whites wanted Blacks to remain enslaved and not because they actually wanted to worship with them. They wanted Blacks to worship them, and if whites were absent they wanted to indoctrinate them so that they would worship like them. This violent revolt was one of the first of many as Blacks struggled for liberation from their white oppressors. Before being hanged, Turner shared his liberation theology with a lawyer named Thomas Gray. "I heard a loud noise in the heavens, and the Spirit instantly appeared to me and said the Serpent was loosened, and Christ had laid down the yoke he had borne for the sins of men, and that I should take it on and fight against the Serpent, for the time was fast approaching when the first should be the last and the last should be the first." [159]

Alexander Crummell (1819-1898) was an American scholar and an Episcopalian minister. Born the son of an African prince and a free mother, Crummell attended an interracial school at Canaan, N.H., and an institute in Whitesboro, N.Y., which was run by abolitionists and combined manual labor and the classical curriculum. In 1897, he founded the American Negro Academy, which was dedicated to the educational, social and financial empowerment of African Americans and was the first major learned society for African Americans.

---

157   Biography Nat Turner. Retrieved from http://www.biography.com/people/nat-turner-9512211 (May, 2016).

158   Charles Marsh, *God's Long Summer: Stories of Faith and Civil Rights*, (Princeton, New Jersey: Princeton University Press), 92-93.

159   Nat Turner and Thomas R. Gray, *The Confessions of Nat Turner*, (Richmond: T.R. Gray, 1832), 9-10.

The Whitewashing of Christianity

Crummell was a pioneer of Pan-African thought, as he saw the image of God in Black people which wasn't affirmed during his time. Pan-Africanism focused on two fundamental aspects: a collective consciousness between various African and diasporic communities and an emphasis on Black autonomy from white hegemony.[160] His Christian faith and affinity for Black people led him to cultivate scholarship and leadership among young Blacks for their empowerment. Crummell was denied admission to the General Theological Seminary of the Episcopal church in 1839 because he was Black. Determined to grow theologically, Crummell studied theology privately and became an Episcopalian minister in 1844. In 1848, he traveled to England to raise funds for a church for poor Blacks and soon thereafter began a course of study at Queen's College, Cambridge (A.B., 1853). After graduating, Crummell went to Liberia as a missionary. He would spend the next 20 years there as a parish rector, professor of intellectual and moral science at Liberia College, and public figure. He became a citizen of the new republic and a strong proponent of Liberian nationalism. In his early years, Crummell was an outspoken advocate for the abolition of slavery and the removal of legal restrictions on Black Americans. He fought for the right to vote and recommended the establishment of African American schools. Later in his career, he wrote and lectured widely against the increasingly entrenched racism of post-Reconstruction America, appealing to educated Blacks to provide leadership.[161]

Marcus Garvey (1887-1940) was a Jamaican political leader and is regarded by some as "the apostle of Black Theology in the United States of America."[162] Marcus Mosiah Garvey, Jr. was born on August 17, 1887, in St. Ann's Bay, Jamaica. A self-educated, brilliant man, Garvey founded the Universal Negro Improvement Association, dedicated to promoting African Americans and resettlement in Africa. In the United States, he launched several businesses to promote a separate Black nation due to the inequitable practices in America. After he was convicted of mail fraud and deported back to Jamaica, he continued his work for Black repatriation to Africa. Garvey was the last of 11 children born to Marcus Garvey, Sr. and Sarah

---

160 Vince Bantu, *Gospel Haymanot: A Constructive Theology and Critical Reflection on African and Diasporic Christianity*, (Urban Ministries, Inc. 2020), 35.

161 Britanica, *Alexander Crummell American Scholar and Minister* https://www.britannica.com/biography/Alexander-Crummell, (January 2020).

162 Randall Burkett, *Garveyism as a Religious Movement*, (Metucher, NJ: Scarecrow Press, 1978), 15.

Jane Richards. His father was a stonemason, and his mother a domestic worker and farmer.[163] He is most notably known because of his intentional affirmation of Black people. Marcus Garvey was an orator for the Black Nationalism and Pan-Africanism movements, to which end he founded the Universal Negro Improvement Association and African Communities League. Garvey advanced a Pan-African philosophy which inspired a global mass movement, known as Garveyism. Martin Luther King, Jr., said that Garvey "was the first man on a mass scale level to give millions of Negroes a sense of dignity and destiny, and make the Negro feel he is somebody."[164] Garvey was one of the first to speak of seeing God through Black "spectacles."[165]

Howard Thurman (1899-1931) was a philosopher, theologian, educator and a civil rights activist. He was one of the first leading African American pacifists.[166] His non-violent tactics shaped Martin Luther King Jr. and he is often ignored for the role his teaching played in Dr. King's life. Thurman's book *Jesus and the Disinherited*,[167] written in 1949, paralleled Jesus' life with the plight of African Americans in America. Thurman used Jesus' poverty as the impetus which enabled him to identify with the poor masses. This is when a hermeneutical perspective that was intentional about taking the African American experience in America began to gain more prominence.[168] Thurman, who influenced many, saw that there was a need to contextualize Scripture to the audience's experience. Since the African American experience primarily seemed valued by African Americans, Black theologians saw a need to show them how Jesus could identify with their struggle and would one day end all suffering.

---

163 Biography, *Marcus Garvey*, https://www.biography.com/activist/marcus-garvey (January 2018).

164 Randall Burkett, *Garveyism as a Religious Movement*, (Metucher, NJ: Scarecrow Press, 1978), 15.

165 Ron Rhodes, *Black Theology, Black Power, and the Black Experience, Reasoning from the Scriptures Ministries*, http://ronrhodes.org/articles/Black-theology-Black-power.html, 2016.

166 Papers Project, *Howard Thurman*, http://www.bu.edu/htpp/, accessed 2016.

167 Howard Thurman, *Jesus and the Disinherited*, (Boston, MA: Beacon Press Books), 11.

168 Albert J. Raboteau, *Canaan Land*, (New York, NY: Oxford University Press, 2001), 110.

The Whitewashing of Christianity

Medgar Evers (1925-1963) sought liberation for Black people through education primarily and not the local church. Evers saw education as the primary means to both educate and liberate African Americans from their oppressors.[169] His assertion was since African Americans had access to education and it was no longer illegal for them to read, they could empower themselves through education and build their own neighborhoods in which they were affirmed and appreciated.[170] Evers preceded Dr. King as a public activist and was effective in his message of empowering African Americans outside of the church.

Martin Luther King, Jr. (1929-1968) was not an outright proponent of "Black liberation theology," but he was a clear proponent of Black people.[171] While there was debate about his non-violent tactics, African Americans did not question his allegiance to see Black people liberated from oppression. Some white theologians labeled King as liberal because he studied Gandhi and Thurman, but it is important to understand that King saw a lack of orthodoxy and orthopraxy from people who professed Christ, his challenge was rooted in the canon of Scripture, and his methods were rooted in reading how Jesus instructed his audience to "turn the other cheek" (Matthew 5:39).[172] His motivation was the gospel which he proclaimed unapologetically. Lastly, there was Albert Cleage.

Albert Cleage (1911-2000) was one of the more militant Black writers of the twentieth century, with most of his writings taking place in the 1960s. Cleage is most well-known for his 1968 publication *The Black Messiah*,[173] which was a collection of sermons to communicate the teachings of Black nationalism, which essentially advocates racial identity and the need for African Americans to have their own; it had aspects of Pan-Africanism which was created by Alexander Crummell, but not with the biblical emphasis as Crummel had. Cleage rejected most of the principles of racial integration because he saw it as harmful for Black people. Cleage thought that if Black people could see Jesus as a Black person they

---

169 Evers-Williams Myrlie, *The Autobiography of Medgar Evers: A Hero's Life and Legacy Revealed Through His Writings, Letters, and Speeches*, (New York, NY: Basic Civitas Books), 162.

170 ibid.

171 Albert J. Raboteau, *Canaan Land*, (New York, NY: Oxford University Press, 2001), 112.

172 ibid.

173 Albert Cleage, *The Black Messiah*, (New York: Sheed and Ward, 1969), 4.

could identify with him better and not be oppressed by the false teachings of racists that used Scripture to oppress African Americans.[174] The African American experience in America and the continual rise of Liberation Thought set the stage for James Cone to speak to the cultural realities that African Americans faced by the culturally imperialistic practices of white theologians who ignored the Black experience in America, while simultaneously benefited from their privilege and whitewashing the Christian faith.

Enter James Cone

James Cone was born in Fordyce, Arkansas, in 1938. He was raised in a town about sixty miles southwest of Little Rock called Beardon. He grew up in a predominantly white neighborhood with about eight hundred whites and four hundred Blacks. In this town Cone's spirituality was shaped and enhanced.[175] In the Black church, Cone encountered the presence of the Holy Spirit and his soul was moved toward aspiration and freedom. The affirmation of his being and the aspiration for freedom was fueled and encouraged at the Macedonia African Methodist Episcopal Church (AME).[176] The Black church played a major role in how he approached, applied, and taught theology. His interpretive lens starts with his experience in the Black church and the questions that his experiences caused him to raise. Growing up and experiencing racism and witnessing African Americans endure racism was the impetus that led him to see a need to emphasize the reality that the gospel is a message of liberation and hope for oppressed people. He says, "Jesus' work is essentially one of liberation. Becoming a slave himself, he opens realities of human existence formerly closed to man."[177] In *The Cross and the Lynching Tree*, Cone addresses how the heinous reality of lynching reminded African Americans that suffering in Christ ends in triumph, while pointing out the blatant hyposcrisy of whites who claimed

---

174 ibid.
175 James H. Cone, *God of the Oppressed*, (Maryknoll, NY: Orbis Books, 1997), 1.
176 ibid.
177 James H. Cone, *Black Theology and Black Power*, (Maryknoll, NY: Orbis Books, 1997), 35.

The Whitewashing of Christianity

to be followers of Christ.[178] He notes that after the Civil War, white Christians participated in the lynching of almost 5000 Black men and women, but did not see the contradictory nature of their actions.[179] Since the cross was necessary for our redemption, the cross provided a source of hope for African Americans, since they could identify with Christ and suffer for Christ. As he recalls the lynching era of 1880-1940, he says, "In that era, the lynching tree joined the cross as the most emotionally charged symbols in the African American community, symbols that represented both death and the promise of redemption, judgment and the offer of mercy, suffering and the power of hope."[180] Cone saw a need for African Americans to be affirmed and treated like people and this was not the case in the world he lived in; thus the need for liberation from cultural, social and political oppression led him to emphasize the liberation nature of the gospel. It was not that he wanted to racialize hermeneutics in general or deny biblical theology, but rather since those spewing theological truth did not take the Black experience into account and oftentimes were functional antinomians preaching grace while attending public lynchings, Cone saw a need to connect Scripture to the issues of Black people. Cone contextualized it for people of his day. Cone saw the duplicity of white Christians of his day and wanted to call them back to Christian ethics and wanted them to stop whitewashing the Bible as if it were written by white people for white people. It was this type of mindset that enabled Martin Luther, the reformer of the 16th century, to preach grace yet be antisemitic. This same duplicity lasted for several hundred years as whites preached Christ yet denied him by their heinous acts. Lynchings were so common in the South that African Americans were expected to accept it. White supremacist and bishop Attiucus G. Haygood actually complained because killing Blacks become so common that it was no longer intriguing. He says, "now-a-days, it seems the killing of Negroes is not so extraordinary an occurrence as to need explanation; it has become so common that it no longer

---

178 James H. Cone, *The Cross and the Lynching Tree*, (Maryknoll, NY: Orbis Books, 2011), 3.

179 James H. Cone, *God of the Oppressed*, (New York, NY: Orbis Books, 2008), 39.

180 James H. Cone, *The Cross and the Lynching Tree*, (Maryknoll, NY: Orbis Books, 2011), 3.

surprises."[181] This sociological and culturally oppressive climate is what led Cone to write *Black Theology and Black Power* in 1969. In it, Cone defines Black Power, not as an escape from Christianity nor as a rebellion against the white race. For him, Black Power was about Black freedom, Black self-determination and Black empowerment in which Black people could determine their own destiny without the approval or validation of white people.[182] In other words, the Black identity wasn't determined by its proximity to whiteness, but rather by God, who created and affirmed their Blackness because He created them (Psalms 139:13).

Cone quotes Paul Tillich to expand on the idea of Black Power being self-determining and self-affirming regardless of oppressive circumstances when he says, "The courage to be, which is the ethical act in which man affirms his being in spite of those elements of his existence which conflict with his essential self-affirmation."[183] The African American struggle is what shaped Cone's approach to theology; this is not at the exclusion of Scripture, but rather in application to Scripture. The term Black Theology came into being because Cone starts with his personal experiences and the plight of African Americans in America because, for him, theology cannot be separated from the ethics of those that claim service to a deity, nor can it be applied in a vacuum.[184] Therefore, Black Theology seeks to reveal how Scripture addresses and comforts the oppressed. Since God is not deistic, but rather intimately involved with his creation, authentic Christian theology cannot afford to be an abstract discourse that lacks passion on the nature of God in relation to humanity; any analysis void of God's involvement with people, in particular oppressed people, is not reliable, in his view.[185] Cone views Blackness as it relates to Black Theology as ontological more than physiological; Blackness is an experience synonymous with struggle and oppression.[186] Therefore, since whites were the oppressors of

---

181 James H. Cone, *The Cross and the Lynching Tree*, (Maryknoll, NY: Orbis Books, 2011), 6.
182 James H. Cone, *Black Theology and Black Power*, (Maryknoll, NY: Orbis Books, 1997), 6.
183 ibid.
184 ibid.
185 ibid.
186 ibid.

The Whitewashing of Christianity

African Americans, they could not be trusted with the final say on theological matters. Cone rejected their whitewashed narrative because it wasn't biblical, orthodox, loving or Christian in any way. In Cone's view, white people used Scripture to protect and preserve their perverse agenda. Culturally oppressive hermeneutics, which presented whites as superior and normative, is why Cone saw a need for continuity between the historical Jesus as written in Scripture and the kerygmatic Christ, because without this continuity, Christianity becomes subjective and enables people to interpret the kerygma (the apostolic proclamation of salvation through Jesus Christ) based on their own existential state. A lack of continuity between the historical Jesus and the kerygma is what allowed whites to enable their condition to determine the meaning of Jesus and Scripture and use it to oppress African Americans.[187] The culturally, politically, and socially oppressive climate that Cone and millions of African Americans were birthed into is what compelled Cone to make a cultural distinction in his theological approach. He saw a need to join culture and theology in a way that would affirm the oppressed and empower them through Jesus' suffering and triumph.[188] His critique of white theologians was similar to that of Dr. King in that he saw white "Christians" as proponents of the antinomian heresy.[189] Not all whites, but any white person that could vocally and passionately claim Christ, yet joyfully attend a lynching, silently watch African American oppression, and sanction separate but equal Jim Crow laws was not bearing godly fruit and therefore was a heretic and not truly redeemed (1 John 4:19-21). Heresy is typically confined to wrong ideas about doctrines; in essence it is about orthodoxy. The way Cone approached heresy included both orthodoxy (right belief) and orthopraxy (right practice); he approached heresy with a complete view that his white counterparts ignored. He also understood heresy as a refusal to do justice, not a social gospel, but rather social engagement fueled by the gospel (Micah 6:6-8, Isaiah 58:1-14, Proverbs 31:8-9, Matthew 23:23-24, Matthew 25, Titus 2:11-13). In Isaiah 1:21-23 the totality of conviction is presented, which involves both belief and practice. Antinomianism is the heretical belief that

---

187   James H. Cone, *A Black Theology of Liberation*, (Maryknoll, NY: Orbis Books, 1970), 119.

188   James H. Cone, *The Cross and the Lynching Tree*, (Maryknoll, NY: Orbis Books, 1997), 38.

189   ibid.

one can essentially live hedonistically because salvation is granted apart from works, but one must not forget that while works do not save, they do reveal if one's faith is genuine (James 1:17). To willfully embrace and propagate the systematic oppression of another race in the name of religion denies and defies that religion. This is what Cone constantly confronted in his books and activism.[190] His writings were rooted in his love for Black people because from his perspective the only people that would love Black people were primarily other Black people. Sadly, when African Americans sought common ground with whites based on both having faith in Christ, they were still met with rejection and hatred within the church. His critique was rooted in the social and cultural realities that he faced.

Cone's Critique of the Reformers

Cone did not disagree with the reasons and essence of the Protestant Reformation of the sixteenth century, but the inconsistency of the Reformers is what bothered him. He points out how the Reformation could aggressively fight for right doctrine, but ignore the right practice of honoring and fighting for the liberation of the oppressed.[191] He points out how the bloody history of antisemitism was not confronted or emphasized during the Protestant Reformation.[192] Cone sees Martin Luther's identification with the oppressors in society as the bridge that enabled him to communicate the state as a follower of God, while simultaneously ignoring the fact that the oppressed were being tormented by the state. The silence of the Reformers on the issue of racial oppression by other Reformers like John Calvin and John Wesley communicates an affinity among Calvinism, capitalism and slave trading.[193] Not much has changed; as it relates to Black and white cultural and ecclesiological relations and the cultural and social challenges that Cone faced still exist today, though not as vehemently.

---

190 ibid.
191 James H. Cone, *A Black Theology of Liberation*, (Maryknoll, NY: Orbis Books, 1970), 35.
192 ibid.
193 ibid.

Not Only Theological, but Culturally Imperialistic

Cone's primary issue was with the culturally imperialistic practices of white Christians, who saw their way of doing things as the way. Cone disagreed and said:

"Because a particular methodology has been used to dehumanize and oppress people of non-European descent for several hundred years, any association with that particular hermeneutical tradition, then, is rendered impotent in an African American, African or Latino setting."[194]

Like Martin Luther, John Calvin and Jonathan Edwards, James Cone was not a perfect theologian and there are aspects of Liberation Theology that aren't consistent with orthodoxy the same way that the reformers ethics were not consistent with orthopraxy. Cone's issue was that of many African Americans of his day: whites determined what was acceptable and what was right, while living totally wrong. This has led to the chasm that still exists in the church today as it relates to Reformed Theology, cultural understanding and racial reconciliation and the culture that accompanies it as discussed earlier, which Cone opposed because their version of Christianity didn't include people who looked like him nor did it address their concerns; it was a whitewashed Christianity void of Black and brown people. White evangelicals of his day presented sovereignty as a reason to endure and accept dehumanization, and when Blacks resisted, they were viewed and labeled as having a low view of God, his sovereignty and or being theologically liberal. This is another example of whitewashing that I believe is unintentional, but no less damaging. It was Black people's understanding of sovereignty that got us through slavery and Jim Crow and when whites ignored this reality by not displaying a lack of compassion and Christian love.

Gayraud Wilmore points out the fact that it was the sovereignty of God that enabled African Americans to endure slavery and Jim Crow and keep their faith in a God that white oppressors presented inaccurately. He says:

> Blacks have used Christianity not so much as it was delivered to them by racist white churches, but as its truth was authenticated to them in

---

194   Rhodes Ron, *Black Theology, Black Power, and the Black Experience, Reasoning from the Scriptures Ministries*, http://ronrhodes.org/articles/Black-theology-Black-power.html Accessed April 2016.

the experience of suffering and struggle, to reinforce an enculturated religious orientation and to produce an indigenous faith that emphasized dignity, freedom, and human welfare.[195]

As pointed out earlier about theologian John Frame, Cone saw the same double standard in Reinhold Niebuhr.[196] Niebuhr took a realist approach to Christian ethics and promoted what he called a transvaluation of values, a term derived from Nietzsche (who disparaged Christianity's care for the weak).[197] Transvaluation for Niebuhr was what the gospel empowers people to do; see themselves as lowly instead of proud, and weak instead of strong. Niebuhr aggressively preached about how the gospel seeks the least of these and unites people, yet he could not identify the theological and cultural hole in his theology because he was a willful victim of his own whitewashing. When it comes to the ethics of some reformed heroes, I'm amazed by the hermeneutical and exegetical gymnastics played to ignore their ethics in favor of their theology. Statements like, "slavery was a cultural thing back then," fornication is a culturally acceptable practice now, should we ignore the biblical ethic in favor of a cultural one? Of course not, but when these men dehumanized people while teaching sound doctrine, many turn their hermeneutical cheeks, thus undermining the orthodoxy they claim to hold dearly. [198] Niebuhr and many others who comfortably separate theology from ethics of the theologian contribute to the issue that whitewashing creates: disunity. Niebuhr, as Cone points out, ignored the plight of African Americans in his research and application. Niebuhr heralded the founding fathers who owned slaves as virtuous and honorable and not villains.[199] Consequently, Cone felt the need to "do his own thing," for his people; Black people and thus Black Theology was needed.

The issue Cone had was not truth relating to biblical orthodoxy, but rather it was the whitewashed version of Christianity presented to him that was culturally

---

195 Gayraud S. Wilmore, *Black Religion and Black Radicalism* (Maryknoll, NY: Orbis Books, 1998), 25.
196 James H. Cone, *The Cross and the Lynching Tree*, (Maryknoll, NY: Orbis Books, 2011), 38.
197 ibid.
198 ibid.
199 ibid.

imperialistic as it related to worship, preaching, hermeneutics, interpersonal relations, and Christian history. When racism is ignored and the culture of another is not considered *cultural dominant, doxological* and *liturgical exclusion, homiletical bias* and *hermeneutical preferences*, we can begin to make ground and expose the exclusionary measures to stay separate and reverse the whitewashed version of Christianity that's been preserved for centuries. We must imagine Cone's world to understand his cultural and theological critique of white evangelicals of his day and how the need to expose whitewashing still exists today.

Correcting Cone

The reality is any movement led by a predominant race is going to have some form of cultural expression, but when that cultural expression becomes dominant and is not simply numerical, but also oppressive, that movement should not be supported. Cone responded to a need that he saw in his community. A need to let Black people know that Yeshua (Jesus) loved them, affirmed them, and could identify with their suffering because he suffered because of the sin of humanity and to redeem humanity. While understanding most of Cone's sentiments considering the time in which he lived, ethnocentrism should not be the only determining lens through which life and doctrine are to be interpreted. This is where we must part ways with some aspects of Cone's hermeneutical application. Cone does not exclude the gospel or orthodoxy entirely, but he promotes Blackness to the point he explicitly says Jesus is Black, which we know that Jesus was indeed a man of color. He says, "The Blackness of God, and everything implied by it in a racist society, is the heart of the Black Theology doctrine of God. There is no place in Black Theology for a colorless God in a society where human beings suffer precisely because of their color."[200] While I agree that Jesus certainly was not a white man and he was definitely a man of color, Black washing the Bible isn't the answer to whitewashing. To make God a God of the oppressed only misses the beauty of the cross. It was on the cross that Jesus said, "Father forgive them for they know not what they do" (Luke 23:34). Yeshua revealed that he did not only come to save the oppressed, but his grace is available for the oppressor as well when the oppressor genuinely repents. Since

---

200   James H. Cone, *A Black Theology of Liberation*, (Maryknoll, NY: Orbis Books, 1970), 67.

Cone begins with the Black experience almost exclusively, he can make that experience the all-determining factor for theology and functionally impose views on Scripture that are not there. Cone's cultural critique and many of his theological, anthropological, social critiques are understood and should be affirmed, since white evangelicals considered their culture as normal and really did not see themselves as having a culture. However, to respond by making God exclusively a God of the oppressed misses the universal invitation of the cross. Any preferential imposition of Scripture will lead to the same abuse of Scripture that white supremacists used to enslave African Americans. God is a God of the oppressed and he extends grace to the oppressor because both need it.

Malcolm Foley of The Witness does a good job explaining the conundrum Cone lived with daily. In explaining both the necessity and difficulty of Cone's perspective he says:

> Therein we see the lamentable necessity of Cone's theology: it sprang out of a mind and an experience that was inevitably shaped by trauma, as the experience of many Black people in America is. To consider the whippings of slaves, the rapes of slave women, the family separation inherent in the slave system, the corkscrew tortures of Luther and Mary Holbert, the burning of Sam Hose, the mutilation of Henry Smith, the indignities of Jim Crow, and the injustice of mass incarceration is to plunge oneself in a pit from which escape is not guaranteed. And yet, if one's theology is not shaped by it and has no answers for it, one's theology is not properly Christian. This is a reality, a history, and a theology that the Christian, especially the American Christian, must wrestle with. They must ask the question: how does a good God sit by and allow innocent Black men, women, and children to be tortured and killed? Black Christians have spent much time and many resources answering such questions. It is time that we were not alone in doing so.[201]

---

[201] Malcolm Foley, "On the Assault of James and Black Liberation Theology" https://thewitnessbcc.com/on-the-assault-of-james-cone-Black-liberation-theology/, (January 2020).

The Whitewashing of Christianity

Liberation was a needed response, but certainly not the only response of Black people and not all aspects of liberation theology should be embraced. Liberation was one response to whitewashed Christianity, but there are more, some Black and brown people internalized the false narrative, which leads to self-hatred.

Discussion Questions

1. Why was liberation essential as a response to oppression?
2. What is the difference between liberation and liberation theology?
3. What aspects of liberation theology are misunderstood by many evangelicals?
4. Can the orthodoxy of reformed theology and the orthopraxy of liberation theology be reconciled? Why or why not?
5. Where are you prone to have blind spots in your own theology and practice?

9

Responses to Whitewashing
Self-Hatred
the Making of a COON

> He gawn stay in the Big House?
> – STEPHEN
> (DJANGO UNCHAINED)

IN 1510, the hateful, diabolical, unregenerate racists found one of their greatest advocates, a self-hating Arab-African by the name of Al-Hasan Ibn Muhammad al-Wazzan al-Fasi. He wasn't born hating himself; he was taught self-hatred, a reality that still exists today. Fasi was captured as he traveled with his uncle, and the well-educated Moroccan youngster would be taught to hate himself and people who looked like him. Pope Leo X of Italy freed Fasi before dying in 1521, converted him to an unbiblical slave version of Christianity and renamed him Johannes Leo. He became known as Leo the African, or Leo Africanus, and he affirmed the delusion Italians had about Africa and Africans with his survey titled *Della descrittione dell'Africa* (Description of Africa).[202] Fasi, later named Leo Africanus, described his native continent of Africa as one being prone to venery

---

202   Ibram X. Kendi, *Stamped from the Beginning: The Definitive History of Racist Ideas in America*, (New York: Nation Books, 2016), 28.

The Whitewashing of Christianity

(sexual indulgence). He also said that the Africans "lead a beastly kind of life, being utterly destitute of the use of reason, the dexterities of wit, and of all arts" and capped it off by saying that they behave themselves as if they had continually lived in a forest among wild beasts.[203] This process still works today, as many Blacks have responded to whitewashing by committing the sin of self-hatred, an affront to the imago dei within people of African descent by people of African descent.

Fasi and people like him have been referred to as coons, a derogatory term that's used to describe a Black person that hates or has extreme disdain for Black people. The term was originally used in 1837 and is said to be from barracoon, from Portuguese barraca "slave depot, pen or rough enclosure for Black slaves in transit in West Africa, Brazil, Cuba." The popularity of the term was boosted by the immensely popular Blackface minstrel act Zip Coon (George Washington Dixon) which debuted in New York City in 1834. But it is perhaps older (one of the lead characters in the 1767 colonial comic opera "The Disappointment" is a Black man named Raccoon).[204] The point in entertainment that was highlighted by Blackface and Black people which presented them as morons was two-fold; to entertain white people and to indoctrinate Black people with inferiority in hopes that they'd embrace it. While many argue about the term and its usage, others prefer the term "internalized racism." Whatever the verbiage used, self-hatred is still prevalent and must be opposed. Another phrase used to describe a self-hating Black person is Uncle Tom. Uncle Tom is the fictitious character in Harriet Beecher Stowe's Uncle Tom's Cabin. The book records a Kentucky slaveholder who plans to sell Uncle Tom and the son of a woman named Eliza Harris. Eliza flees to the North with her husband George Harris, while Tom stays and is sold in the South. Tom ends up saving a little white girl by the name of Eva, who had fallen in a river. Eva's father, Augustine St. Clare buys Tom as a show of "gratitude." While many wrongly assert self-hatred to Uncle Tom, Sambo was the cruel overseer of the slaves who worked for the slave owner Simon Legree and showed vehement hatred for Black people and ended up murdering Uncle Tom after he refused to tell where some women escaped. In a Stephen-esque (Acts 7:54-60) manner, Tom prays for Sambo and Quimbo as they beat him to death. While Uncle Tom's Cabin is considered an anti-slavery book, Stowe still communicated racist ideas

---

203   ibid.
204   Online Etymology Dictionary, *Coon*, https://www.etymonline.com/word/coon (Douglas Harper).

through the characters in her book. Tom embraces Black spiritual superiority as a concession for being intellectually inferior. Stowe claimed that spiritual superiority allowed Black people to have soul. Unfortunately, many Blacks consumed this ideology and spiritually gifted Black people became central to Black identity, while embracing intellectual inferiority. This means that some Blacks embraced racist ideas about themselves. Stowe was also successful in creating a sense of jealousy in white racists, since they believed themselves to be void of the 'soul' that Blacks possessed, they found soul through Black people while self-hating Blacks found intellect through white people. Tom was a symbol Black submissiveness, spiritual superiority and intellectual inferiority. Deifying the race of another or demeaning one's own race can both create and contribute to self-hatred. I think we should think of COON as a process in which one contributes to ongoing oppression through negligence. It's a self-inflicted affliction in which one asserts that giving in to whitewashing and stereotypes will somehow lead to acceptance and self-fulfillment. COONing (Contributing to Ongoing Oppression through Negligence) is the result of a process similar to that of Al-Hasan Ibn Muhammad al-Wazzan al-Fasi, one that involves both displacement and indoctrination.

- **Contributing**—Blacks dealing with self-hatred contribute to whitewashing by denying its existence or remaining silent on clear issues of race and injustice and affirming whitewashing by only heralding white preachers, theologians and scholars as credible. Since the goal is white acceptance and comfort, silence and willful ignorance are deployed to keep the peace, while ignoring their own objectification and tokenism. Clear examples of racial insensitivity said by leaders in churches or seminaries is ignored in the name of keeping peace or avoiding the angry Black man or woman moniker. Black and brown people contribute through silence on social issues that Scripture addresses (police brutality, abortion, sexism, etc.). They also contribute by accepting a token role where they are a face, but not a voice, agreeing when disparities are clear and evident and affirming the delusion about Black people by agreeing that our history is one of emotionalism, not intellectualism. They contribute by accepting the version of Christianity given that almost never mentions people that look like them. They contribute by believing the false narrative that anything of significance as it relates to the Christian faith and history had to have come from white people. While Blacks aren't monolithic and we do disagree and disagreement doesn't make one a

The Whitewashing of Christianity

COON, willful silence can. In many churches and seminaries Blacks dealing with self-hatred hurt reconciliation and ethnic conciliation by refusing to confront ignorance about Black people and by simply smiling and nodding.

- **Ongoing**—these aren't isolated incidents; self-hatred is something that isn't just a past occurrence of slaves, but a present reality of those that deify whiteness. The ongoing nature of ecclesiological coonery is seen by Black people who embrace a whitewashed narrative of the Christian faith and refuse to serve under Black leadership based on the faulty assumption that only white ministers are orthodox and gospel-centered. They wrongly believe that essentially all Black ministers have given in to the prosperity gospel not knowing that this philosophy originates in white circles and was known as New Thought philosophy.[205] To be clear, there's nothing wrong with a Black person having a white pastor, but if the reason is based on a disdain for people who look like them, then coonery is evident and should be shunned for the sin that it is. Sadly, when many Blacks dealing with self-hatred enter and join predominantly white churches, their self-hatred is sometimes celebrated as biblical maturity because they affirm the caricatures many of these churches have about Black people.
- **Oppression**—Blacks dealing with self-hatred also deny oppression and in some cases I would concur that the term is used too loosely, but oppression isn't just in the form of slavery, but applies to inequity. For instance, Black children make up 18 percent of the preschool population, but represent half of all out-school suspensions. This is not solely due to behavior, but to an educational system primarily filled with people teaching children of color, many of whom don't give Black children the benefit that they give to white children.[206] Additionally, Black youth are 18 times more likely to be tried as adults than white children for the same crime. People with Black sounding names have to send out 50 percent more resumes just to get a call back. If a Black person kills a white person, they are twice as likely to receive the death sentence than if a white person kills a Black person, but when these stats and

---

205   David Jones, *Health, Wealth and Happiness: How the Prosperity Gospel Overshadows the Gospel of Christ*, (Kregel Publications Grand Rapids, MI, 2011), 51.
206   Amy Halberstadt, *Future Teachers More Likely to View Black Children as Angry, Even When They're Not* https://news.ncsu.edu/2020/07/race-anger-bias-kids/, July 2020.

the like are mentioned, they are outliers, but the stats on Black depravity are somehow accurate. From access to credit, accumulating generational wealth, engaging with law enforcement, treatment by health care professionals, and even the likelihood of a mother's death while giving birth are affected by our collective racial biases against people of color, and especially African Americans and Native Americans.[207] I'm amazed at how opponents of white privilege can quickly spew stats on the Black community to buffer their points, but ignore stats that reveal that the playing field is still not level and that white people still benefit from a system rooted in oppression. This isn't to say that all whites are racist and that benefitting from the system makes one a racist; it's the denial that I take issue with and while terms can be disputed, facts can't.

- **Negligence**—Blacks dealing with the aforementioned willfully ignore these issues in some cases to receive acceptance. Their negligence isn't due to lack of information, but rather a lack of compassion for people who share their race and/or ethnicity and an internal battle for identity, which should be found in Yeshua, but is instead sought after by aggressively pursuing the acceptance of man.

---

207 Aaron Glantz and Emmanuel Martinez, "Kept Out," Reveal, February 15, 2018, www.revealnews.org/article/for-people-ofcolor-banks-are-shutting-the-door-to-homeownership/. Jamiles Lartey, "Median Wealth of Black Americans 'Will Fall to Zero by 2053,' Warns New Report," The Guardian, September 13, 2017, www.theguardian.com/inequality/2017/sep/13/medianwealth-of-Black-americans-wil-fall-to-zero-by-2053-warns-new-report. Andrew Cohen, "What We've Learned About Racial Disparity in Policing Since Ferguson," The Marshall Project, August 10, 2015, https://www.themarshallproject.org/2014/11/19/what-we-ve-learned-about-racial-disparity-in-policing-since-ferguson. Amanda Holpuch, "Black Patients Half as Likely to Receive Pain Medication as White Patients, Study Finds," The Guardian, August 10, 2016, www.theguardian.com/science/2016/aug/10/Black-patientsbias-prescriptions-pain-management-medicine-opioids. Linda Villarosa, "Why America's Black Mothers and Babies Are in a Life-or-Death Crisis," New York Times Magazine, April 11, 2018, www.nytimes.com/2018/04/11/magazine/Black-mothers-babies-death-maternal-mortality.html.

The Whitewashing of Christianity

A more recent example of a coon in the mainstream was a character by the name of Stephen played by Samuel L. Jackson in the 2012 movie Django Unchained. There's a pivotal scene that captures the essence of coonery and self-hatred (warning vulgarity is used, no surprise from a Quentin Tarantino film).

Calvin Candie : Hello. Stephen, my boy!

Stephen : *[Black house servant exiting the Big House]* Yeah, yeah, yeah. Hello, my a#$. Who dis nigger up on dat nag?

Calvin Candie : Aw, Stephen, you have nails for breakfast? What's the matter? Why you so ornery? You miss me? Huh?

Stephen : Oh, yes, sir. I miss you like a hawg miss slop. Like a baby miss mammy titty! I miss you like I misses a rock in my shoe! Now, I aks you, who dis nigger on dat nag?

Django : Hey, Snowball. You wanna know my name or the name of my horse, you ask me.

Stephen : Just who the hell you callin' 'Snowball,' hoss boy? I'll snatch yo Black a#% off dat nag down here in the mud so fast make yo head spin!

Calvin Candie : Whoa, whoa, whoa, whoa! Stephen! Stephen! Let's keep it funny. Django here's a freeman.

Stephen : Dis nigger here?

Calvin Candie : That nigger there. Let me at least introduce the two of you. Django, this is another cheeky Black bugger like yourself, Stephen. Stephen, this here is Django. You two oughta hate each other.

Stephen : Calvin, just who the hell is dis nigger you feels the need to entertain?

Calvin Candie : Django, and his friend in gray here, Dr. Schultz, are customers. And they are our guests, Stephen. And you, you old, decrepit bastard, you are to show them every hospitality. You understand that?

Stephen : Yes, sir. Him I understands, but I don't know why I got to take lip off dis nigger.

Calvin Candie : You don't have to know why. Do you understand?

Stephen : Yes, sir. I understand.

Calvin Candie : Well, good. They are spending the night. Go open the guest bedrooms and get two ready.

Stephen : [*mortified*] He gawn stay in the **Big House**?

Calvin Candie : Stephen. He's a slaver. It's different.

Stephen : In the Big House?

Calvin Candie : Well, you got a problem with that?

Stephen : Aw, naw, naw. I ain't got no problem with it. If you ain't got no problem with burnin' the bed, the sheets, the pillowcase, and everything else when this Black-ass mother#$%@ gone!

Calvin Candie : That is my problem! They are mine to burn! Now your problem right now is making a good impression! And I want you to start solving that problem right now and get them goddamn rooms ready!

Stephen : Yes sir, Monsieur Candie.

Calvin Candie : Go on, now.

Stephen : Cain't believe you brought a nigger to stay in the Big House. Yo daddy's rollin' over in his god$%* grave, right now. Brought a nigger to stay with us. What kinda sh@% is that?[208]

Notice that Stephen was more offended by a Black man staying in the Big House than he was being a slave. For many Blacks that have allowed whitewashing to cause them to view themselves as inferior, the 'Big House' is the acceptance from and acquiescence to whites based on the faulty belief of inferiority. The 'big house' for Black and brown people who embrace a whitewashed narrative of

---

208   Quentin Tarantino, *Django Unchained* https://www.imdb.com/title/tt1853728/characters/nm0000168, accessed September 2020.

The Whitewashing of Christianity

Christian history isn't hearing well done from Yeshua (Christ), it's hearing well done from white evangelicals, and this well done is often only achieved by pathologizing Black people as Muhammad al Fasi did. This phenomenon is prevalent in seminaries and evangelical circles that have little knowledge of Africa's influence and shaping of the Christian faith nor the historic Black church, and therefore they speak from ignorance and assumption. I've personally experienced Blacks with a disdain for Black leadership based on an assumption that the Black church doesn't have the gospel (direct quote), it's only emotional and void of doctrinal fortitude. This self-hatred is rooted in viewing effectiveness based on proximity to and acceptance from white people; to put it plainly, it's idolatry. What's worse are the white evangelicals who applaud and platform these Blacks as pawns to further communicate a false narrative about the Black church and Black people in general. Rather than being challenged, many whites seek affirmation from Blacks in order to affirm their assumptions, and self-hating Blacks often fit the bill. Little to no research is done when it comes to discrediting the theological prowess and hermeneutical brilliance of the Black church because in their minds, it's non-existent. This isn't always the fault of white evangelicals; after all, it's called **self**-hatred; however, there are environments that are breeding grounds for self-hatred. A careful examination of Fasi's experience parallels that of those who embrace inferiority and therefore internalize racism (a term used instead of the word coon) and view others that look like them through a faulty lens. Fasi shows us how when one is stripped of their history by force and in some cases willingly and consistently given a deplorable view of self that they can embrace it as an identity and degrade anyone that reminds them of the deplorable way that they view themselves. When we're given white as the standard of beauty, scholarship, intelligence, achievement and accomplishment, some wrongfully embrace white as the only means of acceptance, because not too many Blacks can make it to the 'big house' of white acceptance in some evangelical spaces, and if a self-hating Black person does make it to the 'big house,' other Blacks are seen as threats unless they can match or exceed their self-hatred. Blacks that oppose whitewashing and address issues of race committed by whites must be demonized by self-hating Black people because white acceptance is the goal, not the gospel and Christian unity. This is most clearly seen in evangelical circles that celebrate Blacks that pathologize other Blacks. These are the one that are erected as anomalies within Black culture and given platforms to spew self-hatred in order to nurture the delusion many whites have about Blacks and to hang on to the whitewashed version of

Christianity that needs Black advocates to survive. Blacks that do this are guilty of what I call sunken place ecclesiology. The sunken place is a phrase made popular by filmmaker Jordan Peele, who directed, wrote, and produced the movie *Get Out*. The sunken place is a metaphorical place a beleaguered person goes when they have become silent or compliant to their own provocation and interiority complex. Oftentimes, the sunken place is used to describe a person who is ignorant or unwilling to see that they have been conditioned into acquiescence. However, the sunken place can apply to anyone who chooses to stay silent in the face of discrimination or injustice, usually of their own.

Those that embrace sunken place ecclesiology are guilty of believing some if not all of the following:

- The Black church doesn't have the gospel.
- I have to go outside of my race/culture for sound doctrine.
- The Black church is emotional, and the white church is intellectual.
- They (white church) have the lyrics and we (Black church) have the musicians.
- I don't need to be trained within the context I feel called.
- Whatever dominant culture teaches me about my culture is pure and correct and I must question people who look like me.
- I must ignore social issues in the name of being reformed or gospel-centered.

Blacks that embrace the aforementioned will not listen to sermons by Black pastors or read books about the Black church except if it's about the decline of the Black church. They miss the rich gospel-centered homiletical tradition of people like pastor and theologian, Gardner C. Taylor, who saw the gospel throughout all of Scripture. He called it the "scarlet thread," to Taylor, every law, psalm, and prophecy was woven into the larger fabric of Jesus' life, death, and resurrection.[209] Their confirmation bias only allows them to seek affirmation for their disdain with Black people unless they've (Blacks) received a stamp of approval from an evangelical Christian leader, typically a white evangelical Christian leader. It's saddening and sinful because it elevates the approval of men, in most cases the approval of white men above love for the neighbor that bears their skin color.

---

209 Jared E. Alcantara, *Learning from a Legend: What Gardner C. Taylor Can Teach Us about Preaching*, (Eugene, OR Cascade Books, 2016), 38.

The Whitewashing of Christianity

Before we unpack this further, we must examine the striking parallels to Fasi's experience and that of others who commit the sin of self-hatred.

What I'm not Saying

Before explaining self-hatred, I think it's important to be clear on what I'm not saying. I'm acutely aware that when a topic like whitewashing is addressed, opponents will attempt to fill the silence with a narrative as if that's my position. I'm not saying that any Black person that disagrees is automatically a COON; voices of dissent are welcomed and considered when addressed in love. I am saying to deny that self-hatred is an occurrence amongst Black people or any other group is simply unreasonable because depravity can take on any form. I am not saying that Black people should leave white churches simply because their pastor is white. I am saying that if your pastor upholds a whitewashed narrative and presents diversity as silence, assimilation to European cultural norms as tantamount to growth in Christ and complicity, than that's not a healthy place for you to thrive as a Black person and perhaps you should leave based on their lack of empathy, charity and care for an accurate narrative of Christian history, not because of their skin color, but because of a potential lack of gospel-centrality and honesty. I'm not saying that all Black and brown people feel the same about this issue. Black is not monolithic or one thing; however, any person who turns on people who look like him based on personal experiences or colonized discipleship is a person who hasn't considered their own propensity to sin. I am not saying that white people can't critique or rebuke Black people—as stated repeatedly, no one deserves a pass for bad doctrine—I am saying when a white person criticizes the Black church solely based on preferences and seeing things typically associated with white churches as the standard of liturgy, preaching and development, that person needs to repent of elevating their preferences as a prescription for all to follow. Unless there's a text giving a command, this person is exhibiting a sinful favoritism that James clearly speaks against in Scripture (James 2:1).

What is Self-Hatred?

Self-hatred is an extreme dislike or even hatred of oneself or being angry at or even bigoted against oneself. The term is also used to designate a dislike or hatred of a group, social class, nationality, or stereotype to which one belongs. It may be associated with aspects of autophobia, which is the fear of being alone, which is why the Big House even if you're dehumanized in the Big House is better than being alone to the person who's internalized whitewashing and racism. There are three components that lead to self-hatred: displacement, demonization and colonization.

Displacement

Fasi was taken from his native land and then indoctrinated with a view of Black people that he would later embrace as factual. When some (this isn't to paint all Black and brown people in spaces where they are the minority this way) Black or brown people enter spaces dominated by white culture by choice or by circumstance, their response is to minimize friction in order to be accepted and not be seen as angry, unintellectual, liberal or overly emotional. When one is displaced from people who not only look like them but affirm their personhood, it's easy to then allow someone else to define their identity for them. Our identity is supposed to start with our creator (Genesis 1:26-27), but this isn't always the case. Displacement is experienced by many Black and brown people who attend predominantly white seminaries and churches and are flooded with slave-owning theologians as heroes of the faith and not taught about the African heritage of many of the church fathers. Instead, they are asked about the length of services, the assumed lack of gospel emphasis, the spiritual gifts and female preachers looking for affirmation from these displaced Black people in order to justify never considering serving under someone Black themselves—again, this doesn't apply to everyone, but it does apply. Over time, some Blacks, whether consciously or subconsciously, begin to associate the white church as the standard of orthodoxy and the Black church as inferior. This leads to the next step of self-hatred: demonization.

Demonization

Fasi wrote one of the most scathing pieces of literature of his day against Black people as a Black man. It's extremely disheartening to see Blacks who pathologize other Black people celebrated in some evangelical circles. Call Dr. King a Marxist and heretic as a Black man and in some spaces, you'll get a standing ovation. Talk about the German reformer Martin Luther's anti-Semitism, George Whitefield's and Jonathan Edwards' slave-owning and you'll get excuses from the same people who applaud Black people for railroading other Black people. This doesn't mean that Black people should give Black people with bad doctrine a pass. I vehemently oppose the prosperity gospel and any group that supports it because the Bible clearly opposes it (Galatians 1:8), but when a Black person internalizes racism, they turn on people that look like them, because again, their mission becomes white acceptance and the comfort of white people; the Big House. Which means they've demonized Blackness and idolized whiteness, both should be shunned as sinful, because there's only one perfect Savior.

The demonization of Black culture is an extension of Western white cultural captivity, which is indiscriminate in its devaluing of cultural expressions that aren't European. Missiologist Randy Woodley addressed how the conflation of European culture with Christianity historically played out in Native American culture:

> For Native Americans to become Christian has often required us to divest ourselves of most of our cultural distinctives, including language, hairstyle, values and devotional practices. It is assumed that there is nothing in Native American culture worth redeeming. This evangelistic philosophy, brought over to the New World from Europe, made the broad assumption that European culture was "Christian" and that Indians needed to conform to European American culture in order for God to accept them.[210]

Robert Chao Romero addresses Spanish idolization which permeates some within the Latin community, resulting in self-hatred in his book *Brown Church*:

> Idolatry lay at the center of the sistema de castas, and, as evidenced by the racial claims of many US Latinas/os, it still does today. Those from Spain, or those who imagined themselves from Spain, idolized themselves and their culture as the supreme manifestation of the image of God. According to their twisted, unbiblical logic, those from Spain possessed a monopoly on Jesus and cultural civility, and in order to become his follower, one had to first become a Spaniard. They confused and conflated Spanish culture with Christianity and thereby idolized themselves. This idolization of Spanish culture and

---

210   Randy Woodley, *Living in Color: Embracing God's Passion for Ethnic Diversity*, (Downers Grove, IL: InterVarsity Press, 2004), 46.

identity is blasphemy, and continues to pervade Latin American and US Latina/o media, society, and even churches, to the present day.[211]

Sadly, in order to get in the Big House of white acceptance, many people of color align themselves with whites that resist the contextualization or enculturation of Christians of color. This leads to movements that counter contextualization, which are often rooted in secular conservatism which seeks the retention of political power and influence and attracts some Christian leaders of color equally committed to a vision of Christianity in the service of white supremacy.[212]

Colonization

This could be the first step in self-hatred, because typically demonization of one's own race is the result of a colonized mindset, as displayed by Fasi. Colonization is a vicious process in which settlers invade the land of native people in order to displace the indigenous people and dispossess their land through heinous acts of rape and genocide while oppressing the survivors by indoctrinating them with inferiority.[213] Whitewashing is a form of historical and theological colonization, where Africans are removed from the pages of history and whites are celebrated, championed and elevated despite their lack of Christian ethics in many cases. Black and brown people are socially and, in some cases, theologically colonized when they are taught disdain for their own race and culture, traditions and appearance by implicitly being taught that only white men have solid theology through the willful omission of Black contributions to the Christian faith and criticism of Blacks, the Black church, which oftentimes are rooted in assumption and xenophobia, not scholarship. Blacks are told that their music is too loud and lacks a gospel emphasis, their preaching is more style than substance, people responding during a sermon are rude, and that they are too emotional to be taken seriously. For instance, many think that there's an anti-intellectualism, an

---

211 Robert Romero, *Brown Church: Five Centuries of Latina/o Social Justice, Theology, and Identity*, (Downers Grove, IL: InterVarsity Press, 2020), 65.

212 Vince Bantu, *A Multitude of All Peoples: Engaging Ancient Christinaity's Global Identity*, (Downers Grove, IL: InterVarsity Press, 2020), 4.

213 Ekemini Uwan, *Decolonized Discipleship,* http://www.sistamatictheology.com/blog/2018/2/6/decolonizeddiscipleship, February 2018.

anti-church history-ism, an anti-theology-ism, anti-Bible transmission and Bible translation-ism especially true in Black churches based on their experience or what they've heard. They make their experience universal and paint most Black churches this way without knowing Black church history. Sadly, many white evangelicals assume this and look for Black people that will affirm their assumptions about Black churches. Since they are looking for confirmation of their views and not conciliation with other cultures, oftentimes there's no empirical data to support their claims, no books or literary points of reference or quoted historians to factually support their faulty claim, but many feel comfortable making claims about most Black churches without proof of that reality. When it comes to assessing Black people and predominantly Black churches, many are comfortable using assumptions and a few Black "friends" as a credible reference. In many cases it seems the primary reference used are Black people who said that they had a hard time presenting church history to Black people, but the fact that much of this history is whitewashed and people could be rejecting a whitewashed version of church history isn't considered, because after all, if one believes that it's mainly Black people who lack intellect and theology, who are the ones that have "it" (sound doctrine) by and large? Many assign sound doctrine exclusively to their white constituents, of course. While the assumptions of many about the Black church are hurtful, what's even more alarming are the Black people that defend racially insensitive statements and mindsets. People who do this may be more concerned about assimilation more than they are biblical orthodoxy and Christian charity, and they've possibly been colonized to embrace faulty views about themselves not rooted in Scripture. Black and brown people who are self-hating don't realize that in some cases their presence is based on the degree of their acquiescence; their presence in some white churches will last only as long as they agree and don't ruffle any evangelical feathers. In fact, sociologists have shown that some predominantly white Christian churches only allow Blacks that will serve the interests of whites or execute exclusionary race tests to coerce people of color into leaving their space.[214]

Bryan Loritts captures this in his book, *Right Color Wrong Culture*, where he breaks down culture into what he calls C1, C2 and C3:

---

214   Gnenn Bracey and Wendy Moore, *Race Tests Racial Boundary Maintenance in White Evangelical Churches*, (Sociological Inquiry 87, no 2 May 2017): 282.

- C1: a person from one ethnicity who has assimilated into another (e.g., Hellenistic Jews of Acts 6 or, in another of Loritts' examples, Carlton Banks of the TV series "Fresh Prince of Bel Air").
- C2: people who are "culturally flexible and adaptable without being ethnically ambiguous or hostile" (e.g., Paul in 1 Corinthians 9 when he talks about being all things to all people, or Denzel Washington).
- C3: people who are culturally inflexible (e.g., Pharisees, or Al Sharpton).[215]

C1s are the dream of churches, denominations and organizations that want Black faces, but not Black voices. These men and women will simply do all they can to fit in, and while no one person should speak for all Black (or any race) people, the issue is that when they do speak, they affirm the caricatures and stereotypes that some white evangelicals have of Black Christians in social, seminary and church settings. This effect of whitewashing is not the fault of white people, but believers must be aware that there's the potential for some of the Blacks in their social circles and even churches. In other words, self-hatred may have been the motivating factor in them attending a predominantly white church. Many evangelical leaders are unaware that their ethnic members could be dealing with this and their presence in said church, organization or seminary is either to escape an aspect of their identity that they see as reprehensible or become the representative for all things Black when that's not their place, both are equally dangerous.

From C1 to Freedom

If we're ever to realize the hope of encouraging people to pursue and achieve authentic oneness, we must tackle how whitewashing contributes to the divide. As Dr. Tony Evans says, "Blacks and whites don't need to take sides, but need to be biblical." Addressing whitewashing and self-hatred isn't taking sides, but hopefully informing both "sides." After all, we're one according to Ephesians 2, and anything that opposes that oneness should be addressed. I realize that some will label this book as sowing discord, and I won't attempt to change their heart; I'll leave that up to God. My goal is to hopefully assist in understanding some nuances as it relates to race in an ecclesiological and social context. If we can't

---

215   Bryan Lorrits, *Right Color, Wrong Culture: The Type of Leader Your Organization Needs to* Become Multiethnic. Moody Publishers, 2014. 208.

The Whitewashing of Christianity

have such dialogue, then either we're operating in fear or we don't believe that the Bible gives us the ability to address these issues with grace, neither of which I affirm. I think we can and should engage in this discussion honestly with the hopes of co-laboring together as practitioners and not Christian idealists who contend that pretending there are no races is the key to unity. As stated earlier, race may be a social construct, but it's certainly one we can't ignore. The world is watching and as long as we ignore and finger point, they'll see our duplicity and want nothing to do with the God we serve. Dr. Tony Evans addresses both "sides" when he says in *Oneness Embraced*, "White theologians' silence and Black theology's victim mentality promote separatism and oneness becomes more difficult to embrace."[216] I hope this book contributes conversation toward genuine oneness, because in order for this to be attained we (Blacks, whites, Hispanics, Asians, Indians, etc.) must aggressively position ourselves as mediators in this with the end goal being glorifying God. Both "sides" will have to give up some things, but neither should give up everything.

Several years ago, an African American male approached me and apologized for some extremely critical things he'd said about me and my church. He'd only heard about us through others and came to our facility for a concert that we were hosting. Our church is in Raleigh, North Carolina.

He admitted to being critical of our building. Despite it being clean, the grass cut and edges trimmed, he found it wanting because it didn't fit the suburban standard he was used to (his words). After he apologized, I said one of the hardest things I think I've had to say to another believer. I told him to repent for not wanting to be Black. Why would I say something like that?

As he spoke, I noticed he gave tons of reasons for his criticism, but I felt like he never got to the root cause of his disdain. Being teased and called "white" for how he spoke, coupled with his membership at a predominantly white church (nothing wrong with that) and having both parents and being criticized for that, yielded bitterness over his experience with African Americans that was, by and large, negative.

He would later admit his disdain for "his own" as he and I continued to converse. This has been a pattern that I've noticed in my personal experiences with African Americans that have either distanced themselves from African Americans by choice and displaced themselves in majority culture by choice. My experience

---

216   Tony Evans, *Oneness Embraced* (Moody Publishers, 2011), 207.

with him and others tell me he's not the only one whose response to this type of experience (feeling tormented by other African Americans and feeling like majority culture will accept them) was to distance himself from almost all things deemed as Black in the ecclesiological and cultural context, namely how worship is expressed and sermons are preached.

I explained to him that you can't affirm the imago dei and the sovereignty of God, yet wish you weren't Black, criticize most things associated with Black culture and even distance yourself from Black people except for settings stereotypically deemed African American like "the hood" and hip-hop, yet embrace the notion that there's no theological depth, ecclesiological health nor homiletical prowess.

We talked for a while, and he was in tears. I embraced him and challenged him to forgive those that hurt him and to embrace the reality that God wanted him to be African American and that African Americans aren't one-dimensional, contrary to what he'd been presented with by other African Americans from his past and white people in his present.

I didn't tell him to change his dress or speech, but I did encourage him to read a little more on "his" history to understand the contributions of African Americans to theology, science and American history so that he can appreciate his heritage racially, but not limit himself to that.

This isn't the only conversation that I've had like this with African Americans, and I want to submit one question for African Americans in this situation that may be a sign that you're embracing the sin of self-hatred and one question majority culture can ask themselves to help pastor people with this destructive pattern of white acceptance, false identity and self-hatred.

If you're a minority in a majority culture context, whether it's ecclesiological or cultural or both, I want to ask you to ask yourself this question.

Why am I highly critical of Black people?

This question is designed to cause the person to look within before pointing the finger. When one essentially embraces the notion that they are either inferior or rejected by their "own," it's not unusual to embrace those that seemingly embrace you, namely the majority culture, and to be critical of those you feel represent something you now resent: yourself. I'm not talking about heresy as it relates to criticizing African Americans or anyone for that matter—no one should get a pass for that—but if you find yourself making comments like "the Black church lacks

The Whitewashing of Christianity

the gospel" or "I have to go outside my race to get solid teaching" or even "I need to get trained outside my race to get trained properly and then I'll return," this sunken place ecclesiology is rooted in a sinful view of self that embraces inferiority, bitterness, and delusion and is sinful because love keeps no record of wrongs (1 Corinthians 13:5) and self-hatred opposes the idea of loving your neighbor as yourself (Romans 13:9). Not liking your color is not liking how God created you (Genesis 1:26 and Psalm 139). It's highly unlikely that you'll help or actually care about African Americans if you don't want to be around them; no effective missionary has a disdain for the people they are called to reach, but rather they share a genuine concern, love and appreciation (read Acts 17 on how Paul engaged people in Athens). In most cases when African Americans make the aforementioned comments, they are usually speaking from very limited experiences and they don't have much to back up their claims outside of their personal experiences, which aren't totally reliable when labeling an entire race. It's dangerous to ignore and label an entire group of people based on personal experience; that's actually the recipe for embracing and promoting prejudice, which Scripture clearly rejects (Galatians 2:11-21 and James 2:9). If you're a Black person reading this and you're frequently complaining to majority culture about "all Black" churches, you're not being completely honest because there's no way you could have attended them all and I would challenge you the same way I challenged the young man who shared his story with me and encourage you to repent. I would lovingly ask you to pray the prayer David prayed in **Psalms 139:29** when he asked the Lord to "search him." If you can admit that you struggle with lust, a lack of patience, lying, etc. could it be possible that you struggle with self-hatred? Do you see it as a sin? Are you seeking people to affirm your self-hatred? To be clear, I'm not talking about loving yourself more in some esoteric way, but loving and knowing that God created you, your personality and your race for His own glory (Genesis 1:26).

Ask God to reveal possible patterns of self-hatred (displacement and demonization) and talk to others as the younger brother I mentioned earlier shared his struggles with me. If you pray this prayer and seek authentic accountability from those that are brutally honest with you, you may find that your criticism stems from bitterness and not knowledge or concern and you may even be missing out on a group God wants to use you to minister to, but you're presently blinded by your disdain and ignorance and possibly affected by a whitewashed narrative of the Christian faith. While you may verbally affirm your contentment with who you are, you could be functionally communicating that you're Black, but don't want to be. You could be affected by your constant criticism of things pertaining to African American culture and your subsequent affirmation of everything else.

To be clear, I'm not saying that you should only read African American authors exclusively, that you shouldn't affirm non-African Americans in any way, nor am I saying you need to leave your church and join an African American-led one, unless your church is committed to whitewashing. I am saying that this (self-hatred) could be in you and it is sinful and we should all repent of sin and run to Yeshua. Begin to examine whom you read, listen to, associate with and affirm and ask God to reveal potentially sinful patterns. After starting with prayer, I want to encourage you to read books like *Oneness Embraced* by Tony Evans and you'll find that all races have a rich history. Or listen to theologians like Dr. Carl Ellis on orthodoxy amongst civil rights leaders and you'll find out some wonderful things about Christian history. Am I saying to find your identity in your Blackness? No, but I am saying that knowing your history gives you an appreciation and the ability to speak from a more informed perspective outside of your negative experiences, if that has been your experience.

Be careful of the source of your criticism. If it's biblical that's one thing, but honestly every race had and has its share of heretics, prosperity gospel proponents and detractors from gospel-centrality in ministry, not just Black people. In fact, as stated earlier, David Jones in his book *Health, Wealth & Happiness: Has the Prosperity Gospel Overshadowed the Gospel of Christ?* points out how the prosperity gospel started as New Thought philosophy by men like Phineas Quimby long before it had Black proponents.[217] Reject the temptation to pigeonhole one sect and remember Christ redeems people and perspectives and yours may need to change in this area. I hope this both challenges and encourages you on your journey of finding a "place to land" as it relates to discerning where you "fit in" and where your gifts can be leveraged for the gospel, because you're made in His image, not one you construct or an identity fashioned by who others want you to be.

To my white brothers and sisters, I'd ask you to ask yourself this question:

---

217 David Jones, *Health, Wealth and Happiness: How the Prosperity Gospel Overshadows the Gospel of Christ*, (Kregel Publications Grand Rapids, MI, 2011), 51.

Am I promoting minorities too fast for my own affirmation?

There's another side to the perpetuation of African American inferiority and disdain, and it often goes unnoticed. A common thread I've seen in the people I've engaged is that many of them represent about 1-5 percent of the racial make-up of their churches. Again, this isn't necessarily wrong, but how they are treated can oftentimes be dangerous. When some (emphasis on some; I'm not presuming to label all predominately white churches in this way) get an articulate African American male or female sometimes they are quickly elevated to leadership because the church is thrilled to have a non-white person on the stage. This happens because in many cases white evangelicals see the presence of a Black person as a win regardless of the condition of their soul or concerns, In *Rediscipling the White Church*, David Swanson addresses this blindspot when he says, "When white Christianity pursues racial justice and reconciliation, relationships between white people and people of color are the priority. White Christianity is willing to acknowledge that racism has kept people apart, but its focus on personal relationships makes it almost impossible to see the systemic nature of our racialized society. So, Christians of color who are drawn to multiracial churches are often disappointed when they realize that, for most of the white members, their presence alone indicates success."[218] The presence of a non-white person is oftentimes seen as the win instead of discipleship and spiritual maturity.

This can be dangerous, unloving and "tokenistic," especially if the standard for your leadership pipeline is lowered simply because they are a minority. In fact, it's insulting to think that the theological bar needs to be lowered for a Black person. When you do this, this exploits the person and can actually enable their self-hatred because some of the minorities I've talked with are only at predominantly white churches because they've sinfully labeled churches led by African Americans as lacking the gospel because they couldn't get promoted quickly within that context or because their immaturity was confronted and they felt they could hide at predominantly white churches and be promoted because the Black church that confronted them was "holding them back."

---

218 David W. Swanson, *Rediscipling the White Church*, (InterVarsity Press Downers Grove, IL 2020), 31.

You may ask how can I know that someone could be struggling with this? Through patience, relationships, engagement and most importantly, asking the Holy Spirit to lead you as you lead cross-racially and culturally. I don't have a formula because people aren't linear; however, I would say it may be a good idea to reach out to the previous pastor if possible, so that you're not only hearing one side and forming your ideas from that. Additionally, you should look at who you primarily herald and promote to see if you're contributing to whitewashing at your church.

Don't assume that everything that they are presenting is accurate, and ask God if they are affirming negative ideas you may have about Black led churches and if you can be honest about potential prejudices you may have internally. Don't quickly elevate a person simply because of their race and don't think that because they listen to John Piper, can quote John Calvin, read books by Tim Keller and know the Five Solas that they are "ready." I'm sure that you've encountered people from your own race that can do the aforementioned, and they still needed maturity in crucial areas before they could be elevated to leadership. In other words, don't make this decision based on perceived epistemological competency at the expense of his or her sanctification, which takes time to examine through relationships (sanctification is the work of the Spirit that produces godly fruit, which can be examined by the family of Christ). Whatever your standard is, keep it the same and don't make one African American male or female the expert on all things African American. Why, you ask? This will breed arrogance in them if they are the source for all things Black, and potentially enable his or her self-hatred and unintentionally affirm the idea that because of the expediency of his or her promotion that churches from their racial make-up were/are "holding them back." It may help to talk to other pastors about questions to attempt to understand whitewashing as well as self-hatred in more depth. Listen to how they talk about others within their race and listen to what they don't say, namely if there isn't anything positive or affirming, and pastor them before you platform them.

Lastly, ask yourself the question: am I promoting them too fast? This question will demand introspection and reveal maybe even some idolatry of pastoring outside your race for some sort of affirmation that can and should only come from Christ. I would also suggest if possible and I think it is for you to serve under or seek African American leadership so that you can be a practitioner of that which you hope to attain (this may or may not be possible depending on your position and season of ministry). An African American pastor shared this with me. "One of the highest compliments I received was from my white associate pastor after about a year of serving together. He said he was blessed to have an African American man to lead him and wishes more white males would do the same, not because of my title, but because he learned how to become a better husband, father, and pastor, and he learned things that he assumed he knew all along because of his association with Black people in the past, but he now acknowledges that he never really had community with African Americans until now." I think asking this question and being honest with yourself is a start to something beautiful that God wants to do amongst his people—ALL PEOPLE!

I know that some of this is hard, the truth often is, and I'm not implying or suggesting that serving in a context where you're the minority is sinful or makes you a "sell out" or COON, but I am saying that you could be, and it's okay to do the internal examination to see if its true. The church I pastor is predominantly Black with a 25 percent white contingent, but my effectiveness and affirmation doesn't come from having white people join our church, it's from Christ. If you're there (a church where you're the minority), serve well and serve with joy, but if you're experiencing whitewashing, I encourage you to have honest conversations and if there's a refusal to acknowledge God's use of all people, I think you should *Get Out* like the movie. I just hope to start a dialogue about a conversation that is happening behind the scenes that I think needs to be brought to the forefront. Blacks dealing with self-hatred need to be reminded that the "Big House" won't satisfy that longing for acceptance they so desperately crave because it's temporary. While we reject self-hatred, the answer isn't deifying one's race or ethnicity either, we must never make a feature of who we are the foundation of our identity. Seek acceptance from the one who prepared a place of eternity, not a temporary seat at the table. The goal is not the Big House of acceptance; it's the place Yeshua prepared (John 14:3-4).

Discussion Questions

1. Why is self-hatred dangerous personally? Socially? Culturally? Spiritually?
2. How is self-hatred nurtured in some evangelical circles? (Share stories or examples)
3. What are some ways to decolonize discipleship in order to foster self-value?

10

Responses to Whitewashing:
Urban Apologetics

> *Before the religious claims become intellectual or "purely theological" they are first existential.*
> —THABITI ANYABWILE

WHILE LIBERATION HAD SOME HELPFUL COMPONENTS for people of color by affirming their dignity and value before God, and self-hatred is something that should be rejected, there have been biblically saturated gospel movements to oppose the false narrative of whitewashing and one of the most prevalent is the movement of urban apologetics. Urban apologetics is needed because in addition to liberation and self-hatred, rejection is the third response to whitewashing. This is where people of African descent reject the idea that Christianity could ever be a religion that they'd embrace, largely due to the false notion that Christianity was forced upon Black people through slavery and not indigenous to Africans and that the Bible only contains white people—to which they conclude God himself didn't want anything to do with Black people beyond salvation based on verses not understood in context.

What Is Urban Apologetics?

When we say "urban," we simply mean dense ethnic neighborhoods usually in the inner-city and we're also talking about values. Generally speaking, those values are self-expression, success, sexual freedom, spiritual tolerance and social justice. The term apologetics simply means defense of the faith. Apologetics as it relates to the Christian faith highlights how people are trying to find effective ways of defending the faith among people in the inner-city. The objections and issues presented in urban communities differ significantly from those typically presented in books on apologetics. A very different set of religious ideas exists in inner-city neighborhoods which must be addressed. Thabiti Anyabwile says:

> Mainstream texts do apologetics by describing the core beliefs of a faith, comparing those beliefs to Christian claims, and then arguing for the superiority of Christian teaching. This approach assumes that if the Christian faith can be intellectually defended and shown to be stronger than rival claims, then the apologist has successfully defended the faith. What would-be urban apologists soon find out is that the typical approach doesn't work with a lot of people. There's a simple reason for this: Black religion in urban centers was developed to answer a very different set of questions than the major world religions. The questions answered by Black religions and cults have a great deal to do with the sojourn and suffering of Black people in the United States. Before the religious claims become intellectual or "purely theological" they are first existential. If we fail to understand this dynamic and genius of Black religion, then we will fail the apologetic task at the start.[219]

Urban apologetics is a specialized branch of apologetics that takes into account the unique experience of people of African descent in America and urban environments to address how they view Christianity as a faith not indigenous to people of color in order to engage them with the gospel and accurate history. As stated earlier, whitewashing contributes to lostness, and many people are turning

---

219   Thabiti Anyabwile, *Urban Apologetics 1: Introduction*, https://thefrontporch.org/2017/10/urban-apologetics-1-introduction/, October 2017.

away from the Christian faith due to its perceived emphasis on whiteness and the almost exclusive use of white people in terms of how it's presented. This is why U.A. also confronts BRICs (Black religious identity cults) and WRICs (white religious identity cults). In order to correct the false notion that Christianity is a white man's religion with an emphasis on whites flourishing at the peril of Blacks, U.A. addresses the devaluing of Black and brown people (imago dei and dignity) as it relates to justice and inequality by confronting, rebuking and opposing white supremacy, whitewashing and how it has negatively affected how people of color in particular view the Christian faith. U.A. doesn't only focus on race; it's a gospel-centered movement rooted in orthodoxy, but addresses the void in current apologetic movements and engages areas of emphasis which rarely address the issues, ideals and religious groups that primarily affect people of color.

What Urban Apologetics Is Not

U.A. should not be confused with Afrocentrism, a word coined by Dr. Molefi Asante, former professor of African American studies at Temple University and author of *Afrocentricity: The Theory of Social Change*. Afrocentrism is about centering Africa and Africa-descended peoples in their worldview, much the way Europe has always been at the center of the worldview of European peoples. Afrocentrism taught that Black people should see the world as Black people. The goal of U.A. isn't deifying nor denying Blackness, but affirming their value, providing all people but primarily people of color with an accurate view of themselves rooted in their Creator, not their detractors.

The rise of urban apologetics has sparked a movement of people to recapture the African essence of Christianity as an indigenous faith for and shaped by people of color. From books, to blogs, to YouTube channels, to classes, to conferences which emphasize aspects of Christian history that have been intentionally ignored, God is using men and women who care about truth in its entirety as it relates to Christian history. This movement will aid in moving the church toward authentic oneness instead of a whitewashed version of Christianity being presented as factual. Urban apologists lovingly push back against this narrative by calling out whitewashing for what it is, dishonest, but while whitewashing must be addressed, the heart of apologetics is evangelism. What many fail to understand is something I've stated repeatedly: whitewashing contributes to lostness and this is something we all should care about, especially those that claim the Christian faith. Urban apologists are letting people of color know that God cares and uses them and has used them in His plan of redemption, despite the flood of white images and historical omissions. God is using this gospel-centered movement in several ways:

1) Reminding the world of Africa's involvement in the shaping of the Christian faith

Since institutions of higher learning are by and large guilty of perpetuating and propagating a whitewashed version of Christianity through false imagery, willful omissions and using scholars who were indeed racist, urban apologists are addressing the effects of this with love and precision while not ignoring how discrimination wasn't limited to social assimilation, but education as well. The prominent distinguishing factor of African Americans is the history of social, economic and political oppression that they have experienced based upon color discrimination which has led to systemic and institutional racism, violence, and discrimination, but it has also contributed to the widespread ignorance of African American influence in this country.[220]

U.A. refuses to allow a European historiography that exclusively acknowledges its own cultural and historical contributions at the expense of others, which assumes that the resulting ethnocentric position represents the only history worth engaging and elevating. Such philosophy only reinforces the false assumption that Black history is substandard to other cultures in general, but to the dominant culture in particular.

2) Challenging seminaries that continue to present a whitewashed version of Christian history

Books assigned in Christian seminaries still present practically all of the African church fathers as white men. Just peruse Saint Vladimir's Press and see almost every African church father presented as white. This isn't accidental, and the consequences are that Black and brown students find themselves either wondering if they had a place in history or being historically ill-equipped to engage people who say that Christianity is a white man's religion, because functionally

---

220   E. B. Lane, *The African American Christian Man: Reclaiming the Village*, (Dallas: Black Family Press, 1997), 156.

it is based on how many conservative evangelical seminaries present Christian history and people within Scripture. To prevent this phenomenon from continuing, urban apologists explain how many graduates will find themselves largely unequipped to minister in minority contexts because they lack a socio-historical lens and how seminaries contribute to this. We challenge seminaries to change their images, include Africa in their lectures, and while we request this in love, we won't wait for a response in order to communicate an accurate narrative because souls are at stake. We'll provide resources to equip people to address the false claims of associating Christianity with racial oppression and degradation.

3) Confronting the idea that Christianity was forced upon Black people

"We're (Blacks) only Christians because of slavery…" This phrase is heard repeatedly because whitewashing has presented the Christian faith as one by and for white people. This has caused many to believe that Christianity for Black people starts with the Trans-Atlantic Slave Trade. While men like Tertullian, Athanasius, and Augustine of Hippo were instrumental in the development and spreading of Christianity throughout the world centuries before the Trans-Atlantic Slave Trade, U.A. is intentional about informing people that these men were not white Europeans! Since Christianity went from Israel to Africa to the rest of the world, our ancestors include African Christians that precede the slave trade! We let people that are unaware know that there are Africans in the Bible who were instrumental in church history. By informing people that Scripture is filled mostly by people of color, we attack the notion to the contrary to restore dignity to Black and brown people by helping them see how God is where their dignity starts. The events and writing of the Bible took place in the Middle East, and white Europeans weren't a majority in that region of the world, so it's geographically and historically inaccurate to think otherwise. One of the most famous stories of God's power and deliverance, the Exodus, took place in Africa (Egypt). A Cushite (Ethiopian) man helped the prophet Jeremiah when he was being oppressed (Jeremiah 38:7-11). An African man from Cyrene named Simon helped Jesus carry His cross (Mark 15:21). Phillip shared the message of Jesus with the Ethiopian eunuch, who then took the Gospel back to Ethiopia and to the queen (Acts 8:26-39). This caused Christianity to spread rapidly throughout Ethiopia, possibly making it the first ever Christian nation. Given the fact that the earliest followers of Christ believed their movement to be for the Jews, they did not preach to non-Jews initially. However, early disciples came to the realization, by the work of the Holy Spirit and searching the Scriptures, that the gospel of Christ was for non-Jews as well who were commonly referred to as Gentiles. What we have with the Ethiopian eunuch in Acts chapter 8 is a testament to this shift in thinking, as this was the first mention of the conversion of a non-Jew in the New Testament. With that said, this would not be the only "first" of church history that involved Ethiopia. The Christianization of Ethiopia is generally attributed to Fromentius, who was a Christian that ended up shipwrecked in Ethiopia and then was made to serve in the royal court. It was through Fromentius' influence that the king became Christian and then declared Christianity over the nation. This occurred in the fourth century, making Ethiopia the first ever Christian nation. Many argue that Armenia was the first Christian nation, but that is based on their oral history and can't be substantiated beyond that. For Ethiopia, on the other hand, there is archeological evidence like the coin of King Ezana.

When we look at the historical and biblical record, we see that true Christianity, instead of being forced on Black people during slavery, was in fact gladly and enthusiastically embraced and spread by and through our African ancestors centuries before American slavery. So, when people say that it was "forced upon us," we gladly let them know that if you want an indigenous African traditional religion, look no further than Christianity. Again, slave owners did not "beat Christianity into slaves," but rather attempted to beat inferiority into the mind of slaves.

4) Creating theologically rich resources to equip the body of Christ for theological, social and cultural engagement

There is a growing list of urban apologists contributing to apologetics, evangelism, theological training and history. If you want to address topics from theodicy to race to eschatology, *Urbanlogia* by Damon Richardson, *The Jude 3 Project* by Lisa Fields, *Tru-ID* Podcast by Adam Coleman, *Thrive in the City* by Dr. Eric Mason, *Faithful to God* by Mike Pereira, *The King Movement* by Chris Broussard, *Face to Face* by Dr. Sarita Lyons, *The Front Porch* by Thabiti Anyabwile, *The BK Apologist* by Alfredo Valentin, *Miss Tytus2*, *The Bodega Ladies* and *Whole Brother Mission* by Maliek Blade are all providing video, audio and written content in order to engage issues and ideologies that oppose Christian orthodoxy. I was honored to create a resource with Lamont English entitled *Is Christianity a White Man's Religion?* It's a pamphlet that addresses both the existential and historical issues that an urban apologist must engage. We made this resource free and encouraged people to not only give this resource at Black barber shops and hair salons, but also seminaries and liberal PWIs (predominantly white institutions).

5) Providing Worldview Analysis

An extremely important contribution of Urban apologists is in the area of worldview analysis. If you go back far enough, groups like Mormons and Jehovah's witnesses were strange/unfamiliar groups that the church had to learn about in order to defend the faith against them. There are all sorts of worldviews that the church is currently unprepared to engage effectively because they are neglected or outside the scope of Western evangelicalism (i.e. Hebrew Israelites, Kemetics, Moors, Nuwapians). Urban apologists are on the front lines of identifying these groups, cataloguing their beliefs, and crafting argumentation to combat deception coming against the church from these groups. One of the main arguments opponents of Christianity make is that there's nothing unique about Yeshua's atoning death for sins and that Yeshua is a copy of pagan and/or African gods and mythology. Many of them use Bart Ehrman as a primary source to substantiate their claim. Perhaps they should read Bart Ehrman, who wasn't a Christian before making such claims. Dr. Ehrman said:

> So far as I know, there are no parallels to this central Christian claim. What has been invented here is not the Christian Jesus but the mythicist claim about Jesus. I am not saying that I think Jesus really did die to atone for the sins of the world. I am saying that the Christian claims about Jesus's atoning sacrifice were not lifted from pagan claims about divine men. Dying to atone for sin was not part of the ancient pagan mythology. Mythicists who claim that it was are simply imagining things. My main objection to this line of argumentation, however, is the one with which I began. There certainly are similarities between what pagans were saying about their divine men and what Christians were saying about Jesus, as we have seen in the case of Apollonius.

But parallels are not as close and as precise as most mythicists claim. Nowhere near as close.[221]

6) Contextualizing Apologetics

There is a broader apologetics community that has, thus far, been largely unaware of the specific apologetics needs in the African American/African context. Some of the arguments they use can be effective in our context with some modification. For example, mainstream apologetics often focuses on atheism and agnosticism. While atheism appears to be on the rise in African American circles, it isn't the biggest bully on the block yet, and there's a need for intentional engagement of these worldviews in a contextualized way. So for urban apologists we often have to take arguments that are directed against atheism and demonstrate further how those arguments also cut against the false conceptions of God that these other worldviews are pushing in our community.

7) Addressing the pseudo scholarship of those who present Christianity as a white man's religion without source evidence

Walter Williams' book *The Historical Origin of Christianity* is often cited by Afrocentrists as the game-changing history book to debunk Christianity. Williams has been a prominent lecturer in Afrocentric circles, but when you read his books, you'll notice a glaring issue. *The Historical Origin of Christianity* lacks footnotes, or endnotes, or some kind of notes and as one reads, you'll find what I found: no notes. He attempted to address this issue; in his revised edition, eighth printing, 2011, he admitted to this apparent deficiency. There was a note on the bottom of the acknowledgments page that read: NOTE: The author is aware of the absence of footnotes. A bibliography has been added for reference purposes. The bibliography consisted of a mere twenty-five books and the major claims Williams

---

221 Bart D. Ehrman, *Did Jesus Exist? The Historical Argument for Jesus of Nazareth*, (New York: HarperOne, 2012), 215.

makes are found in none of them.²²² It's interesting that proponents of views like Williams' are willing to accept outlandish claims without historical proof; this is a form of faith, faith in the views of a man whose evidence and scholarship is lacking.

George G. M. James' book *Stolen Legacy* makes outlandish claims as well. James claimed, among other things, that Aristotle stole his ideas from the Library of Alexandria when he arrived there with Alexander the Great.²²³ Urban Apologists encourage people to not only read but read critically. For instance, James had to be unaware that Alexandria was built on Alexander's orders, which is why it bears its name and its famous library was constructed long after both Alexander and Aristotle were quite dead. It's impossible for him to steal ideas from a grave. Additionally, he claims that the Romans set up Christianity as a state religion to rival the mysteries because they were jealous of the lofty cultural system of the Black people. What's interesting about James' book is that with all of his talk about Egyptian mysteries, you'd think he'd primarily have Egyptian sources, but what you'll find is that he relies heavily on the Freemason historian Charles H. Vail. What many that follow the teachings of men like Walter Williams, George G. M. James, Dr. Ray Hagin, and the like don't realize is that they are regurgitating the teachings of white Egyptologists like Gerald Massey, Kersey Graves, Alvin Boyd Kuhn and Godfrey Higgins.²²⁴ That's right: these Afrocentric men are using white men with pseudo scholarship who aren't taken seriously by credible scholars as sources to oppose Christianity.

8) Addressing the claims that the Bible is tainted and can't be trusted

We address this claim in six primary ways: history, manuscripts, church fathers, consistency, eyewitness accounts, and the inclusion of women.

---

222 Albert McIlhenny, *Afrocentric Ideology and Church History*, (Albert McIlhenny, 2016), kindle location 186.

223 George G. James, *Stolen Legacy*, (Allegro Editions, 1954), 40.

224 Albert McIlhenny, *Afrocentric Ideology and Church History*, (Albert McIlhenny, 2016), kindle location 277.

The Whitewashing of Christianity

Historically

Scripture accurately records geographical places like Israel, Egypt, and Babylon, as well as historical figures like Herod, Pontius Pilate, Nebuchadnezzar, Xerxes, and we have archeological evidence to support the Bible's claims like Cyrus Cylinder in 1879, the Dead Sea Scrolls in 1947, the Pool of Siloam in 2004, Egypt's invasion of Israel (1 Kings 14:25), the Assyrian siege of Lachish (2 Kings 18-19), the trade relations between Israel and Sheba (1 Kings 10), the Babylonian conquest of Jerusalem, and the reigns of Kings Omri, Ahab, Uzziah, Hezekiah, Ahaz, Jeroboam II, and Jehoiachin (1 and 2 Kings)—all are recorded in the Bible and all have been confirmed by archaeology.

Manuscripts

There are over 5800 Greek manuscripts; in second place is Homer's Iliad with less than 2000 copies, then the works of Aristotle and Herodotu.[225] When people say that the Bible is tainted, they don't realize the historical absurdity of that statement. To rewrite the Bible and taint it, "they," whoever "they" are, would have to rewrite over 5000 manuscripts, change all of them without sharing them with people who believed in the inerrancy of Scripture, and get them back to where they stole them without the benefit of text messaging or Uber and place their tainted versions of the Bible over several continents by foot or camel. There are Syriac, Coptic and Latin writings of Scripture that "they" would have to rewrite as well. They would have to rewrite the Greek manuscripts and match the lies of the other languages in order to "taint the Bible."

Church Fathers

Church fathers and other historians contain quotes from Scripture which speaks to the historicity of Scripture. Justin Martyr's writings have **330** New Testament quotes, Hippolytus has **1378** NT quotes, Irenaeus has **1819**, Clement of Alexandria has **2406** NT quotes, Eusebius has **5176** NT quotes, Tertullian has **7258** NT quotes, and Origen has **17,992** NT quotes.[226]

---

225 Josh McDowell, *Evidence that Demands a Verdict: Life-Changing Truth for a Skeptical World*, (Nashville, TN: Harper Collins , 2017), 64-65.

226 Josh McDowell, *Evidence that Demands a Verdict: Life-Changing Truth for a Skeptical World*, (Nashville, TN: Harper Collins , 2017), 64-65.

Consistency

There are three primary languages within Scripture: Hebrew, Greek and Aramaic. The three primary continents are Africa, Asia, and Europe, with over 40 authors who wrote over 1500 years telling one singular story. They prophesy or were eyewitnesses to one beautiful truth: He came, He died, He rose!

Eyewitness Accounts

1 Corinthians 15 talks about how Jesus appeared to Cephas, the twelve and more than 500 other witnesses. If you're a non-believer reading this, keep in mind that if you refute any Scriptural references because you don't ascribe to Christianity that I've provided tons of historical evidence as it relates to non-biblical authors who quote Scripture and reference the Bible historically.

Inclusion of Women

The Gospels of Matthew, Mark, Luke, and John (Matthew 28:1; Mark 16:1-2; Luke 24:1; John 20:1) make it a point to tell us that the first people to report that the tomb of Jesus was empty were women. Not men. Women. In the first century, a woman's opinion was not viewed as credible testimony in court. (Just read the Jewish historian, Josephus, or the Jewish Talmud to verify this fact.) A woman's opinion didn't matter. But the Bible says it does. The last group of people we would expect to find the empty tomb was the first group to whom God looked and used: women.

9) Addressing the claims that Bible is a book of allegory

Many opponents to Christianity within the Conscious Community, hoteps and those who claim to be ex-pastors cite Galatians 4:24 in order to say that Abraham never existed and that the entire Bible is allegorical, based on what Paul wrote to the church at Galatia.

Galatians 4:24 says, "24 Now this may be interpreted allegorically: these women are two covenants. One is from Mount Sinai, bearing children for slavery; she is Hagar."

Notice Paul says, it may be "interpreted allegorically." This is NOT an indication that he's addressing their existence, but rather what their existence points to, which is why he talks about how to interpret their experience. Paul is saying that these historical figures point to a larger redemptive story. Now what about the word "allegory"? Great question. There are two types of allegory:

1. **Philonic Allegory**, which was introduced by the African philosopher Origen. This is parabolic in nature, where people are used to point to a bigger point. Examples of this are the prodigal sons (yes, I meant 'sons'; they both were lost and the wild one responded to grace, while the older brother was paralyzed by moralism). The Old Testament book that's filled with it is the poetic book, Proverbs. Proverbs displays emblematic parallelism which is a poetic device often used in the book of Proverbs where symbols or metaphors are placed side by side for deeper meanings. So the Bible does at times use people that didn't exist to communicate eternal truths (ex. the prodigal sons), but this is not the case with Galatians 4.

2. **Typological Allegory** (or simply put, typology), which is what Paul is employing in the Galatians 4 text, is when historical figures and their stories point to something deeper than their experience. Here, Paul takes three historical people who existed (Abraham, Hagar, and Sarah) and uses them as symbols for a couple of things:

1. Law of Moses (the Old Covenant).
2. Liberation in Christ (the New Covenant of grace, NOT getting rid of The Law).

Paul's use of the word allegory reveals that our relationship with God is one of freedom and not bondage. This is why we are children of the divine promise by faith in Christ, as Isaac was to Sarah; they needed faith to believe they could have children in their old age, not of bondage. We are not children of man's bondage, as Ishmael was to Hagar symbolically. The Holy Spirit led Paul to see the symbolic significance of this historical event and the historical people involved and he used it to illustrate our (believers in Yeshua) position in Christ.

So when opponents attempt to use Scripture without examining its context, their objections consistently fall short. The aforementioned does make something crystal clear for people of faith, which is this: the days of blind faith are over (they should have never existed), and the rise of social media scholars and Google experts should motivate us (people of faith) to dig deeper to engage, grow deeper in our walk with Yeshua and learn apologetics, because souls are at stake. We will be fine, but we need to steward this time well and lovingly engage those that oppose our faith. Many of their questions are valid questions and we shouldn't dismiss them as heathens or hopeless. Remember, we were ALL once in their shoes in varying forms (1 Corinthians 6:11).

10) Debunking the myth that Jesus was created at the Council of Nicea

Dr. Umar Johnson, Dr. Anthony Browder, and countless others have asserted that either Christianity was created, Jesus was invented or that Christianity was Europeanized at the Council of Nicea. They rarely cite sources for their claims; the truth is Christianity existed long before the council met. The truth is Christianity wasn't created at Nicea, it was debated at Nicea. As stated earlier, Constantine issued the Edict of Milan in 313 which legalized Christianity twelve years before the council met, which would be impossible if Christianity wasn't already in existence. What they fail to realize is that the two debating about the essence of Jesus were both African men: Athanasius, who presented the reality that Jesus was not a created being and he was indeed both human and divine, and Arius, who presented the heresy known as Arianism, which denies the deity of Christ. Arius' doctrine of a created Son having a beginning before creation had been discussed and condemned at an African synod in Alexandria, Egypt in 321 by Bishop Alexander and by Bishop Hosius of Cordoba in Antioch (Syria) in the Asian continent earlier in the year of 325, before Nicea. Apologist Damon Richardson points out several aspects of what really happened at the Council of Nicea:

> The Christian faith had already spread to Nicea, centuries earlier through Pauline evangelism in Asia Minor. The Greco-Roman city Nicea was geographically situated in the continent of Asia, not Europe, whereas today it sits between the two continents as the Turkish city Iznik. According to Eusebius of Caesarea, most of the 318 bishops were from the East (Africa and Asia), and it was held in Nicea for Constantine's convenience because his headquarters was nearby Nicomedia, where Constantine's friend and confidant Bishop

The Whitewashing of Christianity

Eusebius of Nicomedia, an Arian sympathizer, presided, NOT for the Europeanization of Christianity. Hence European influence would have been minimal. It was NOT determined here that Jesus was the One and Only begotten Son of God. This position was defended here as the earliest church in the first century through the Gospel writings of John, believed that Jesus was monogenes that is with respect to the Son's unique relationship to the Father (John 1:14, 18; 3:16, 18; 1 John 4:9). The New Testament from which Alexander and Athanasius argued taught explicitly that Jesus, God the Son, was pre-existent, eternal (uncreated), Creator, and pre-eminent (Supreme) above all creation. The very notion that The Council of Nicea represented the invention of Jesus as God and the Europeanization of Christianity is originally the white man's idea.[227]

11) Getting Christians to stop answering fact-based questions with faith-based answers

Christians are making the claim that Christianity is the only faith for over six billion people in the world. If we're going to make that claim, we need to be able to defend it when challenged. Questions about slavery, allegory, archeological evidence and the like are fair questions, but for decades, Christians have avoided these questions or answered them with Christianese and cliches and the end result has been people assuming that Christianity is simply blind faith. The Bible itself rejects that notion, 1 Peter 3:15 says "to give a reason for the hope that is within you…" This means that faith and reason can and should coexist. If you're a believer in Christ and you're reading this, know that your faith has what we call in urban circles receipts. Meaning we have references, primary sources, archaeology, manuscripts and much more. Blind faith is weak faith, and Christians must not be mediocre in their knowledge of God, history or their response to challenges against what we believe. When someone asks if the letter 'J' wasn't invented until the sixteenth century then how could his name be Jesus? That's a fact-based question. Don't dance around and say, "Things I used to do

---

227 Damon Richardson, *Urbanlogia Ministries*, https://urbanlogia.org/pages/damion-richardson, accessed March 2021.

I don't do no more, places I used to go I don't go no more..." While that may be true, it doesn't address the core concern of someone who asked a legitimate question and may make an eternal decision based on your response. While conversion is completely up to God (John 6:44), how we represent Him is up to us and it matters. Don't make something up if you don't know how to respond. Simply say, "I don't know" and use it as an opportunity to grow deeper in your faith and get back with the person. So how should we respond to the letter 'J' question? Simply put, while the J didn't exist, the 'j' sound did. For instance, the words cat and circle both start with the letter 'C,' but have two different sounds. Gian Giorgio Trissino (1478—1550) was an Italian grammarian known as the father of the letter J. Trissino made a distinction of the letters 'I' and 'J.' Prior to this distinction, the letter 'I' had the 'j' sound. In fact, if you research what was known as the Table Alphabeticall (yes, spelled with two l's), you'll see that Jesus and Jehovah were spelled with the letter "i" at the beginning, but maintained the sound of what we now call the letter 'J.' The issue in part is knowing the difference between translation and transliterating. Translating is the process of decoding words or text from one language to another. Transliterating is a type of conversion of a text from one script to another that involves swapping letters. So while the J wasn't invented until the sixteenth century, the 'j' sound did exist, and so did Jesus. UA refuses to run from challenges and we refuse to answer fact-based questions with faith-based answers. While we address historical concerns, make no mistake about it; we're passionate about our faith, which is why we study the Scriptures and history in order to address the core concerns of those that have legitimate questions about Christianity.

12) Addressing evangelical silence on social issues

One of the disheartening aspects of a fallen world is the fact that lives aren't valued equitably, if at all. What's worse is when people who claim Christianity as their theological home neglect to show compassion and care for people. This is most notably seen in how many evangelicals respond to unarmed Black men being killed at the hands of law enforcement. When we all witness a Black or brown person murdered at the hands of police, many evangelicals have responded with silence or changing the subject to Black-on-Black crime, abortion and fatherlessness. While those are all poignant issues, it's demoralizing to hear conservative talking points instead of Christian compassion from many white evangelicals. What many of the people who bring up Black-on-Black crime don't realize is that the Black church has led marches, rallies, provided gang counseling, established after school programs and created neighborhood watches and more for decades to address violence within the Black community. These efforts weren't and aren't called The Stop Black-on-Black Crime Rally but rather Stop the Violence or Hope for the Block or they didn't have names or news cameras to capture their efforts, but rather people who are going out sharing their faith and being a tangible display of the gospel. What's interesting is that they'll appeal to Scripture while actually avoiding it and failing to properly apply it. They'll apply dignity to aborted babies, but not to unarmed men and women. They miss that human dignity starts at creation, not salvation, all image bearers are valuable to God and deserve dignity, honor and respect because they are made in His image (Genesis 1:26-27). This reveals that many of them are pro-birth, not really pro-life, because a biblically informed life ethic cares about lives in and outside of the womb. When confronted, many of them label people who call out their duplicity Marxist, liberal, Critical Theory or Critical Race Theory proponents, race baiters, or social justice warriors, as if somehow using social justice warrior pejoratively denies the potency of those that obey the Scriptures by speaking up for the voiceless (Proverbs 31:8-9), when the truth in many cases is that they've given in to secular conservatism and have made patriotism a fifth gospel. While they call people who understand that faith and works commingle (James 2:26) social justice warriors, they are themselves social 'inacticians' or social 'inactivists' who think that faith is inactive. This is what Thabiti Anyebwile calls the philosophical fallacy where evangelicals appeal to the government being ordained by God in Romans 13:1-2 as a means for inaction, but this isn't exegetically faithful. They pick and choose what aspects of that chapter fits the narrative they embrace. It's not only the American government under God's jurisdiction, but all governments. Would they approve everything done in nations under communism? Would they approve the governmental control of all nations? It's highly unlikely. The role of the government is to reward the good and punish wrongdoing. Is the government perfect and do they administer perfect justice? Of course not. For instance, there are several examples of people of God going against the governing authorities because of their treatment of people or their denial of God's sovereignty:

- **Shiphrah and Puah** feared God more than they feared the king and resisted his order to kill male born babies, and it was their bravery that allowed Moses' birth to occur (Exodus 1:15-18).
- **Hananiah, Mishael and Azariah** refused to bow to Nebuchadnezzar's statue and God supported them. (Daniel 3:12).
- **Esther** appeared before the king illegally and God was with her, because Haman was going to do an injustice against His people by committing genocide (Esther 4:15-17).

When it comes to police brutality specifically, we're told these are isolated incidents or to just "get to the gospel" or "just preach the gospel" as if the gospel is silent because they are. Which displays the reality that those that use that phrase to ignore injustice actually have a truncated gospel. Yeshua says, "All authority has been given to me in heaven and on earth." This means he's not just the king in heaven, but that he's the king here, too. His word says to mourn with those who mourn and weep with those who weep (Romans 12:15). His word says to act justly (Micah 6:8), and this isn't exclusive to lives in the womb or religious freedom, but rather it applies to all of God's image bearers. A glaring hole in those that deny or ignore police brutality is their claims of total depravity or original sin. If one affirms total depravity, then they can't deny that total depravity can play out in the form of a white man in a blue suit pointing a Black gun at an unarmed Black man. To be clear, when urban apologists confront police brutality it's not just police brutality against Black and brown people; it opposes all abuses of power, which should be confronted, but we're not aloof to the racial disparities as it relates to this subject. There's another glaring hole in their theology, and that's how Paul handled his own encounter with abuse. Read what Luke writes in Acts 16:19-23 after a woman who was enslaved is freed by the gospel and her owners could no longer own and oppress her:

Acts 16:19-24 (CSB)

19 When her owners realized that their hope of profit was gone, they seized Paul and Silas and dragged them into the marketplace to the authorities. 20 Bringing them before the chief magistrates, they said, "These men are seriously disturbing our city. They are Jews 21 and are promoting customs that are not legal for us as Romans to adopt or practice."

The Whitewashing of Christianity

22 The crowd joined in the attack against them, and the chief magistrates stripped off their clothes and ordered them to be beaten with rods. 23 After they had severely flogged them, they threw them in jail, ordering the jailer to guard them carefully. 24 Receiving such an order, he put them into the inner prison and secured their feet in the stocks.

Why was Paul beaten?

- **Seeking justice**—the slave girl was set free, magistrates (officers) and the crowd beat Paul (Acts 16:19-22) as a result of her gaining freedom.
- **Disrupting an unjust system**—the girl's owners were allowed to own her (Acts 16:20), which is an affront to her as an image bearer and opposed the biblical ethic on humanity from which Paul operated.
- **Not being seen as a citizen**—Paul had dual citizenship (Acts 22:28), but they found that out later and attempted to release him silently.
- **The Gospel**—the gospel was the reason he was beaten. The slave girl heard the gospel along with Lydia and the Philippian jailer, and she (slave girl) was no longer a slave to men; the gospel freed her spiritually and naturally. So when people say just preach the gospel, they miss that Paul was beaten because of preaching the gospel, which addressed the slave girl's spiritual status and social status.

Paul was stripped and beaten and the magistrates, στρατηγοι (strategoi), the original Greek word translated "magistrates," can mean either military officers in charge of military units or civilian officers who administer the law in a region. Therefore Paul was a victim of police, magistrate or officer brutality, and this is recorded in Scripture. How did Paul respond? Did he just "get to the gospel" and ignore the injustice he encountered? Let's see:

Acts 16:35-40 (CSB)

35 When daylight came, the chief magistrates sent the police to say, "Release those men." 36 The jailer reported these words to Paul: "The magistrates have sent orders for you to be released. So come out now and go in peace." 37 But Paul said to them, "They beat us in

public without a trial, although we are Roman citizens, and threw us in jail. And now are they going to send us away secretly? Certainly not! On the contrary, let them come themselves and escort us out." 38 The police reported these words to the magistrates. They were afraid when they heard that Paul and Silas were Roman citizens. 39 So they came to appease them, and escorting them from prison, they urged them to leave town. 40 After leaving the jail, they came to Lydia's house, where they saw and encouraged the brothers and sisters, and departed.

Paul clearly understood himself as an image bearer and wasn't silent about the injustice he encountered. Once they found out that he had dual citizenship, they attempted to sweep their abuse of power under the rug and release him silently, but Paul refused. He says, "They beat us in public without a trial, although we are Roman citizens, and threw us in jail. And now are they going to send us away secretly? **Certainly not**! On the contrary, let them come themselves and escort us out." So Paul didn't "just get to the gospel," as if the gospel means ignoring injustice; he demanded justice and a public acknowledgement of their wrongdoing. Addressing social issues does not mean that we neglect the Great Commission of discipleship. As Justin Giboney says, "If the Great Commission becomes secondary, or if Christianity is understood primarily as a means of accomplishing social or political goals, then we've handed to Caesar what belongs to God" (Matthew 22:21).[228]

To evangelicals that remain silent or ignore these issues I ask, if Paul wasn't silent, why are you? Paul encouraged the Corinthian church to imitate him as he followed Christ (1 Corinthians 11:1) and he tells us to imitate Christ as children (Ephesians 5:1). Evangelicals should follow his lead and not be silent and take meaningful action against injustice. While police brutality isn't the only issue, it is an issue that shouldn't be ignored. Urban apologists are committed to a biblical view of justice that cares about all life.

---

228   Justin Giboney, *Compassion & Conviction: The And Campaign's Guide to Faithful Civic EngagementI*, (InterVarsity Press Downer Grove, IL, 2020), 8.

13) Debunking the Assertion that Yeshua is a Copy of Horus

From the video known as Zeitgeist to proponents of Kemet, many have asserted that Yeshua is a copy of Egyptian mythology and therefore not worthy of worship or credence. They claim that everything related to Yeshua's birth mirrors Horus' birth and that the Christian God copied the Egyptian myth. This erroneous view has gained tons of popularity from opponents who want to disprove Yeshua's existence or make the deities worshipped in antiquity as superior or equal to Yeshua.

Horus is one of the oldest recorded deities in the ancient Egyptian spirituality and is often depicted as a falcon or a man with a falcon head. Horus was believed to be the god of the sun and of war. Horus was said to be born of Osiris and Isis, who originally ruled over a world that they created. Osiris's brother Set killed Osiris for having sex with Set's wife Nephthys. Before Isis could resurrect Osiris, Set had Osiris's body cut to pieces and scattered them either across Egypt or the four corners of the earth. Nephthys and Isis found all of Osiris's body parts except for the one important piece needed to impregnate her; his penis, Isis used her goddess powers to temporarily resurrect Osiris and fashion a golden phallus. She was then impregnated, and Horus was conceived. Osiris descended into the underworld to reign as Lord of the Dead. Set vowed to find and banish this man, at which point Isis revealed her true identity. Ra gives the throne to Horus because of Set's vow. Horus then restored prosperity to Kemet and later had four sons.

When one reads the Kemetic sources you'll find significant differences between Horus and Yeshua, which reveal that Yeshua's historical account is not a copy of Kemetic sources:

- The depiction of Horus reveals four sons of Horus and six semi-gods, but nothing adding up to 12 disciples as recorded in Scripture (Matthew 10:2-4).
- Horus is one god among many because aspects of Egyptian spirituality were polytheistic, whereas Yeshua is the one and only son of God and Christianity is a monotheistic faith (Deuteronomy 6:4).

- Horus wasn't a supreme being as Yeshua is as Horus was under the authority of Ra, whereas Jesus holds all authority as God incarnate[229] (John 1:14, John 8:58, Colossians 1:15, Titus 2:13).

When one examines Isis, we see that she was a goddess, while Mary is a human who gave birth to Yeshua as a result of the Holy Spirit (Matthew 1:18).

Isis essentially resurrects Osiris' penis after assembling his body to become pregnant, which doesn't mirror the virgin birth in which Mary conceived Yeshua (Matthew 1:23).

There's no credible historical record of an Anup the Baptizer as many claim.

The contention between Seth and Horus does not parallel God and Satan, because they believed that reconciliation between Seth and Horus was possible, whereas Satan is eternally banished into the lake of fire (Revelation 20:10).

This isn't an exhaustive list of the concerns and worldviews that urban apologists address. The point is urban apologists address these concerns in order that those opposing Yeshua will come to faith in Him by responding to the gospel. Rather than affirming, embracing or internalizing whitewashing, urban apologetics gives credence to the contributions of Black and brown people to Christianity and Western civilization and the world, and reverses the effects of whitewashing by affirming Paul's great call for racial, social, gender, and cultural equality (Gal. 3:28) in the name and power of Yeshua.

Discussion Questions

1. What resources have you been exposed to in the past for apologetics?
2. How does understanding the needs of the urban context shape your understanding of the needs and engagement of that context?
3. What do you need to do to be better equipped in urban apologetics?
4. Are there social issues that you've failed to apply the gospel to? If so, what issues?

---

229 Tony Evans, *Theology You Can Count On*, (Chicago: Moody Publishers, 2008), 193-197.

11

A People From All People

*I'm closer to a white brother that knows Christ,
than I am a Black brother that doesn't.*
– Dr. Eric Mason

IF YOU MADE IT THIS FAR in this book you may be wondering how is there a hopeful future? Whitewashing has had centuries of a head start and it seems insurmountable to curtail, so why even try? You may even be thinking if some white people could be this diabolical, how could we ever truly be united or be "brothers and sisters in Christ" when they won't acknowledge us? As hopeless as it may seem, I know that we're not without hope because of who the source of our hope is. If death, the grave, hell, and sin have all been defeated (1 Corinthians 15:53-55), then whitewashing will not prevail even when it seems to. So where is hope found in all of this? It's in the one who embodies and upholds justice. If unity and truth is up to us, we're doomed, but thank Yahweh it isn't. I said that the gospel is what motivated me to write this book and it's the gospel of Yeshua that is the source of my hope.

I sat and listened to a man I admire and who has mentored me in many ways as he said one of the most profound statements that I've heard on how the gospel unifies. It was the Frequency Conference, and Dr. Eric Mason shared about how he still believes in unity despite the countless attacks he's faced from evangelicals who opposed him personally. He expressed his commitment to unity rooted in the gospel. As he continued his message, he talked about the power of the blood of Christ and how his blood transcends race. "No matter how frustrated I get or how much injustice I witness, I'm still committed to Christian unity with my white brothers and sisters and all people, the reality is based on the blood of Christ and this is hard, I'm closer to a white brother that knows Christ, than I am a Black brother that doesn't…" This indeed is one aspect of the power of the gospel, it unifies, but as stated at the start of this book, **reconciliation is impossible without confrontation.** Dr. Mason refused to allow the stench of whitewashing to cloud the way he sees all white people nor to embrace the notion that they are beyond grace because he's a recipient of grace, too, and any person that claims faith in Christ should do the same. This is where some hoteps, Afrocentrists, kemetics, Black humanists and the like propose forgiveness as a reason to not follow Christ and assert why Christianity isn't good for Black people, but this is hotep hypocrisy. One glaring reason this is hypocritical is because to deny forgiveness is to deny an attribute of faith that many of the ancestors they claim to herald held. We've seen the overwhelming Black and brown presence in the Bible, established the reality that many of the Jews were people of color, and referenced several Black and brown people who influenced and shaped the Christian faith long before the slave trade. To ignore these Black people because one has a disdain for Christianity is to do two things:

1. It denies the contributions of Blacks in favor of embracing a whitewashed narrative in order to wrongly assign whiteness to Christianity.
2. It plays into the hands of white supremacy by intentionally ignoring and embracing the narrative of white racists about Christianity.

The aforementioned undermines some of the overall unified elements of Afrocentrism, which are Black empowerment and ancestral acknowledgment. Wrongly castigating Christianity undermines their own movement and beliefs. Before you leave "the white man's religion"—which it is not—I ask that you do three things:

1. Check the sources of the people you're getting your information from. Look for primary sources and not just google research and YouTube videos. In other words, do personal research.
2. Do unbiased research by reading authors that oppose your assertions, if you only read people that agree with you about Christianity being a white man's

The Whitewashing of Christianity

religion, you're not allowing your views to be challenged, and if you're certain of your convictions, then they should be able to withstand opposition.

3. Ask God to reveal himself to you. I know you're probably thinking that doesn't make sense if one doesn't believe, but keep in mind I'm talking to some people on the verge of leaving, which means they are in the faith, but wrestling with their faith. Consider what's been presented in this book and realize that Yeshua loves you and died to save you.

I have several hopes which led me to write this book.

Hope 1—Loving Confrontation

The good news is that there's a diverse, concerted effort to undo the damage that whitewashing has caused humanity and the way people view the Christian faith. Thankfully, this issue isn't seen as a Black issue or a non-issue by all. Matt Chandler, pastor of The Village Church in Texas, addressed issues of race in a message from the MLK50 Conference titled *Gospel Reflections from the Mountaintop* in Memphis, Tennessee. He confronted the inconsistencies among his God-fearing flock when it comes to racial issues. He said:

> If I preach the sermon out of the book of Isaiah on justice, my inbox would fill with their glee that I would broach the subject. But if I applied it to the subject of race, then all of a sudden, I was a Marxist, or I've been watching too much of the liberal media. If I spoke on abortion, I was applauded as courageous, as a ferocious man of God, and yet when I would tackle race, I was being too political. If I quoted the great reformer Martin Luther... never did I get an email about his blatant anti-Semitism. But let me quote the great reformer Martin Luther King Jr., and watch my inbox fill with people asking me if I'm aware of his moral brokenness... I think there is a cascading effect

and it starts with ignorance... They don't know what they don't know and they are part of a system that encourages their not knowing.[230]

As he continued, he addressed the whitewashing of Africa by addressing his white counterparts and the education system on how it portrays Africa not as a continent of rich history and ingenuity, but rather one of jungles and poverty.

> They would lead me to believe that Africans were just running around in the jungle, with no homes, cities, architecture or culture. They are wearing leaves, and have spears. They are basic and uneducated. I am not taught about their architecture or engineering, although I will be taught about pyramids, but we want to make sure that northern Africa is not the same as Africa. There is nothing about how the majority of white men and women are educated that would lead us to believe that Africans and African Americans are intellectual, innovative or creative except a couple a y'all in sports or entertainment."[231]

Chandler is confronting something that, while uncomfortable for some, is necessary for authentic unity. We must not see whitewashing as a Black issue; it must be an issue of The Church because it's false and denies the beautiful mosaic of God's family.

There are brothers and sisters of different hues willing to confront whitewashing and evangelical silence in love. They are willing to endure the backlash and mischaracterization from those that think the gospel somehow ignores issues that aren't theological in their eyes, when the gospel is a message that confronts the issue of sin with the hope of acceptance in Christ. As more and more people are willing to confront these issues with love and place purpose over popularity, we'll move closer toward authentic unity.

---

230 Leonardo Blair, *Matt Chandler Calls on White Pastors to Help Fight Miseducation of White America on Blacks,* https://www.christianpost.com/news/matt-chandler-calls-white-pastors-help-fight-miseducation-of-white-americaon-Blacks-222479/, April 2018.

231 ibid.

Hope 2—Honest Conversation

We have to be able to dialogue without leaving the room when voices of dissent are expressed. Having conversation about these issues in homogenous settings is unlikely to produce any lasting change. I'm grateful for my brothers and sisters who don't look like me but are willing to listen and change, and I'm willing to extend the same respect because all sides have blind spots. This means our posture can't be to sit down and shut up but rather to disagree without being disrespectful, even when these conversations are hard or frustrating at times. A posture that says, sit down and shut up is the antithesis to what the Prophet Isaiah teaches in Scripture: "Come now, let us reason together, says the Lord…" Isaiah does not tell one person to "shut up and listen," but challenges all people to "reason together"[232] (Isaiah 1:18). We (believers and followers of Yeshua) must refuse to give into 'cancel culture' and writing people off because recipients of grace have no right to permanently cancel anyone. Yeshua has canceled our eternal debt and that cancelation must keep us from canceling others (Colossians 2:14). Additionally, while proponents of biblical justice are wrongly labeled proponents of Critical Theory and Critical Race Theory, we must reject CT and CRT because it makes the issue color of someone's skin and not the condition of their heart. The issue with whitewashing and white supremacy is not their white skin, but rather their deeds being evil (John 3:19), which wrongly assigns superiority to those with white skin. I'm hopeful that we can get in rooms and discuss the heinous nature of whitewashing and ways to undo it as we move forward. President of the Southern Baptist Convention JD Greear is one of many leading the charge of having dialogue that's not built for comfort, but for change. He led and moderated *Undivided: Your Church and Racial Reconciliation*. Greear focused on why Southern Baptists need to discuss race relations and how the church can improve in that area. The Southern Baptist Convention has a long history of racism that still exists today, but concerted efforts are being made to address the sins of the past and chart a new way forward. He addressed the effects of hundreds of years of living in what he characterized as a "racialized society" and acknowledged that "we've got to lament that we live in a racialized society where this is even a ques-

---

232 Tim Stanton, *Critical Theory vs Critical Thinking*, https://freethinkingministries.com/critical-theory-vs-criticalthinking/?fbclid=IwAR2nKx-gzAsN2NdsYVR0o5MxWYhG8KpD_vALt4VUvN4ZiK2QvOSe6f7KUE, June 2020.

tion… and it really shouldn't be a question, but sins have consequences. Sins from the past have consequences in the present."[233]

As a gospel-saturated, concerted, unified effort is made to realize what Scripture displays, I remain hopeful that we'll get there.

Hope 3—Conciliation

In *Removing the Stain of Racism from the Southern Baptist Convention*, Dr. Jarvis Williams notes:

> The category of race has a broader use in the Bible than in modern terminology. One important distinction is that the biblical category of race was not constructed with pseudoscience for the purpose of establishing a racial hierarchy. Racial categories were employed apart from any consideration of biological inferiority rooted in whiteness or Blackness. In fact, Genesis 11:6 in the Septuagint identifies humanity as one genos (race/kind/class/group). The Greek term ethnos (nation, Gentile) overlaps with genos. Both terms function as racial categories.[234]

Whether you see race as a social construct or not, the reality is that the differences are evident, but don't have to be divisive, in order to move forward we must champion what D.A. Horton calls ethnic conciliation, Horton says, "Ethnic conciliation is accomplished when we affirm (not ignore or idolize) the ethnic heritage of every human being and seek to remove animosity, distrust, and hostility from our interpersonal relationships."[235]

This affirmation needs to become the norm and not the exception, and whitewashing highlights one ethnicity at the expense of all the others. My hope is that

---

233 Diana Chandler, *Greear on Race: Past Sins, Present Consequences*, http://bpnews.net/53121/greear-on-race— past-sins-present-consequences, June 2019.

234 Jarvis J. Williams and Kevin M. Jones, *Removing the Stain of Racism from the Southern Baptist Convention: Diverse African American and White Perspectives*, (Nashville: B&H Academic, 2017), 27.

235 D.A. Horton, *Intensional: Kingdom Ethnicity in a Divided Word*, (NavPress, 2019), 12.

the conciliation will be realized as thoughts, trends and methods that oppose it are both confronted and resisted.

Hope 4—Color Engagement > Color Blindness

The gospel isn't colorblind; it's color-engaging. Many would assume that the answer to whitewashing and racial disparities is a colorblind society that doesn't see color, but it isn't, the gospel is the answer. I'm hopeful for a gospel-rich color-engaging gospel that doesn't need to be blind to color, but rather one that celebrates differences and displays the courage to confront issues that threaten unity and degrade entire people groups. While well-intended by some and diabolically used by others, color blindness oftentimes becomes truth blindness. As Thabiti Anyabwile says, "The color-blind approach proceeds on a misdiagnosis of the problem. Seeing color in the physical sense of seeing is *not* the problem. Unless one is actually blind, we all see color. Admitting that people have skin pigments of varying hues and that sometimes those hues cluster into what the Bible calls families, clans, kinsmen, and nations is *not* the problem. Again, that's self-evident. Anyone denying these things (and I'm not aware of any who does) is simply being delusional or dishonest."[236] God created color, ethnicity by creating all people in His image (Genesis 1:26). A kingdom ethic is one that sees the differences within humanity as one aspect of the creative genius of a God who can create something from nothing. My hope is the colorblindness will be rejected and color-engaging accepted as a true kingdom approach to humanity. After all, John sees every tribe, tongue and nation in the book of Revelation (Revelation 7:9). Scripture isn't color-blind and neither should followers of Yeshua be colorblind either.

Hope 5—Funding More Black and Brown Missionaries

Oftentimes when missionaries go to foreign countries, they hand out Bibles. This is great, but that's not the only thing they hand out. The curriculum provided usually has exclusively white imagery. This contributes to the global spread of whitewashing and creates more work for indigenous people who have some of the same challenges Black and brown missionaries have in America by associating

---

236 Thabiti Anyabwile, *When Color Blind is Truth Blind* https://www.thegospelcoalition.org/blogs/thabitianyabwile/color-blind-truth-blind/, May 2018.

Christianity with whiteness. One of the visions of the church I pastor is to sponsor 100 Black and brown missionaries over the next 10 years. We're funding Black missionaries in Ghana right now and assisting in building a special needs school. A hundred may seem small, but I'm hoping more churches will follow our lead by intentionally funding Black and brown missionaries to go into the mission field. This isn't to disparage missionaries of other colors, but to be intentional championing missions while opposing whitewashing by equipping Black and brown missionaries with the rich testimony of Black and brown people that have contributed to faith and theology. This is often left out when white missionaries enter these countries, and this must be curtailed. The percentage of Black and brown missionaries is extremely low. There are a myriad of reasons for this, but we must take an active role in funding Black and brown missionaries globally for the spread of the gospel first and foremost, but also for indigenous people to see people that look like them and appreciate some of their cultural norms while affirming their dignity and presenting accurate church history. Leaders like Lloyd Chin, who works with organizations like World Venture and Black led organizations like Vision 938 under the leadership of Byron Johnson are leading in this effort, but more collaboration is needed.

Hope 6—An Increase of Black and Brown Presidents of Seminaries

Dr. Doug Logan, President of Grimké Seminary and Professor of Urban Ministry, started Grimké Seminary, named after pastor and theologian Francis Grimké with a mission to train pastors and planters who are characterized by theological clarity, cultural engagement, and missional innovation. Born October 10, 1850 to a slave mother, Nancy Weston, and her owner, Henry Grimké, Francis Grimké was the son of an aristocratic slaveholding family in Charleston, South Carolina and a relative of the famous abolitionist sisters Angelina and Sarah Moore Grimké. Grimké distinguished himself as a highly intelligent scholar at Lincoln, where in 1870 he graduated as class valedictorian.[237] In 1871 he began studying law at Lincoln, and in 1872 he moved to Washington, D.C. to continue pursuit of a law degree at the historically Black college Howard University. While at Howard

---

237   Thabiti M. Anyabwile, *The Faithful Preacher*, (Crossway Books Wheaton, Illinois, 2007), 113.

The Whitewashing of Christianity

University, Grimké felt God calling him to Christian ministry. He left Howard in 1874 to pursue theological education at Princeton Theological Seminary under the leadership of Charles Hodge. Grimké graduated from Princeton in 1878 and soon after began his public ministry at the affluent 15th Street Presbyterian Church in Washington, D.C. On December 19 of that same year Grimké married Charlotte Forten, granddaughter of influential businessman, activist, and abolitionist James Forten, Sr. of Philadelphia. Grimké knew the contradiction between profession and committed action. He witnessed the lash applied to enslaved Africans and the inhumane cruelty of selling "brothers" to the highest bidder. That the particular band of "brothers" known as Christians could be capable of the same treacherous hypocrisy was plain to Grimké as he observed the silence and inaction of both white and Black churches in the face of racial injustice. Consequently, he dedicated himself to expositing the role of the church in the world.

Existing seminaries need to move toward diversity at the executive level of their institutions because there are tons of qualified people of color to help shape and enhance curriculum, activities, community engagement and more. While schools need to change, what I love and admire about Dr. Doug Logan is the fact that rather than requesting a seat at the table, he created his own table and is inviting and equipping others, Dr. Logan says:

> As an African American pastor, it has long been my desire to train pastors, particularly those called to the urban context. Wherever I have been called to serve, I have invested in trying to bring this vision to fruition. I was involved early on with two different urban training school start-ups in Philadelphia. Neither was able to become the established institution I envision. Because of this, I jumped from school to school, eventually finding myself at a traditional seminary. Along the road, I always felt that my education lacked the necessary components to comprehensively train leaders in the complexities of urban mission. Throughout my time in seminary, leading seminars, and serving on the Board of Trustees of my wonderful alma-mater, Lancaster Bible College/Capital Seminary and Graduate School I was driven by my passion to train urban pastors. I can distinctly remember a conversation I had with my dear friend, Mez McConnell, pastor of Niddrie Community Church in Edinburgh, Scotland. As we shared our struggles of trying to develop urban training in existing

institutions, we found a common vision. Sharing a dinner of fish and chips, Mez said to me, "Pastor Diddy, you know what? If they won't invite us to their table, then we're gonna leave their dining room, go to our house, and build our own table. But, we're not going to do like they did. We're going to invite them to our table and show them what the Great Commission looks like in education and mission." Mez stood up from the table and concluded, "Doug, we have to build. We can't wait for them to care about what God has called us to." Ever since that dinner, Mez's comments have been stuck in my head, reinvigorating my vision to build an urban focused seminary. Since that point, God has called me to raise up a team of pastors and theologians to bring about my vision for a new seminary. A seminary that would invest in places where Black and brown people live, both in the United States and around the world. A seminary that would be accessible and affordable for the urban poor while offering rigorous theological education and contextualized urban ministry training. A seminary that would produce ethnically diverse leaders who in turn would impact both the church and other educational institutions. Grimké Seminary was established in June 2019 after years of working with dear brothers, partners, and friends from my local church in Richmond, VA, the Acts 29 Network, and around the world. Through Grimké, we have not just built a table but have laid it with a rich feast of the Apostle Paul, Athanasius, Charles Haddon Spurgeon, Martin Luther King, Jr., and so many others so that generations will be able to come, feast, and be nourished so they can be equipped to lead the urban church. Paul writes in 2 Timothy 2:2: "and what you have heard from me in the presence of many witnesses entrust to faithful men, who will be able to teach others also." As Grimké's first president, my prayer is that Paul's commission is fulfilled in the mission of Grimké seminary as we labor to train faithful pastors and church leaders for every context and every generation.

Doug has created a school that equips and acknowledges the rich history of our faith, one that embraces a narrative of how God uses all people in his redemptive plan. This needs to happen more, and I hope that this will be a trend that continues, especially since education is being taught beyond the classroom and is becoming more and more mobile which breeds innovation and advances opportunities for people to hear from Black and brown educators.

Hope 7—Change

I've had countless conversations with ethnic minorities who talk about the need for diverse authors, theologians, speakers, etc. to be highlighted, empowered and heard in seminaries and conferences, not because they are Black, but because of their expertise, but oftentimes, it doesn't go beyond a conversation. My hope is that syllabi that doesn't include one voice of an ethnic minority will no longer be a common practice, conferences will not pigeonhole Black and brown people to one area of expertise by having them talk about race, but not hearing them address apologetics, theology, church history, philosophy, epistemology, soteriology, etc. and all pastors, not just Black and brown pastors will actively talk about the African presence within Scripture and history from their pulpits and this will be done with love and joy. My previous hopes are only realized if change is applied. Change must start within, as the philosopher Miroslav Volf said, "We struggle to have the right view of our neighbor because I exclude the enemy from the community of humans and myself from the community of sinners."

What should we do?

1. Let's pray, hope for and apply intra-racial (or ethnic) confrontation as Paul a Jew confronted Peter a Jew in Galatians 2:11-13. As long as diversity, culture and whitewashing are an issue of Black and brown people exclusively, many white evangelicals may fall subject to seeing homogenous churches and superficial relationships with people outside of their race as okay, while still promoting a whitewashed version of the faith. We have to challenge all people to see this as a gospel and heart issue that should be aggressively confronted with grace and not use grace as a license for things to stay the same.
2. Let's challenge seminary presidents, professors and executive staff at churches to divest themselves of promoting whitewashing functionally by continuing to display white imagery of Black African people and presenting almost everyone in Scripture as white. Additionally, these schools need

to opt to join churches in which they can serve under qualified minority pastors and encourage their student body to do the same. We need more practitioners and less talkers in this area in order to create a new normal of people thinking beyond homogeneity as it relates to their ecclesiological experience and how they think of Christian history.

3. We need to be intentional about mentioning the African and ethnic heritages of many of the church fathers, martyrs and monks who existed long before the Protestant Reformation and the slave trade. Since whitewashing has been accepted and ignored for centuries in order to present a fuller narrative of Christian history that isn't exclusively white, having Christians of all hues knowledgeable and intentional about communicating this will be helpful within the body of Christ and the world that's watching.
4. Let's believe in the gospel! The truth is, if we aggressively pursue this, we'll see that some of our churches and seminaries aren't on board and they need to be identified and prayed for and confronted lovingly on the fact that the gospel unites, not separates.
5. Let's pursue biblical justice!—**How do we act justly?** In Micah 6:6-8 (CSB), we read: 6 What should I bring before the Lord when I come to bow before God on high? Should I come before him with burnt offerings, with year-old calves? 7 Would the Lord be pleased with thousands of rams or with ten thousand streams of oil? Should I give my firstborn for my transgression, the offspring of my body for my own sin? 8 Mankind, he has told each of you what is good and what it is the Lord requires of you: to act justly, to love faithfulness, and to walk humbly with your God.

I believe we can do this in four ways:

1. We should be eager to do good works in light of Yeshua's finished work!

Titus 2:11-13

11 For the grace of God has appeared, bringing salvation for all people, 12 instructing us to deny godlessness and worldly lusts and to live in a sensible, righteous, and godly way in the present age, 13 while we wait

for the blessed hope, the appearing of the glory of our great God and Savior, Jesus Christ. 14 He gave himself for us to redeem us from all lawlessness and to cleanse for himself a people for his own possession, eager to do good works.

This isn't guilt, this is a desire to do justice based on God delivering justice to all humanity.

2. We should pursue justice because Christ pursued us first!

Isaiah 1:16-17

16 "Wash yourselves. Cleanse yourselves. Remove your evil deeds from my sight. Stop doing evil. 17

Learn to do what is good. **Pursue justice**. Correct the oppressor. Defend the rights of the fatherless. Plead the widow's cause.

We don't withhold justice for personal comfort!

Matthew 23:23-24

23 "Woe to you, scribes and Pharisees, hypocrites! You pay a tenth of mint, dill, and cumin, and yet you have neglected the more important matters of the law — justice, mercy, and faithfulness. These things should have been done without neglecting the others. 24 Blind guides! You strain out a gnat, but gulp down a camel!

3. We remember the injustice done against God by us!

In verses 6-7 of Micah 6, they asked four questions:
What should I bring before the Lord when I come to bow before God on high?
Should I come before Him with burnt offerings, with year-old calves?
Would the Lord be pleased with thousands of rams or with ten thousand streams of oil?
Yeshua endured every form of injustice, yet He remained faithful for God's glory and our redemption, this is the foundation of pursuing biblical justice. The

fourth question in Micah 6:6-8 was, "Should I give my firstborn for my transgression, the offspring of my body for my own sin?"

We don't have to give up our firstborn to sacrifice because God gave up His!

Here are some honest heart questions evangelicals need to ask to see if they are promoting a whitewashed narrative of the Christian faith or a kingdom one:

Christians: Am I unwilling to admit that prejudice can exist within me? Have I embraced the caricatures of Black and brown people and trust them as factual? Do I believe surface level interactions with people of different ethnicities constitute true friendship? Are my ethnic 'friends' only the ones who agree with me? When I think of Christianity and the Bible do I automatically see images of white people? If so, Why? Does our children's curriculum only display images of white people?

Churches: Are Black and brown people only promoted if they pathologize people of their ethnicity or race? Do we value Black and brown faces numerically, but not their voices socially, structurally and theologically? Have we conflated patriotism with the gospel? Is conservatism presented as biblical Christianity? Is abortion addressed and confronted, but police brutality ignored?

Engaging Women

Are Black women excluded as examples of biblical femininity? Are the voices of Black women only heard if they are agreeable? What is your immediate response when a Black woman says or does something impactful? Do you find yourself surprised or shocked when a Black woman says something insightful? Are we actively supporting and empowering women in our church?

Seminaries and Institutions of Higher Learning:

Are we presenting everyone in Christian history as white in our books, brochures and online content? Are the images used to depict people from Scripture almost exclusively white? If the books used display African people as white, is this publicly rebuked to the class? Are students challenged to read authors of ethnicities, genders, and theological orientations different from those of the professor? Are all the preachers presented as examples white? Are proponents of slavery rebuked or presented as products of their culture?

Conferences: Is it assumed that race and music are areas of expertise that Black and brown people speak on at conferences? Are ethnic minorities asked to teach on topics like theology, apologetics, church history, theodicy, philosophy, etc.? Are ethnic minorities at the decision-making table prior to the conference being completely planned? Are Black and brown people given opportunities beyond singing at the conference? Are Blacks seen as entertaining fillers, but not theological contributors?

Ephesians 2 is clear that the dividing wall of hostility has been torn down, walls of racism, sexism, ageism and any other ism you can think of has been torn down. When we see these walls attempting to be resurrected by any of these isms, there must be a unified effort of the body of Christ that reminds people that through Christ, we truly are one, after all, the biblically reality is that God through His infinite wisdom and power has created a people, from all people. I think CS Lewis said it best:

> There are no ordinary people; you have never talked to a mere mortal. Nations, cultures, arts, civilizations—these are moral, and their life is to ours as the life of a gnat, but it is immortals with whom we joke, work, marry, snub, and exploit. Immortal horrors or everlasting splendors, this does not mean that we are to be perpetually solemn; we must play, but our merriment must be of that kind which exists between people who have from the outset taken each other seriously. No flippancy, **no superiority**, no presumption. We have never met mere mortals. Every person we have ever looked upon, smiled at, frowned at, greeted, encouraged, insulted, slandered, touched, is a person bearing the marks of divine likeness and the imago dei.[238]

Discussion Questions

1. What are clear steps of action that you will take due to the knowledge you have gained?
2. In what ways have you been the most impacted by this book?
3. What steps can your church take to move toward presenting the Christian faith accurately?

---

238   C.S. Lewis, *The Weight of Glory*, (New York: Harper One, 2001), 45-46.

Conclusion

> *My master is yet alive.*
> – Josiah Henson

WHEN WE THINK ABOUT PEOPLE of African descent engaging in religion and spirituality, the thirst for lost identity often harbors with it a side effect that seems to be increasingly problematic. Whitewashing contributes to this identity crisis because it affirms the suspicion many have about the Christian faith and its effectiveness for people of color. While whitewashing has attempted to erase the Black and brown contributions to the Christian faith, God has always had a plan that included us, and this can't be denied. Shedding light on what is perceived to be European created, but actually African influenced, frees us to accurately examine our historical roots, which are vast, but include Christianity long before slavery, so we can dismiss the notion that Blacks embraced the Christian faith by force and address concerns that assert that associating oneself with Christianity is somehow an alignment with oppression. As apologist Adam Coleman says, "There seems to be a burgeoning problem in the Black community: People are coming to the erroneous conclusion that Christianity is 'The White Man's Religion' and thus there is incompatibility between being Black and being a Christian. As a result, many people of African descent are sadly either leaving the Christian faith or being hardened in their hearts toward receiving the gospel of Christ. The perception that there is some sort of 'Uncle Tomness' to being both Black and Christian has driven many people of African descent into the arms of other belief systems

The Whitewashing of Christianity

that are thought to be more in line with African heritage. In times past the Louis Farrakhans of the world would say something along the lines of, 'Christianity is the white man's religion so you need to join the Nation of Islam.' This argument has since become more nuanced: objectors allege that Christianity is the white man's religion so Blacks need to join either the Nation of Islam, Hebrew Israelites, Moorish Scientists, Egyptian/Kemetic Spiritualists, African spiritualists, or be an atheist. A concoction of apostasy, Afro-centrism, alternative religions, and a hint of pan-Africanist ideology is offered as the antidote for having betrayed one's African ancestors in taking on the slave-master's religion."[239]

    I get it, I understand the trauma of what is the Black experience in America and I have personally experienced racism and I've had to counsel my daughter through verbal attacks from white classmates, but Yeshua hasn't been a contributor to oppression but rather a place of refuge (Psalms 16:1) and because of his strength I refuse to live a life of bitterness and hatred. If you're one who believes in our African ancestors, how can you ignore the contributions of countless African men and women who trusted Christ long before the plantation? The question is will you only acknowledge the ancestors that fit a narrative that ignores African Christianity? If so, you're guilty of buying into the white man's narrative that you claim to so vehemently oppose, but you don't have to do this. Yeshua has always had a place for Black and brown people at His table. He's never excluded us from His plan of redemption and He's been with us before our collective struggle began on the soil of America. Not only does He understand our struggle, He entered into our struggle. Scripture declares that for the joy set before Him, Yeshua endured the cross (Hebrews 12:2), what was His joy? First and foremost the Father's glory, but also our redemption. His redemption wasn't reserved for one group of people, but it's for all people and that includes you. You no longer have to assign Christianity to the 'white man' because he could never nor is any man powerful enough to monopolize the gospel. Your redemption is not in the hands of a white man, but in the hands of the God-man and He says once you're in His grip no one or nothing can snatch you out of His hands (John 10:28). So, you have a choice, will you continue to buy in and perpetuate a false whitewashed narrative of the Christian faith or

---

239   Adam Coleman, *Introducing the Conscious Community Part 1*, https://freethinkingministries.com/introducingthe-consciousness-community-part-1/ September 2016.

will you place saving faith in Yeshua? I hope for the latter. You've been presented with Scripture, history and sociology and I hope that if you made a decision to reject based on the false premise that God doesn't want or care for people with melanin, my prayer is that you'll divest yourself of that lie and come home. Not only has Yeshua prepared a place for you (John 14:2), but He has secured eternity for you and you no longer have to question His love for you or our people. In fact, His resurrection guarantees eternal security for everyone who trusts him by grace and through faith. This resurrection power was not lost by our ancestors, most notably, Marcus Garvey said this about Yeshua's resurrection in 1922:

> The Lord is risen! A little over nineteen hundred years ago a man came to this world called JESUS. He was sent here for the propagation of a cause—that of saving fallen humanity. When He came the world refused to hear Him; the world rejected Him; the world persecuted Him; men crucified Him. A couple days ago He was nailed to the cross of Calvary; He died; He was buried. To-day He is risen; risen the spiritual leader of creation; risen as the first fruit of them that slept. To-day that crucified Lord, that crucified Christ sees the affairs of man from His own spiritual throne on high. After hundreds of years have rolled by, the doctrine He taught has become the accepted religion of hundreds of millions of human: beings. He in His resurrection triumphed over death and the grave; He by His resurrection convinced humanity that His cause was spiritual. The world felt the truth about Jesus too late to have accepted His doctrine in His lifetime. But what was done to Jesus in His lifetime is just what is done to all reformers and reform movements. He came to change the spiritual attitude of man toward his brother. That was regarded in His day as an irregularity, even as it is regarded to-day. The one who attempts to bring about changes in the order of human society becomes a dangerous imposter upon society, and to those who control the systems of the day. The desire to enslave others. It has been an historic attitude of man to keep his brother in slavery—in subjection for the purpose of exploitation. When Jesus came the privileged few were taking advantage of the unfortunate masses. Because the teaching of Jesus sought to equalize the spiritual and even the temporal rights of man, those

The Whitewashing of Christianity

who held authority, sway and dominion sought His liberty by prosecution, sought His life by death. He was called to yield up that life for the cause He loved—because He was indeed a true reformer.[240]

To my white brothers and sisters who will read this, I'll say this, they are watching. Who's watching? Your children, your youth group, your mentees, your coworkers, your fellow congregants and the next generation of leaders and cultural influencers. They read what you post about people of color. They hear some of the podcasts you listen to. They hear your dinner table conversations and prayers. Do your prayers include comfort for the Black mother whose son was shot while playing with a toy gun? Or does your prayer ignore her cries and focuses on Black-on-Black crime? Are your prayers consumed with love of country, but not compassion for your Black and brown neighbor? Do your prayers present the immigrant as your neighbor? Are your prayers more conservative than they are Christian, because we shouldn't conflate conservativism with the Christian faith? Is the narrative you present them filled with only white faces? They are watching AND listening to both your voice and your silence, which either perpetuates or exposes whitewashing, but more importantly, God is watching. In order to capture a true gospel-centered community, Black and brown people can't be the only ones championing this effort to correct the false narrative that whitewashing has perpetuated for centuries. I'm grateful for the countless advocates that I've met who are willing to have tough conversations and are willing to lose speaking engagements, funding and access to 'elite' circles for the sake of unity and solidarity when they go beyond the conversation and on to action to undo the effects of centuries of racism and whitewashing. This is another reason why I remain hopeful; there are white brothers and sisters at the church I pastor who've displayed a willingness to learn and the boldness to confront race at their schools, dinner tables and extended family gatherings. I have pastors who've called me for counsel and admitted areas of ignorance but refused to remain ignorant and I've watched them lament as they lost members who they thought were committed to Christian truth only to find out that they were more committed to conservative talking points. I've seen this struggle firsthand and they didn't shrink back under the pressure when it would have been easier for them to, but this is what it means to be a true advocate. True advocacy doesn't stop when things become difficult and inconvenient, and I'm grateful for a diverse group of true

---

240 Marcus Garvey, *Selected Writings and Speeches of Marcus Garvey*, (Mineola, NY: Dover Publications, 2015), 66.

advocates. I pray for genuine repentance and true advocacy where we can lock arms and pursue gospel-centered diversity that honors all people and every contribution to the Christian faith and history. My challenge isn't intended to produce or incite white guilt, that doesn't produce any long-term changes nor is it biblical or effective, in fact, it's manipulative, however, if we truly believe what Yeshua says about his brothers and sisters being the ones who does the will of the Father (Mark 3:35) when I say my white brothers and sisters, I mean it, through Yeshua a family is formed and family members can and should challenge each other. In case you missed the connection, the aforementioned are discipleship issues that the body of Christ unified around the gospel must confront within our own ranks, so while I must confront my white brothers and sisters in certain areas, the issue isn't just on them, it's our issue.

I remain hopeful when it looks like there is no hope because I have too many examples from Scripture and history to be hopeless, even in the face of whitewashing, I remain hopeful and active. If you think the task of undoing whitewashing is insurmountable, I encourage you to look back. The prophet Habakkuk does this in Habakkuk 3 when he says, "God is from Teman…" (Habakkuk 3:1). He talks about God coming from Teman, which seems a little weird, right? You'd expect it to say that God comes from heaven to earth to save His people, which He does in Christ, but in this passage, it's poetically written with the history of God's faithfulness in mind. This is why Teman is mentioned, because Teman is a place where God delivered His people. Teman is the southern region, it literally means south because it's located far south of Israel. Teman was a district of Edom, located to the southeast of Judah. So what does this mean? Habakkuk is looking back to when God delivered His children from Egypt and led them in Sinai. Looking back reminds me of other aspects of history that seemed like they would never change or be undone. If you were to talk to people prior to Juneteenth (2-years after the Emancipation Proclamation was signed), many would've said slavery will never been undone, but those who held on to hope and fought back, many of whom were Christians and didn't live to see it, but fought for those who would experience the reality of their hope. If you would have talked to people prior to the passing of The Civil Rights Act they would've said that Jim Crow would never be undone, and Blacks would never be able to vote, and discrimination would continue to be upheld legally, but those that held on to hope were agents of change and I'm a beneficiary of their faith and hope. If you were to talk to people prior to Brown vs. The Board of Education, many would say that integrated schools would never happen, and people fought vehemently so that it wouldn't, but people who put their faith and hope in action worked and, what seemed impossible happened. So, yes, I remain hopeful, but my hope isn't uninformed, lifeless or inactive, but rather it's life-filled, informed and active. My hope isn't in people, but in God, the same God Habakkuk trusted in the midst of impending judgment. This same God that got Black people through slavery, Jim Crow, the Tuskegee Experiement, $3/5$ Compromise, Black codes, segregation— this same God who was with us then is with us now. My hope is in a God who transcends race and prejudice and sovereignly unifies and mends what seems irreparably broken. He (Yeshua) led me to write the book to both expose and repair because after all, reconciliation is impossible without confrontation and reconciliation was initiated by Yeshua on the cross and His sacrifice makes reconciliation with mankind possible. Yeshua confronted the most important issue needing confrontation which exists within the thread of humanity, sin. His confrontation of sin on the cross makes redemption and reconciliation with God and humanity possible.

I want to end with a story that reminds me of the power of God despite attempts to dehumanize and degrade Black and brown people. Josiah Henson (1789-1883) was born into slavery in Charles County, Maryland, on a farm owned by Francis Newman. As a child, he was sold to Isaac Riley, who later appointed him superintendent of the farm at an unusually young age because of Henson's strength and intelligence. At age twenty-two Henson married a slave woman whose name remains unknown. They had twelve children, four while enslaved.[241]

There's a story of Henson returning to the place where he was once enslaved after securing his freedom. Upon his return to a place that did not value his person or regard his humanity, his 'master' had died and his former master's wife said to Henson, "Sy, your master has died." Josiah Henson looked at her and said without hesitation, "**No, madam, my Master is yet alive.**" Even during slavery Black people rejected the idea that God wanted them enslaved in perpetuity and that whites were better than them. They knew that God is a God who will not allow oppression to go unpunished and will not let a narrative that excludes the myriad of people He's used in his plan to go ignored. Whitewashing will not erase the multi-faceted ethnic imprint used by God to spread His message, because our true master is yet alive.

---

241 Jared A. Brock, *"Josiah Henson: The Forgotten Story in the History of Slavery"* https://www.theguardian.com/books/2020/jun/19/josiah-henson-the-forgotten-story-slavery-uncle-tom-s-cabin, accesed July 2020.

Afterword

Dr. Vince L. Bantu

MY FAMILY AND I LOVE TO TRAVEL and we recently visited the gorgeous Sequoia National Park in Central California. We were blown away by the massive Sequoia tree—the largest living organism on earth and one of the oldest. While the size of these massive trees is certainly their most famous characteristic, I was struck with the specific and limited conditions necessary for their generation. Giant Sequoias only grow naturally along the western slopes of the Sierra Nevada Mountains in Central California due to the specific mineral composition, elevation, sunlight exposure and surrounding plant life. These magnificent creations of *'Egzi'abher* (Eth: "Lord of the land" i.e. "God") can only grow under these specific environmental circumstances; they wouldn't survive apart from these conditions. This made me begin to reflect on how all of creation functions similarly—the creation of *'Egzi'abher* is beautifully diverse and was intended to be unified, interdependent and distinct. The Giant Sequoia is a specific type of tree that requires certain surroundings and has unparalleled individuality, yet it is still part of the larger tree family. In the same way, the covenant People of *'Egzi'abher* are one People and yet we are intended to be different and diverse. We cannot, and therefore ought not intend to be the same. The universal *Bisrat* (Eth: "good news" i.e. "Gospel") that transcends all differences is planted within our culturally-specific communities and it grows in unique, distinct and united ways. While the message

The Whitewashing of Christianity

of the *Bisrat* is the same for all, our theology, worship and ministry are all culturally situated and are meant to be distinct. The creation, revelation, salvation and consummation of *'Egzi'abher* are universal and beyond human cultural specificity; the theological and liturgical efforts of believers are human responses to divine revelation and are therefore, *always* culturally specific. Pastor Jerome Gay has drawn our attention to one of the most extensive obstacles to the biblical vision of the global Church: whitewashing.

I was lecturing on church history at a predominately white, Reformed school and one of the white male students asked me after the lecture, "Dr. Bantu, don't you think that God in His providence chose the white race to be the primary stewards of the Gospel because He knew they would be best suited to the task?" I imagine the likelihood of this student—who was also an ordained minister—having been expressly taught such a concept verbatim to be very low. I also know that this student has been taught such a dangerously unbiblical way of thinking in thousands of less direct ways. Within the academic context, the fact that the overwhelming majority of administrators, faculty, staff, students, and required authors are white *actively* promotes this way of thinking—to say nothing of the fact that the theological and ministerial frameworks that are taught are rooted solely in Western linguistics, philosophy and social organization. Many *Nazrawi* (Eth: "Nazarenes" i.e. "Christians") of color have also embraced self-hatred, rejected culturally-relevant expressions and have promoted Eurocentric Christendom. Across the globe for the past 1,700 years, *Nazrawi* have not heeded the Word of *'Egzi'abher* in Acts 10:15: "Do not call anything impure what *'Egzi'abher* has made clean." What Pastor Jerome has done is to draw our attention to the contributions—ancient and modern—to the spread of the *Bisrat* of Yeshua by members of the Body that have lacked attention (1 Corinthians 12:23-24). The seed of the *Bisrat* is planted in every diverse type of soil in humanity and the result is a tapestry of various types of trees, each with our own distinct beauty that magnifies the same Creator in a multitude of ways. Contextualized worship, ministry and theology are fundamental to communicate the biblical truth that the *Bisrat* is for everyone (1 Corinthians 9:22-23). Today, this is especially true for ethnic groups who have been told that the *Bisrat* is not for them (or that it is conditional upon cultural assimilation).

I was speaking at an HBCU on early African Christianity and during the Q&A, a young Black man stood up and declared that the information presented during the lecture had caused him to rethink his commitment to the Kemetic/

Conscious community. Similarly, I was teaching at a seminary in Australia to a class of Aboriginal ministry leaders who taught me about the devastation wrought upon their communities by white Australian Christendom (*terra nullius*, White Australia Policy, Stolen Generations, etc.). The students expressed the empowerment of learning about the early legacy of the *Bisrat* in African, Middle Eastern and Asian communities and that this inspired them to continue to craft a distinctly Aboriginal theological voice. As Pastor Jerome has stated eloquently, to place emphasis on the contributions of people of color to the spread of the *Bisrat* is not tantamount to cultural idolatry or anti-whiteness. Rather, the ministerial methodology of urban apologetics continues the biblical tradition of placing greater emphasis on parts of the Body that have lacked it towards the goal of the advancement of the *Bisrat*. As we continue to sow the seed of the Bisrat throughout the world until the glorious return of our King Yeshua, let us plant well. Let us reject a whitewashing method that raises one plant as superior to others and ultimately leads to the withering of a Westernized seed that isn't suitable to non-Western soil. Let us sow appropriately to the context in which the Creator has made us as we grow into the fullness of His image in which He has created us.

Bibliography

Alexander, Michelle. *The New Jim Crow.* (New York: The New Press). 2012.

Anyabwile, Thabiti M. *The Faithful Preacher* Crossway Books Wheaton, Illinois 2007.

Anyabwile, Thabiti. "When Color Blind is Truth Blind." https://www.thegospelcoalition.org/blogs/thabiti-anyabwile/color-blind-truth-blind/ May 2018.

Athanasius & C.S. Lewis. *On the Incarnation: The Treatise De Incarnatione Verbi Dei.* (Crestwood, NY: St. Vladimirs Seminary Press) 2003.

Bantu, Vince. *A Multitude of All Peoples: Engaging Ancient Christianity's Global Identity* (Downers Grove, IL: InterVarsity Press). 2020.

Bantu, Vince. *Gospel Haymanot: A Constructive Theology and Critical Reflection on African and Diasporic Christianity* (Urban Ministries, Inc. 2020).

Bantu, Vince. "Is Christianity a White Man's Religion?" [audio podcast] retrieved from http://www.jude3project.com/podcast/whitemansreligion?rq=vince%2-bantu. The Jude 3 Project. June 2016.

Becker, Doug. "Does the Bible Condone Slavery?" https://emergencenj.org/blog/2019/01/04/does-the-bible-condone-slavery. January 2019.

Bialik, Kristen. "5 Facts About Black Americans." https://www.pewresearch.org/fact-tank/2018/02/22/5-facts-about-blacks-in-the-u-s/, February 2018.

Bradley, Anthony. *Aliens in the Promised Land: Why Minority Leadership Is Overlooked in White Christian Churches and Institutions.* (Phillipsburg: NJ: P & R Publishing). 2013.

Bradley, Anthony. *Liberating Black Theology: The Bible and the Black Experience in America.* (Wheaton, IL). 2010.

Brecht, Martin. *Martin Luther, Volume 3: The Preservation of the Church, 1532-1546.* (Minneapolis: Fortress Press). 1993.

Burkett, Randall. *Garveyism as a Religious Movement,* Metucher, NJ: Scarecrow Press, 1978.

CARM Reformed Theology. Retrieved from http://carm.org, April 2012.

Carr, Simonetta. "More on The Black Dwarf" http://simonetta-carr.blogspot.com/search?q=black+dwarf, June 2011.

Cartlidge and Elliott, 53–55. See also *The Two Faces of Jesus* by Robin M.

C.F. Keil and F. Delitzsch *"The Pentateuch" in Commentary on the Old Testament* (Grand Rapids: Wm. B. Eerdmans). 1987.

Chandler, Diana. "Greear on Race: Past Sins, Present Consequences." http://bpnews.net/53121/greear-on-race— past-sins-present-consequences. June 2019.

Cleage, Albert. *The Black Messiah.* (New York: Sheed and Ward). 1969.

Coates, Ta-Nehisi. *Between the World and Me.* (Melbourne, Australia: The Text Publishing Company). 2015.

Colorism https://www.dictionary.com/browse/colorism, accessed October 2020.

Coon Online Etymology Dictionary 2019. https://www.etymonline.com/word/coon. (Douglas Harper).

Cone, James H. *A Black Theology of Liberation.* (Maryknoll, NY: Orbis Books). 2010.

Cone, James H. *Black Theology and Black Power.* (Maryknoll, NY: Orbis Books). 1997.

Cone, James H. *God of the Oppressed* Maryknoll, NY: Orbis Books 1997.

Daniels, David. "The African Roots of the Reformation." [audio podcast]. Retrieved from https://podcast.apple.com/us/podcast/african-roots-reformation-special-guest-dr-dadid-daniels/id978012810?i=1000394480912. The Jude 3 Project. November 2017.

Debow J.D.B. *De Bows Review and Industrial Resources, Statistic, Etc.* New Orleans and Washington City, 1857 (article).

Django Unchained https://www.imdb.com/title/tt1853728/characters/nm0000168, accessed September 2020.

Douglas, Kelly Brown. *Stand Your Ground.* (Orbis Books). 2015.

Ehrman, D. Bart. *Did Jesus Exist? The Historical Argument for Jesus of Nazareth.* (New York: HarperOne). 2012.

Ellis, Carl F. *Free at Last?: The Gospel in the African American Experience.* (Downer Grove, IL 1996.

Eliot, T.S. *Christianity in Culture.* (Mariner Books, Orlando, FL). 1977.

Emmerson, Michael. *Divided by Faith: Evangelical Religion and the Problem of Race in America.* (Oxford University Press). 2000.

Evans, Tony. *Oneness Embraced.* (Chicago, IL: Moody Publishers). 2011.

Fields, Lisa. *Through the Eyes of Color.* (Jude 3 Project: Jacksonville, FL). 2019.

Foley, Malcolm. "On the Assault of James COne and Liberation Theology." https://thewitnessbcc.com/on-the-assault-of-james-cone-Black-liberation-theology/. (The Witness BCC). January 2020.

Ferguson, Everett. *Church History, Volume One: From Christ to the Pre-Reformation.* (Grand Rapids, Michigan: Zondervan). 2013.

Frame, John. *The Doctrine of the Christian Life.* (Phillipsburg, New Jersey: P&R Publishing). 2008.

Freedom from Religion Foundation, Chris Rock https://ffrf.org/news/day/dayitems/item/22283-chris-rock, February 2021.

Grant, Ernest. "Whitewashed Christianity." https://thewitnessbcc.com/whitewashed-christianity/. The Witness. October 2016.

Garvey, Marcus. *Selected Writings and Speeches of Marcus Garvey.* (Mineola, NY: Dover Publications). 2015.

Gnenn Bracey and Wendy Moore. *Race Tests Racial Boundary Maintenance in White Evangelical Churches.* Sociological Inquiry 87, no 2. May 2017.

Glaude, Eddie S. *Democracy in Black.* (New York: Crown Publishers). 2016.

Gold, Hadas. "Megyn Kelly: Jesus and Santa were white." *Politico* December 2013 https://www.politico.com/blogs/media/2013/12/megyn-kelly-jesus-and-santa-were-white-179491.

Halberstadt, Amy "Future Teachers More Likely to View Black Children as Angry, Even When They're Not." https://news.ncsu.edu/2020/07/race-anger-bias-kids/ July 2020.

Harris, Forrest E. *What Does it Mean to be Black and Christian?: Pulpit, Pew and Academy in Dialogue,* Sunday School Pub Board 1996.

Hays, J Daniel. *Racial Bias in the Academy Still?* (Ouachita Baptist University).

Haynes, Stephen R. *Noah's Curse: The Biblical Justification of American Slavery.* (New York: Oxford University Press). 2002, loc. 2737, Kindle.

Horsman, Reginald. *Race and Manifest: Destiny The Origins of American Racial Anglo-Saxonism* (Cambridge, MA: Harvard University Press, 1981).

Horton, D.A. *Intensional: Kingdom Ethnicity in a Divided Word.* (NavPress). 2019.
Ingram, Christopher. "Three Quarters of Whites Don't Have Any Non-White Friends." Washington Post, August 25, 2014, www.washingtonpost.com/news/wonk/wp/2014/08/25/three-quarters-of-whites-dont-have-any-non-white-friends/?utm_term=.b994b0930aa1.
James, George G. *Stolen Legacy.* 1954.
Jensen, *Bible Review*, 17.8, October 2002, and *Understanding Early Christian Art* by Robin M. Jensen, Routledge, 2000.
Johnson, Umar. https://www.drumarjohnson.com/#bio, accessed February 2021
Jones, David *Health, Wealth and Happiness: How the Prosperity Gospel Overshadows the Gospel of Christ* (Kregel Publications Grand Rapids, MI). 2011.
Jones, Tabatha L. Jolivet *White Jesus: The Architecture of Racism in Religion and Education* (Peter Lang Publishing 2018).
Keller, Tim. *Center Church.* (Grand Rapids, MI: Zondervan). 2012.
Kendi Ibram. *Stamped from the Beginning.* (New York Nation Books). 2016.
Lane, E. B. *The African American Christian Man: Reclaiming the Village.* (Dallas: Black Family Press). 1997.
Lewis, C.S. *The Weight of Glory.* (New York: Harper One). 2001.
Little, Anita. "The Women of Queen & Slim Survive at All Cost." https://www.elle.com/culture/a29339190/lena-waithe-jodie-turner-smith-melina-matsoukas-queen-and-slim-interview-2019/. October 2019.
Loritts, Bryan. *Inside Outsider.* (Grand Rapids, MI: Zondervan). 2018.
Loritts, Bryan. *Letters to a Birmingham Jail.* (Chicago, IL:Moody Publishers). 2014.
Loritts, Bryan. *Right Color, Wrong Culture: The Type of Leader Your Organization Needs to Become Multiethnic.* (Moody Publishers). 2014.
Mason, Eric. *Woke Church: An Urgent Call for Christians to Confront Racism and Injustice.* (Chicago, IL: Moody Publisher). 2018.
McCray, Walter Arthur. *The Black Presence in the Bible: Discovering the Black and African Identity of Biblical Persons and Nations.* (Chicago, IL: Black Light Fellowship). 1990.
McDowell, Josh. *Evidence that Demands a Verdict: Life-Changing Truth for a Skeptical World.* (Nashville, TN: Harper Collins). 2017.

McIlhenny, Albert. *Afrocentric Ideology and Church History.* (Albert McIlhenny). 2016. Kindle.

McWilliams, James. "Bryan Stevenson on What Well-Meaning White People Need to Know About Race." Pacific Standard, updated February 18, 2019, https://psmag.com/magazine/bryan-stevenson-ps-interview.

National Archives, Declaration of Independence: A Transcription https://www.archives.gov/founding-docs/declaration-transcript accessed February 2021.

Moore, Russell. *The Gospel Life: The Gospel & Racial Reconciliation.* (Nashville, TN: B&H). 2016.

Oden, Thomas. *How Africa Shaped the Christian Mind.* (IVP Books). 2007.

Oden, Thomas. *The African Memory of Mark: Reassessing Early Church Tradition* IVP Academic 2011.

Painter, Nell. *The History of White People.* W.W. (New York: Norton & Company). 2010. Kindle Edition.

Piper, John. "Did Moses Marry a Black Woman?" 9 Marks. February 2010 https://www.9marks.org/article/did-moses-marry-Black-woman/.

Pruitt, Sarah. "The Ongoing Mystery of Jesus's Face." March 27, 2019. https://www.history.com/news/what-did-jesus-look-like.

Raboteau, J. Albert. *Canaan Land: A Religious History of African Americans.* (New York, NY: Oxford University Press). 2001.

Rhodes, Ron. "Black Theology, Black Power, and the Black Experience, Reasoning from the Scriptures Ministries." http://Home.earthlink.net/ron-rhodes. 2016, April 25.

Richardson, Damon. Urbanlogia Ministries, https://urbanlogia.org/pages/damion-richardson, March 2021.

Robert Lewis Dabney. Retrieved from http://www.confederatepastpresent.org/. 2016, May 3.

Romero, Robert *Brown Church: Five Centuries of Latina/o Social Justice, Theology, and Identity* (Downers Grove, IL: InterVarsity Press). 2020.

Sermon Index: "Partiality." https://www.sermonindex.net/modules/articles/index.php?view=article&aid=34571, accessed March 2021.

Skinner, Tom. *How Black is the Gospel?* Fourth Printing. 1970.

Swift, David. *Black Prophets of Justice: Activist Clergy Before the Civil War.* (Baton Rouge, LA: Louisiana State University Press). 1989.

Skot, Welch. *Plantation Jesus.* (Herald Press). 2013.

Stanton, Tim. "Critical Theory vs Critical Thinking" https://freethinkingministries.com/critical-theory-vs-critical-thinking/?fbclid=IwAR2nKx-gzAsN2Nd-sYVR0o5MxWYhG8KpD_vALt-4VUvN4ZiK2QvOSe6f7KUE June 2020.

Tatum, Beverly Daniel. *Why Are All the Black Kids Sitting Together in the Cafeteria? And other Conversations about Race.* (New York: Basic Books). 1997.

Taylor, Jessica "Citing 'Two Corinthians,' Trump Struggles To Make The Sale To Evangelicals" https://www.npr.org/2016/01/18/463528847/citing-two-corinthians-trump-struggles-to-make-the-sale-to-evangelicals January 2016.

Tisby, Jemar. *The Color of Compromise.* (Grand Rapids, MI: Zondervan). 2019.

Thurman, Howard. *Jesus and the Disinherited.* (Boston, MA: Beacon Press Books). 1976.

Walter, Elwell. *Evangelical Dictionary of Theology.* (Grand Rapids, MI: Baker Publishing). 2001.

Washington, M. James. *The Essential Writings and Speeches of Martin Luther King Jr.* (New York, NY: HarperCollins Publishers). 1986.

Wilkerson, Isabel. *The Warmth of Other Suns.* (New York: Random House). 2011.

Williams, Jarvis J. and Kevin M. Jones. *Removing the Stain of Racism from the Southern Baptist Convention: Diverse African American and White Perspectives.* (Nashville: B&H Academic). 2017.

Williams, Reggie L. *Bonhoeffer's Black Jesus: Harlem Renaissance Theology and an Ethic of Resistance.* (Waco, TX: Baylor University Press). 2014.

Wills, Gregory A. *Democratic Religion: Freedom, Authority, and Church Discipline in the Baptist South.* (New York, NY: Oxford University Press). 1997.

Wilmore, Gayraud S. *Black Religion and Black Radicalism: An Interpretation of the Religious History of African Americans.* (Maryknoll, NY: Orbis Books). 1998.

Woodley, Randy. *Living in Color: Embracing God's Passion for Ethnic Diversity.* (Downers Grove, IL: InterVarsity Press). 2004.

Scripture Index

Genesis
1:26, 58, 168, 175, 176, 195, 207
1:27, 15
2:11-14, 43
2:13. 46, 130
9:25, 63
10, 130
10:6, 47, 130
25:1, 44, 131
25:13, 131
50:11, 131

Exodus
1:9-10, 39, 135
1:15-18, 196
1:16, 45
1:22, 45
2:19, 44, 130
3:7-9, 91
5:6-9, 40
6:25, 131
20:5, 63
20:6, 64
21:16, 88, 91

Numbers
12:1, 45, 131
12:2, 46
22:5, 131

Deuteronomy
6:4, 110, 199
7:6, 37
15:12-18, 94
23:3, 46
23:6, 46
23:15-16, 94

2 Samuel
18:19-33, 85

1 Kings
9:20-21, 63
10, 190
14:25, 190

2 Kings
18-19, 190

1 Chronicles
9:20, 131

Esther
4:15-17, 196

Psalm
16:1, 217
45:3, 50
78:51, 46, 130
105:23, 46, 130
106:21-22, 47, 130
120:5, 131
139, 175
139:13, 150
139:14, 30
139:29, 175

Proverbs
31:8-9, 195

ISAIAH
1:16-17, 212
1:18, 205
1:21-23, 151
42:11, 131
53:2, 7, 49
58:1-14, 151

JEREMIAH
13:23, 82
38:7-11, 184
38-39, 82
43:7, 218
46:9, 83, 153
50:6, 37

EZEKIEL
34:23-24, 37

DANIEL
3:12, 196

MICAH
5:4-5, 37
6:6-8, 151, 212, 213

HABAKKUK
3:1, 220

MATTHEW
1:1, 47, 48
1:1-6, 28
1:1-16, 128
1:18, 200
1:23, 200
5:3, 38
5:39, 147
10:2-4, 199
15:24, 37

22:21, 198
22:36-40, 34
22:37, 107
23:23-24, 151, 213
25, 151
28:1, 191
28:19-20, 14, 15

MARK
3:35, 220
6:34, 37
7:8, 76
12:31, 34
14:27, 37
15:21, 185
16:1-2, 191

LUKE
3:23-28, 48
3:32, 47
23:34, 155, 213
24:1, 191

JOHN
1:11-12, 48
1:14, 193, 200
3:16, 193
3:19, 205
4:9, 193
4:22, 37, 48
6:44, 194
8:58, 200
10:11-16, 37
10:28, 217
14:2, 217
14:3-4, 180
20:1, 191

ACTS
1:8, 14, 15
2:10, 13, 15
6, 172
7:54-60, 159
8, 7, 13, 16
8:26-36. 13
8:26-39, 186
9:3, 49
10:15, 225
10:34-35, 16
11:26, 25
13:1, 13, 131
13:1-3, 25
16:19-24, 196
16:20, 197
16:35-40, 197
17:26, 30
21:38, 131, 132
22:28, 197

ROMANS
1:16, 37
2:6-11, 37
5:12, 15
5:18, 16
12:15, 197
13:1-2, 195
13:9, 175

1 CORINTHIANS
6:11, 192
9, 172
9:22-23, 225
11:1, 198
13, 34

13:5, 175
15, 191
15:53-55, 201

GALATIANS
1:18, 25
2, 25
2:11, 25
2:11-13, 213
2:11-21, 175
3:28, 200
4, 192
4:24, 190

EPHESIANS
2, 173, 217
2:8-9, 71
5:1, 198
6, 93
6:5, 63
6:5-6, 93, 95
6:6, 95

PHILIPPIANS
2:3, 34
3:20, 73

COLOSSIANS
1:15, 200
2:14, 54, 205

1 TIMOTHY
1:8-10, 92

2 TIMOTHY
2:2, 212

TITUS
1:13, 9
2:11-13, 151, 212
2:13, 200

HEBREWS
7:14, 48
11:31, 47
12:2, 217,
13:20, 37

JAMES
1:17, 152

2:1, 36, 167
2:1-13, 35
2:2-5, 38
2:26, 195
2:4, 38
2:9, 31, 175

1 PETER
3:15, 193
5:4, 37

1 JOHN
2:2, 15
4:19-21, 151
4:20, 31, 64
4:20-21, 92
4:9, 193

REVELATION
1:14-15, 5
1:14-16, 49
2-4, 16
5:9, 16
7:9, 22, 207
20:10, 200

Subject Index

A
Adam, 42, 43, 50, 107
Albert Cleage, 147
Alexander Crummell, 55, 144, 147
American Revolution, 51, 62
Anglo-Saxons, 41, 42, 56, 58, 59, 89
Animism, 15
Antebellum, 23, 93
Antioch, 13, 16, 25, 128, 193
Aristotle's Climate Theory, 21
Athanasius, 22, 23, 108, 112, 122, 123, 185,, 193, 194
Augustine, 2, 13, 16,, 20, 50, 66, 68, 77, 126, 159, 185

B
Basil the Great, 20
Bathsheba, 47, 128
Biological determinism, 41
Black Religious Identity Cults, 22, 183
Black Theology, 145, 150, 151, 154, 155
Brown v. Board of Education, 139
Byzacena, 20

C
C1, 172, 173
C2, 172
C3, 172
Canaanite, 37, 47, 131
Cappadocian Fathers, 20
Chattel slavery, 21, 46, 62, 79, 90, 94, 96, 97, 99, 100, 102
Church Fathers, 31, 34, 45, 198, 282, 312, 321, 322, 361
Civil Rights, 12, 105, 106, 109, 168, 184, 189, 190, 213
Class, 39, 46, 61, 89
Colonization, 80, 168, 170, 171
Color Blindness, 209
Color Engagement, 209
Conciliation, 161, 171
Constantinople, 106
COON, 158, 159, 160, 161, 163, 165, 167, 179
Councils of Nicea, 106
Curse of Ham, 21, 144
Cushites, 23, 43, 82, 83, 84, 85, 131
Cyprian of Carthage, 114
Cyril of Alexandria, 128

D
Declaration of Independence, 62, 88, 139
Demonization, 168, 169, 170, 176
Diaspora, 11, 19, 25
Didymus the Blind, 20, 80
Displacement, 160, 168, 176

E
Egyptian, 40, 42, 43, 44, 45, 47, 64, 81, 84
Emancipation Proclamation, 62, 100, 136, 137, 142
Ephesus, 106, 128
Esther, 52, 98, 197
Ethiopian, 7, 13, 15, 16, 43, 47, 60, 80, 81, 82, 83, 107, 130
Ethnocentrism, 29, 155
Eurocentric, 24, 225
Evangelicals, 29, 33, 34, 35, 36, 52, 57, 67, 70, 71, 72, 73

F
Fanaticism, 24
Federalism, 62

G
Gender, 16, 39, 105, 201, 216
George Whitefield, 89, 96, 97, 99
Gospel, 101, 106, 110, 122, 132, 138, 142, 145, 147, 148
GotQuestions.org, 11, 12, 16, 17
Gregory of Nazianzus, 20
Gregory of Nyssa, 20

H
Hamitic, 28, 44, 47, 106, 128, 130, 131
Hananiah, Mishael and Azariah, 197
Hegemony, 41
Herod the Tetrarch, 25
Homogenous, 30, 32, 33, 207, 213
Howard Thurman, 146
Historical Whitewashing, 22, 56
Humanism, 10

I
Ignatius, 13, 16
Injustice, 17, 33, 39, 62, 97, 101, 135, 141, 156
Intra-racial, 25, 213
Ireneus, 13
Islam, 1, 14, 15, 16, 26, 107
Israelites, 37, 40, 41, 43, 47, 85, 91, 94, 135, 187, 219, 85, 91, 157, 167, 187

J
James Cone, 134, 135, 136, 143, 148, 153, 156
Jim Crow, 70, 135, 143, 151, 156
John Calvin, 67, 68, 77, 141, 152, 153, 178
Jonathan Edwards, 89, 96, 98, 102, 153, 169

K
Kushite, 7

L
Lactantius, 118
Liberation, 143, 144, 146, 147, 148, 149, 151, 152, 153
Library of Alexandria, 12, 20, 80, 189
Libya, 15, 16, 20
Lucius of Cyrene, 25

M
Manaen, 25
Man-stealing, 91
Manuscripts, 112, 189, 190, 194
Marcus Garvey, 145, 220, 221
Martin Luther, 66, 67, 74, 77, 79, 107, 139, 140, 149, 152, 169, 205
Martin Luther King Jr., 14, 89, 140, 146, 147, 205, 212
Marxist, 169, 196, 205
Mauretania, 20

Medgar Evers, 146,
Monolithic, 17, 24, 42, 43, 161, 167
Mosaic Law, 91

N
Nat Turner, 143
Nubia, 2, 7, , 26, 43, 80, 82, 83, 106, 108
Numidia, 27

O
Oppression, 8, 10, 39, 61, 91, 109, 135, 139, 142, 163
Origen, 2, 20, 50, 64, 191, 192, , 46, 97, 121, 148, 200, 201

P
Pachomius the Great, 120
Pan-Africanism, 54, 144, 146, 147
Perpetua and Felicity, 116
Pharaoh, 40, 41, 44, , 59, 135
Philonic Allegory, 192
Plessy v. Ferguson, 139
Protestant Reformation, 21, 66, 67, 79, 107, 140, 152, 213
Publius Cornelius Tacitus, 41, 59
Puritans, 20, 51, 59

R
Race, 59, 61, 73, 76, 81, 91, 105,128, 135, 155,160
Racial Ignorance, 32, 39
Racial Indifference, 32, 34,143
Racial Insensitivity, 32, 35, 44, 143, 160
Racism, 32, 39, 41, 46, 48, 58, 67, 70, 75, 78, 81, 135
Rahab, 47, 128, 131
Rastafarianism. 15
Reconstruction Era, 137
Reformed Theology, 65, 67, 68, 70, 153
Reinhold Niebuhr, 154
Religion, 2, 23, 53, 79, 90, 100, 135, 182, 186
Romanita, 41
Ruth, 42, 43, 46, 47, 70

S
Salvation, 71, 101, 135, 151, 181, 196, 214, 225
Secularism, 10
Self-hatred, 73, 156, 158, 159, 160, 161, 163, 165, 166, 167,
Shenoute of Atripe, 124
Shiphrah and Puah, 197
Simeon, 13, 25, 131
Sphenisciformes, 28
Sunken Place, 166, 175

T
Tamar, 47, 128
Tertullian, 2, 13, 16, 49, 80, 110, 185, 191
The Ethiopian Coptic Church, 13
Thermuthis, 44, 45
Trans-Atlantic Slave Trade, 2, 90, 91, 93, 94
Triennial Baptist Convention, 14
Tyconius, 20, 80
Typological Allegory, 192

U
Urban Apologetics, 181, 182, 201, 226

W
White supremacy, 8, 19, 20, 24, 36, 41, 42, 48, 54, 56
whitewash, 56, 57, 64, 73, 89, 98, 100, 106, 107
WRIC, 183

About the Author

JEROME GAY JR., WAS RAISED in Southeast Washington, DC and moved to the Raleigh, NC in 1997 to attend Saint Augustine's College for his undergraduate studies, where he graduated with a Bachelor of Arts in Communications. While there he founded a campus ministry that emphasized the gospel and biblical orthodoxy in the urban context. The ministry grew campus wide with many trusting Christ as Savior, upon graduating he served as an elder for several years and after fervent prayer was led to plant Vision Church in October of 2010.

Pastor Jerome serves as the Pastor of Teaching and Vision at Vision Church. Jerome has a vision to see gospel centered churches and leaders raised up within the urban context and sent out to plant other gospel-centered churches. Jerome is married to Crystal Gay and the father of Jamari Gay and son Jerome Jordan Gay III. He is also the author of several books, *The Whitewashing of Christianity: A Hidden Past, A Hurtful Present and a Hopeful Future, Renewal: Grace and Redemption in the Story, Talking to Your Children about Race, Church Hurt and African Heroes: Discovering our Christian Heritage*. Jerome is also the founder and President of The Urban Perspective.

Jerome has his Master's Degree in Christian Studies and Ethics from Southeastern Baptist Theological Seminary.

More By Jerome Gay Jr.

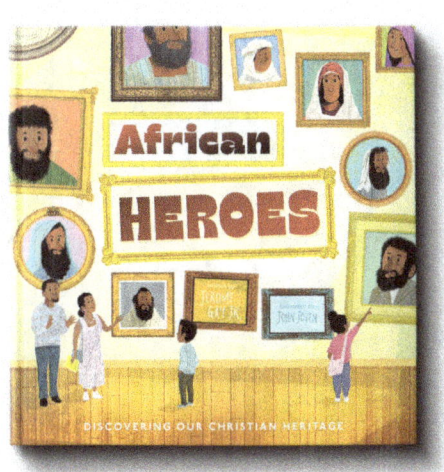

www.ingramcontent.com/pod-product-compliance
Lightning Source LLC
Chambersburg PA
CBHW071957070526
44583CB00015B/1232